PELICAN BOOKS

A 584

THE CITY

PAUL FERRIS

THE CITY

PAUL FERRIS

PENGUIN BOOKS

Penguin Books Ltd, Harmondsworth, Middlesex
AUSTRALIA: Penguin Books Pty Ltd, 762 Whitehorse Road,
Mitcham, Victoria

—

First published by Gollancz 1960
Published in Pelican Books 1962

—

Copyright © Paul Ferris, 1960

—

Made and printed in Great Britain
by Richard Clay & Company, Ltd, Bungay, Suffolk

Set in Monotype Times

CONTENTS

The Radcliffe Report referred to throughout is the report of the official Committee on the Working of the Monetary System, Cmnd 827, published by the Stationery Office in 1959. Chapter 7 draws freely on the Proceedings of the Bank Rate Tribunal, also published by the Stationery Office.

1

A VIEW OF THE CITY

A LOT of money is made in the City of London. A lot of trade is financed there. A lot of lives are spent there, and at one time it must have been possible for a partner or a chairman to grow old and mellow there without feeling that he occupied the specific role in British society of 'City man'. He couldn't avoid the feeling nowadays. The City is looked at, quoted, laughed at, put on a pedestal, gossiped about, threatened, and defended – all by men with hot breath who see with delight, bewilderment, or disgust that the City has come through the upheavals of the forties and fifties with most of the pieces intact.

Caution is needed. When I talked to a banker about a little finance company I had been to see that day, which charged interest on unsecured loans at a rate of 2 per cent per month – 24 per cent a year, and they insisted it wasn't extortionate – he asked where the company had their offices. I said they had an accommodation address, the one they used in advertisements, in the West End, but operated mainly from a house with a small brass plate and curtains on the windows in the suburbs. He held up his hand and lectured me on the dangers of referring to such firms as part of 'the City'. He agreed that 'the City' was a convenient shorthand way of saying 'British banking, merchanting, and financing', but said that one had to draw the line somewhere. City men are touchy – like the Institute of Directors, who, goaded by unfavourable publicity for tycoons, ran a survey which showed that only 6 per cent of directors were chauffeur-driven, only 30 per cent smoked cigars and attended business lunches more than twice a week, and only a third arrived at work later than 9.30 a.m.

Even stockbrokers, traditionally hard-bitten, are easily upset.

I met a broker for lunch in a Lyons café, where he ate a chop and drank orange squash so as to leave his head clear for the afternoon's trading. A Right-wing newspaper had just suggested, in one of the City columns that have grown longer and fruitier in recent years, that stockbrokers should take less time over lunch. The broker was angry and hurt at the same time. 'It isn't fair,' he said. 'They keep coming at us. Nothing's too small to have a go at. *I* take forty minutes for lunch – I wonder how long that newspaper chap takes.' Presently he was reminded of the Labour Party's demands for a capital-gains tax (this was before short-term speculation became taxable), and he was off again, grumbling that the papers wrote a lot of nonsense about the way the tax worked in the United States. He pointed out that, anyway, every time he bought or sold for a client, more or less, there was stamp duty to be paid, and that was money in the Government's pocket, wasn't it, so why bother with a tax on capital gains?

He kept talking about 'us', meaning the Tories – it didn't occur to him that I might not be one of us, and somehow I never got round to telling him. It would have bothered him, like something nasty in his coffee. There are Left-wing people at self-employed and boardroom levels in the City; but not many, and they keep it to themselves. To be a responsible person in the City is to be automatically of the Right, just as to be a Socialist is to accept as a matter of course that there is a perpetual mess in the City, and particularly around the Stock Exchange, that needs clearing out. Like all tightly organized communities, the City reacts sharply, assuming that anyone who goes against it is a villain, a red, a bolshie – you still hear this archaic word used, even by young City men.

Although the Stock Exchange is the principal Aunt Sally, there's no shortage of symbolic wickedness throughout the system for those who want to have a go at it. Take the grouse obsession. Grouse shooting is expensive because of the cost of renting moors, but it seems a reasonably harmless occupation. In 1957, when a major sterling crisis blew up in the summer, some of the officials and bankers involved were taking holidays and shooting grouse. In September the Bank Rate – what Americans call the discount rate, the basic national rate of interest – was raised dramatically to help ease the pressure on sterling. News of the rise was alleged by Labour M.P.s to have leaked out the day before, enabling a few insiders to make a small fortune. There was a Government inquiry (the story is told in full in Chapter 7) and everyone was exonerated. Much incidental light was thrown on the workings of the City; and merchant bankers, the class that came in for the most publicity, are still inclined to freeze up if you ask them about the tribunal. But whatever cupboards the inquiry may have opened, the fact that a few merchant bankers were discovered on a Scottish grouse moor seems harmless enough (there is an argument that says steps to prop up sterling should have been taken earlier – but that's another matter). Yet 'grouse' has become a term of sarcastic reproach. There were at least five references in the Bank Rate debate in Parliament. Mr Grimond, leader of the Liberals, said he didn't see it was any more wicked to talk on a grouse moor than in the tea room at the House of Commons or in a coffee house – 'Banks may be inefficient,' he said, 'but this doesn't prove it.' But two years after, in a debate on private industry, they were at it again – 'The public had no idea that such important decisions were considered partly on grouse moors,' and so on. Grouse will never be the same again.

It's easy to believe that all take-overs are harmful, every compensation for a retiring director a disgraceful golden handshake, every twitch of the stock market a result of hard-faced speculation on the end of a private line, all smoked salmon eaten by men in striped trousers part of the great expenses fiddle. Similarly, for its apologists the self-evident truth about the City is that it protects freedom and the £ sterling, ensures a free market in every commodity and half the stocks under the sun, and generally helps to expedite civilization. The one point on which everyone will agree is that the City is a great place for power. Typical of the intellectual radical's approach are the views of Professor Titmuss of the London School of Economics, who singled out insurance companies in a paper on *The Irresponsible*

*Society.** Finding that the last decade has 'witnessed something of an explosion in the accumulation of immense funds in
the hands of private insurance companies and pension trusts',
he sees a 'major shift in economic power in our society'. It
represents 'power concentrated in relatively few hands, working
at the apex of a handful of giant bureaucracies, technically supported by a group of professional experts, and accountable, in
practice, to virtually no one'. A lot of the critics are vaguer than
this; but what none of them fails to notice is the *concentration* of
the City.

Everything about its past has contributed to concentration –
even the arrangement of bricks and mortar. Roman London
covered 325 acres. By Norman times it had more than doubled,
but in the 900 years since then the boundaries of the City of
London have scarcely changed. 'London' has sprawled in all
directions, and the sights the visitors see are mainly in the West
End. But the City, the original London, now given over almost
entirely to the finance and commerce which have accumulated
there around the Thames, has retained its identity: with a Corporation, Lord Mayor who is a national figure, private income,
and elaborate protocol for ceremonial occasions. It adjoins the
north bank of the river, from Fleet Street in the west to Aldgate
in the east; but the financial district, the inner square of banking,
Stock Exchange, and insurance with which this book is concerned, is a much smaller place, little more than a quarter of a
mile each way, with the Bank of England not far from the centre.
The Bank's prison-like walls, high attic windows, and aerials
dominate a bleak stretch of tar macadam and pavement where
eight roads meet: Princes Street, Threadneedle Street, Cornhill,
Lombard Street, King William Street, Walbrook, Queen Victoria
Street, and Poultry. On a Saturday afternoon when the City is
deserted, an energetic man with a bicycle could ring the door-
bells of a dozen international bankers, a dozen of the little-
known but indispensable bill brokers, and tap the frosted glass
of a few stockbrokers just for luck, all within the space of ten
minutes.

* Published by the Fabian Society, London, 1960.

This concentration contributes to the City's feeling of clannish-ness, its resentment when outsiders meddle. So does the common background of so many City men. There must be an affinity between men who have been to the same public school, or public schools which produce the same way of speaking and encourage the same way of thinking. At and near the top of office after office are men who went to the same ten or twelve schools. Any-one without their background is immediately aware how similar they seem – no doubt he exaggerates the similarity, but the long, easy vowels and the commanding style of speech do provide a uniform stamp. There's also the manner: a little casual, a little amateurish, never taking things too seriously: the English sense of detachment, of considering it bad form (another phrase still heard in the City) to get all earnest and worked up about a matter of principle. After spending most of my time for six months in the City I could vouch for the accuracy of this anonymous description of public schoolboys at Oxford University, quoted by John Vaizey in *The Establishment*:*

Physically they seem to be bigger than the rest of us with especially long legs. Their faces tend to be long and lean, or fleshy; in every case they seem to be permanently twenty-five years of age. Their hair is longish and either very fair and straight or dark and curly; their lips are slightly bulging; their voices loud and confident or soft and penetrating. They are always very well-shaven; never blue-jowled or side-boarded; they tend to look very clean and to smell of Imperial Leather soap and bay rum.

The only difference is that by the time they reach the discount house or merchant bank, their age has jumped up to a per-manent thirty-five; and the hair is now kept short around the neck.

Many City men are from families which have been similarly engaged for up to 200 years. Names like Baring and Mullens are as much a part of the City as the Bank of England. The *University and Left Review* once printed a list of City names, showing multiple directorships – like those of Lord Kindersley, of Lazard Bros., Bank of England, Bank of London & South America,

* Published by Blond, London, 1959.

Royal Exchange Assurance, Rolls Royce, and British Match Corporation (they missed out the most important, S. Pearson; the Left never knows quite enough about the City). The City regards this interest in directorships with deep suspicion; it likes to dismiss it as the pointless curiosity of a lunatic fringe, partly because the facts about power are always glossed over by the powerful ones, but partly because there is genuine surprise, among the City's ostriches, that anyone should bother to record such facts. Adverse comment on the number of peers who grace the boardrooms is another matter for surprise. Why should it worry anyone that when Alliance Assurance merged with Sun Insurance in 1959 (one of five major insurance mergers that year), the former was reported to contain an earl, a duke, three viscounts, two barons, and four knights, the latter two barons, a marquis's son, and one knight? Why shouldn't men of ancient lineage like Lord Dynevor, the Earl of Rosebery, and the Duke of Devonshire sit on boards like anyone else? Sometimes the innocence is painfully contrived; but not always.

After all, the City *works*, and has done for a long time. More than eighty years ago Bagehot could say that it represented 'by far the greatest combination of economical power and economical delicacy that the world has ever seen' and that 'our people are bolder in dealing with their money than any continental nation'. Things have changed since then, but a large proportion of international trade is financed in London. The merchant bankers may be only a shadow of what they were, but they still go about their business with *élan*, financing anything from a steelworks in the East to a whaling expedition. More currencies are exchanged, one for another, than in any other foreign exchange market. Nowhere can money be lent and borrowed so easily as through the discount houses around Lombard Street. London is the centre of gold and silver dealing. Lloyd's is still the best name in insurance. The credit of London remains the highest in the world – however tired you get of hearing that an Englishman's word is his bond, London's custom of verbal contracts is one of the planks of its reputation.

It may be the honouring of a bill of exchange; it may be

simply a matter of oiling the wheels, the kind of imprecise service they're very proud of. I met a bank official fresh from an afternoon's work on the telephone, where he had been soothing the fears of irascible Continentals. He was from the overseas department of a domestic bank – a 'joint-stock' or 'clearing' bank, not one of the merchant houses. A freighter sailing from Genoa harbour, in Italy, had struck and damaged a pier. The ship was fit to sail but the port authorities wouldn't release it without a promise of indemnity. It was after three in the afternoon; for various reasons it was essential the ship should be away by four o'clock, but a guarantee from the local agent of the shipping company wasn't enough. A chain of phone calls and cables was needed to circumvent the authorities' fear of being left with a hole in the pier that no one would pay for. The agent phoned his head office in Milan. Head office phoned their bank in another part of Milan, who phoned their London agent – the clearing bankers – to say the shipping company was trustworthy, with sufficient money to pay for holes in twenty piers, and an insurance policy against such accidents with a local insurance company. The London bank rang the underwriters at Lloyd's, who already knew what was happening from their agent in Genoa, and said they would indemnify Lloyd's if necessary because they had been promised indemnity by the bank in Milan, which had the local insurance company to rely on. The underwriters cabled their promise to pay if the worst came to the worst and the whole affair turned out to be some nightmare of intrigue and double-dealing, the promise was delivered to the authorities, and the ship was allowed to sail, just on four o'clock. It goes to show how suspicious people can be, but for London the point is that it was necessary to include Lloyd's in this chain of promises, though Lloyd's were on the other side of Europe and there was only an hour to spare.

The same banker told me a story about the Suez crisis of October 1956, a reminder that to talk of the City as a single-minded unit can be misleading. When Britain invaded Egypt and relations between the two countries were broken off, a number of confirmed credits were outstanding on behalf of British exporters to Egypt. These credits would arise when an Egyptian importer instructed a London branch of his Egyptian bank to honour bills of exchange drawn by the British exporter – the idea being, as explained in Chapter 3, to let the exporter get his hands on the money as soon as the goods are delivered to the docks. A London bank, by adding its name to the bill, would 'confirm' the bill's promise of credit. When the crisis came, phone calls went out from the Bank of England, acting on Treasury orders, telling banks to freeze these credits. It was a cutting-off-the-nose-to-spite-the-face operation, since the money had been or was being provided by the Egyptians, so that the result would simply have been to stop British firms getting it. The result would also have been a jolt to the City's reputation. The banks said it was out of the question, since they had joined with the Egyptians in guaranteeing the bills. For a few hours the arguments went on; then the banks got their way. So here was a sharp line down the City, dividing the central bank from the rest, who according to my banker were more concerned for the City's reputation than the Bank of England was itself (though he agreed it was good for business as well as good for tradition to see that clients were paid).

But the most noticeable thing about the City remains its unity. Like sheep around a shepherd the banks cluster near the Bank of England, presenting a very different picture from a hundred years ago, when a journalist could write that 'The lenders of money in Lombard Street are all within a stone's throw of one another, but the Channel might run between instead of a dark, narrow little street, for all the interchange of information and assistance that goes on.' Lombard Street is still dark and narrow, but its occupants have long since been welded together. The Baring Crisis of 1890, when the powerful merchant banking house of Baring Bros. nearly failed for more than £20,000,000, was checked largely because, for the first time in a major crisis, everyone cooperated. The crash could have brought down half the City; but the Bank of England – then and for years to come a privately owned concern – was allowed to take the leadership, and the foolish Barings were fished out of the pit. It put the seal on the leadership of the Bank, as well as marking the City's final emergence from the jungle of every man for himself.

Whether or not the City remains a jungle in less blatant ways, it has acquired respectability in its own eyes and the eyes of most outsiders. The Committee of Lloyd's, the Council of the Stock Exchange, the Accepting Houses Committee, the Discount Market Association, are plump with good intentions, and they and many other bodies seek, and usually manage, to impose strict professional standards on their members. When the official, corporate voice of the City is heard, it is in such publications as *Notes on Amalgamations of British Businesses*, brought out by the central institutions because people were worried by the number of take-overs. It didn't actually use such rude words as 'take-over' and 'bid', but contented itself with laying down vague and commendable principles. On the whole the City is unnecessarily coy. Some of its apologists talk as if young men went on the Stock Exchange in order to ensure a free market in shares, not to make money, and it's a relief to hear the City defended on really practical grounds, say as an earner of overseas currencies. Various estimates drift through the bankers' journals, generally between £125,000,000 and £150,000,000 a year. The £125,000,000 figure would be made up: merchanting £30,000,000; profits of British banks overseas and acceptance-credit commissions earned in London, £25,000,000; overseas insurance, £40,000,000; all other brokerage services, £30,000,000. These earnings are often made the principal argument for maintaining sterling as a great international currency, since London is the centre of the Sterling Area, and, it is reasoned, if there were no sterling then the world would stop coming to London. The Radcliffe Report refuted this when it said: 'The invisible earnings of what is loosely described as "the City" are substantial, and may reach a total of about £125,000,000. But [calculations] do not demonstrate that these earnings would be perceptibly less if the settlements that now take place in sterling came to be made, under a different system of payments, in some international currency such as "bancor". These earnings and the international use of sterling are not so much effect and cause as the common outcome of the same set of circumstances: the nineteenth-century development of the non-European world round a largely British core and the growth of institutions, business connections, and trade centring on London.'

Nothing, you hear the voices saying, is sacred any more: I had that passage pointed out to me with disapproval by a banker as if it was being deliberately offensive not only to sterling but to John Bull and the British way of life. There are some pretty heavy nostalgias in offices where, if they can't remember it themselves, they know what a heyday their predecessors enjoyed before the first world war ended Britain's primacy in commerce. Yet the decline in Britain's status has made the City more, not less, ingenious. It remains an invigorating place. Even the traditions are vigorous. The Bank of England has been guarded by a troop from the Brigade of Guards since an outbreak of rioting in 1780. At the end of each afternoon an officer, three N.C.O.s, twelve guardsmen, and a drummer march to the Bank from the other side of London, causing minor traffic disruptions on the way, and mount guard all night. Once, the War Office, trying to save money, wished to discontinue the guard. The Bank was appalled. The Governor made a fuss, and the idea was dropped. City men approve of that. It catches a City attitude, just as the sudden twist of an alleyway, untouched by bombing, catches some appealing fragment of the past, a wall broken by low windows of frosted glass, and gold letters announcing *Jelly* (*Invalids*). *Wines. Liqueurs. Iced Punch. Soups.* Outside the Threadneedle Street branch post office, where a plaque that must have been there many years promises 'Direct Telegraphic Communication with the chief provincial towns', I saw a middle-aged man with a florid face, rippling watch chain, and striped trousers, a dying cigar between his red rubber lips, stop on his way back from lunch to buy a copy of the *Evening Standard*. He stood looking at the financial page, then made a sour face, crumpled up the paper and let it fall to the pavement, squashed the butt under his heel, and headed for the Stock Exchange. He was too good to be true: a City cliché come to life. Later that afternoon I was in the visitors' gallery of the Stock Exchange, where you stand behind glass and look down on the floor, but I couldn't see him anywhere; probably he was something neutral like a life insurance underwriter or a cocoa merchant.

It was a hot afternoon, and some of the brokers had replaced the jackets of their dark suits with light linen coats. At one end of the gallery a girl was painting the scene in oils on a small canvas. A dark, elegant young man of about twenty was standing by her, pointing out people he knew down below – he seemed to be cousin or brother or nephew to half the Stock Exchange. His suit was near-black; his shirt had narrow blue and white stripes, and his collar was white and glassy. 'I think chaps without their jackets look scruffy,' he said at one point – I had taken my jacket off and was carrying it over my arm, and the interesting thing, I thought, was that when he turned a moment later and caught my eye, I was the one who blushed. He was so beautifully self-assured – no wonder, if you hate the City, you really do hate it hard. There are intellectual grounds for castigating the City and what it represents, but emotional attitudes are generally mixed up with them. I began and ended my research with a moderate bias against it; on the way, though, I acquired respect for the City's hard core of reality. They know what they're doing. Every morning the bill brokers set out on foot to make their rounds of the banks, wearing top hats. I told one of them that I found this strange. 'It may be a fact,' he said, 'that men wearing top hats and talking to other men wearing top hats don't run the country. But men talking to other men do.' It was the unanswerable voice of those who believe in themselves.

2

STOCK MARKET MEN

THE stockbroker's manager, sitting between a teapot and a calculating machine, was explaining the paperwork involved in the purchase of a block of shares for a client. When the shares were bought the stockbroker's contract department prepared a slip with details, which went to the machine room, who prepared a proper contract note. This went to the client. In God's good time a transfer deed arrived from the broker who sold the shares – a foolscap sheet written in the grey tones of the law ('. . . hereinafter called the said Transferee' etc) – and this deed went off to the client. After the client had signed it and had it witnessed, back it went to the stockbroker. He sent it to the company whose shares they were; the company sent a transfer receipt, and later, perhaps much later, the transfer receipt was exchanged by the company for the share certificate, a pretty document which the client could keep in his safe – always assuming that by this time he hadn't sold the shares again. A man owns his shares from the moment his stockbroker buys them on the floor of the Stock Exchange. But a long paper tail wags behind each transaction, and if a man is buying and selling all the time, the situation is always a few jumps ahead of the paperwork.

Complications visible to the client are matched by complications within the Stock Exchange. Like the problem of how a newspaper arranges the type in its pages so as to make each column fit exactly, the way each purchase of shares is married to a corresponding sale seems too good to be true. Among the ten thousand shares quoted in London, there are in fact a number which may take months to find; but most shares keep coming on the market. In the active ones, a single day's business may mean a chain of buying-and-selling operations within the Exchange itself. Members, whether dealing for themselves or for their clients, may do dozens of transactions in the same shares within a few hours. A block of shares may pass quickly through the hands of a succession of speculators. It would be fantastically complicated to treat each of these transactions as a full-scale purchase, with all the attendant paperwork of contract notes and transfer deeds. So the Stock Exchange has an internal system which short-circuits the operation, and leaves the ultimate end-of-the-day buyer to collect his shares from whoever made the original sale. The members who have been involved in the intermediate stages sort out among themselves the marginal amounts of a few pence or shillings per share which are their profit or loss on the deals.

A large part of the equipment of a Stock Exchange firm seems to consist of ledgers, where men with steel pens scratch away endless entries. Though some partnerships have started hiring computers, mechanized accounting still has a long way to go in the smaller offices; while the central departments of the Exchange which coordinate business ran on clerk-power until mechanization began in 1960. Like British Railways, the Stock Exchange suffers from its early start in the field, from having grown rigid in its ways before the beginning of the century. 'It works,' said the office manager, 'but it's daft.'

Although the next ten years will see the systems of settlement and transfer simplified, the pleasures of antiquity tend to put a brake on progress. The Stock Exchange has no charter and no standing as a company or a public corporation; but like every City circle, it immediately communicates the whole weight of its tradition to the new member, making him wary of altering the way it works in case the magic is lost. Long after the second world war, the Exchange conformed to the stranger's idea of Olde England. By the early 1960s there were plans for a new Exchange to replace the existing structure – a building discreet to vanishing point, screened by an outer shell of insurance companies, shops, and blank walls, with small entrances and a warren of offices around the central trading floor. The visitor would notice prices chalked on boards, attendants called waiters (from the eighteenth-century coffee-house beginnings) dressed in picturesque clothes, and a surprising ignorance of the amount of business handled: the daily *Official List*'s itemizing of transactions in each share can be and usually is inaccurate, and in any case gives no indication of the *size* of transactions. The pre-reconstruction visitor would also observe poor ventilation, manually-operated lifts, and a fine collection of speaking tubes.

One curiosity is likely to be permanent – the jobbing system. It is, however, a very functional curiosity. The Stock Exchange has about 3,350 active (and 150 inactive) members, but only 2,600 are stockbrokers. The remainder, a body of men with, on the whole, sharper wits, are the stockjobbers. Jobbers don't deal with the public. They are the middlemen, the specialists, the dealers-in-shares on their own behalf instead of (like brokers) on behalf of clients. A broker will buy or sell any shares on request; a jobber deals in a specific variety – chemicals or industrials or stores or hire-purchase. Brokers live on commission (though the jam on the bread may come from speculation on their own behalf); jobbers operate as principals and live by taking a 'turn', a margin of profit between the price at which they buy and the price at which they sell. Within the Exchange is a tangled skein of dealing – broker to jobber, jobber to jobber, broker to broker. A little library research produces a picture of the typical small investor asking his broker to buy 500 Courtaulds (for some reason they always buy Courtaulds in the textbooks), the broker stepping briskly into the House, the jobber being approached, the deal being clinched, and the jobber being promptly approached by another broker with an order to buy 500 Courtaulds for *his* client to round it all off. It may be oversimplified, but the textbooks know what they're doing; to trace each deal as it splits into segments which become parts of other deals would be almost as dangerous to the reason as trying to follow specific banknotes as they pass in and out of a bank's tills. A large parcel of shares bought by a jobber may be broken into many smaller parcels before he's rid of it. All he cares about is to balance his 'book', to see that he is buying and selling roughly the same number of shares.

Jobbers spend most of their working day inside the Exchange, occupying the few square feet of paper-littered floor reserved for their market. When business is good they stand. When it isn't they sit on a polished wooden bench, fixed to one of the floor-to-ceiling pillars or set down like a small island in the open floor-space. Jobbers are there all day, waiting for something to happen – unlike brokers, some of whom never go near the inside of the Exchange. A few of these absentee brokers will be rolling middle-class stones who have been found a safe niche, or men of distinguished background brought in for prestige. Others will be senior stockbrokers who have something better to do than stand and trade – Authorized Clerks (that is, clerks who are authorized to deal in the Exchange) can do it just as well. These brokers spend their time in carpeted rooms behind doors marked *Partners Only*. The conscientious man will want to keep up with the deluge of chronicles, gazettes, guides, bulletins, charts, surveys, reports, and indices; someone has to compose the market slips, which are pamphlets for the grinding of investment axes, and there are the lengthy reviews of industries and companies to compile, with the aid of back-room statisticians, for wealthy clients. Some brokers specialize in handling and advising on share issues. Representatives of banks and discount houses look in for a chat and are looked up in turn so that 'City opinion', that interesting silt of rumour, gossip, half-truth, and intuition, can be kept well stirred. Keeping in touch is a semi-social routine, with clients who may be anything from the investment managers of insurance companies who think nothing of selling a million pounds worth of stock in an afternoon, down to that much-talked-about man of the sixties, the small investor. ('Frankly,' said Lord Ritchie, chairman of the Stock Exchange, in 1959,* 'if a man has £25, he has no business to buy stocks and shares. But if, after he has bought his house and taken out an insurance policy he has £100 to spare, he can write to the Secretary of the Stock Exchange and we shall be pleased to help him.' The small investor is not the most popular figure in the City. Brokers' commission varies with the price at which the share stands, and

* In an interview with the *Sunday Times*.

of course with the number dealt in. On a £50 deal in shares worth 12s. 6d. each, commission is 12s. 6d.; so the brokers' lack of enthusiasm is understandable. Firms have been known to refuse business where commission is less than £5.)

A jobber's office is more casual than a broker's – the bosses don't arrive there until after the House closes at 3.30. There are starchy jobbers, but not many. Their side of the dealing makes more intellectual demands than the brokers': the typical jobber is as sharp as a razor, with no time for standing on ceremony. Going on the Stock Exchange is regarded as a reasonably elegant way of earning a living, but the elegant thing to be is a broker rather than a jobber. Among 2,500 or so partner-members – the rest are 'associated' with firms without being partners – the roll of peers and honourables (younger sons of earls, and sons of all other peers below the rank of marquis) is small: any half-dozen merchant banks could better the twelve or thirteen peers which is all it can boast, together with seventeen or eighteen honourables. And even this small total of aristocrats goes mainly to the brokers: jobbers, with close on a quarter of the members, have to make do with two or three aristocrats out of thirty.

The essence of the jobbing system is that when the broker asks him to make a price, the jobber doesn't know if he is going to be asked to buy or sell. He can begin by refusing to deal, or widening the gap between his prices to a point at which he knows no one is going to do business. Assuming he wants to deal, he quotes the broker two prices: the lower the one at which he'll buy, the higher the one at which he'll sell. Having quoted the price, the jobber is compelled to deal as long as the quantity isn't unreasonable. Usually the broker will have indicated whether the deal is, in rising order, 'small', 'fairly big', 'large', 'lumpy', or 'a line'. If the broker is satisfied he says 'I buy' or 'I sell' whatever the quantity is. The jobber repeats it. Each writes it down in a tatty notebook, and the 'bargain' is complete. There are strict conventions. If no business results from the jobber's quote, he can say, 'I'm off', which wipes the slate clean, and they have to start again. The same thing happens if the broker walks away without dealing – he can't come back in ten minutes, having been comparing prices with the rest of the jobbers in that market, and carry on where he left off. Compromise, intuition, and leg-pulling, designed to trap the unwary broker into disclosing his intentions, are all elements in dealing, and everyone needs to be honest. The motto of the Stock Exchange is '*Dictum meum pactum*' – 'My word is my bond' – and opportunities for rascally fellows to pretend they said something else would, if many rascals were about, soon paralyse trading. The temptation to pretend they weren't there at all did in fact prove too strong for a small minority in 1959, one of the busiest years in the history of the Exchange, and resulted in the distressing business of the badges. Under such hectic conditions as those of the 1959 share boom, a throng of brokers and clerks around a jobber in a popular share can produce enough bedlam for a broker to say next day, if prices have moved against him and he has lost on the deal, that he didn't deal at all. There would be no point in denying a deal if it were on behalf of a client; it would have to be on one's own behalf. Clerks can't deal for themselves, which leaves the finger pointing at the members. Jobbers complained, and the result was that one morning in November, everyone appeared with regula-tion metal tabs in their lapels, each bearing the firm's name. 'Why not top hats with name bands?' one member asked bitterly. But a broker said one jobber had lost £6,000 since the start of the year as a result of deals that were denied by brokers when their clerks got together to compare notebooks in the Settling Room next morning. No member, even if he so wished, can take another member to law to enforce a claim: Rule 75(3) forbids it.

Stock Exchange publicity naturally doesn't go out of its way to mention such goings-on, and contrives to go to the other extreme by producing floods of alkaline solution to neutralize the acid of its critics. The foreword to a booklet called *The Stock Exchange: Some Questions and Answers* insists that 'the Stock Exchange is a national institution, standing apart from political controversy', which is a nice piece of wishful thinking. The basic premise of all the publicity, that the Exchange is simply a place in which to buy and sell shares, and that without this facility neither the State nor industry could be financed, is reasonable enough, except for the doctrinaire anti-capitalist. But the plain statements always come embedded in yards of self-justification. There is now a pleasant public gallery looking down on the floor of the Stock Exchange, with a small theatre attached in which a publicity film called *My Word Is My Bond* is shown free, six times a day. It was some time before I could see it because a general election was pending, and Conservative Association parties were turning up in strength. When I did get in one afternoon it was unfortunate that no sooner had the coloured curtains embroidered with the ubiquitous *Dictum Meum Pactum* folded back than the film broke – a party of schoolboys laughed delightedly, while a single young City man, bowler under his seat, stared in front with an expressionless face. It was also unfortunate that a minute later, before the film restarted, the door opened and a well-dressed middle-aged woman was seen arguing with one of the elegant young ladies in attendance. 'Would you mind coming out?' said the young lady. 'It happens to be full.' 'I suppose if I was a tourist from Soviet Russia it wouldn't matter,' said the woman in a furious voice. 'It's absolutely disgraceful!' The door thudded shut, the boys giggled, the City man gazed ahead, and a moment later the film came on – technically expert, with some clever camera-work and editing, but festooned with such dialogue as:

It looks like a market place.

That's exactly what it is!

Ye olde stockbrokers at Jonathan's Coffee House, *circa* 1760, were all right for a dash of colour, but the small investor's earnest admission at the end, 'I hadn't realized the Stock Exchange really is necessary,' and the close-ups, the music, the 'Word is my bond' routine, the vibration in the voice as it intoned 'This mutual trust . . . . A simple statement – so deep in moral obligation' all belonged to the most flaccid kind of TV commercial.

Individual brokers and jobbers, unless forced on the defensive, are more agreeable than their publicity. Shorn of the trimmings, a career on the Stock Exchange is seen as a straightforward means of earning a respectable living without necessarily being one of the City élite. About half the members begin as clerks; they pay, or their firm pays for them, an entrance fee of 500 guineas, and two partner-members must put up a £300 surety apiece for four years. The other half go in more expensively, buying membership outright; there is an entrance fee of 1,000 guineas, three four-year sureties of £500 and a nomination has to be purchased from a retiring member who himself used this way of getting in. There is a market in nominations, handled as a sideline by a couple of jobbers, and the price to a new member may be anything from £1, where a father is handing over to his son, to £2,000 when the Exchange is booming and demand is high. In the spring of 1959 nominations could be bought for less than £200; by the autumn, after six months of boom, they were costing up to £1,975, though a few weeks later they drifted down to the £1,600 mark. (In New York these would be regarded as giveaways: a Wall Street stock seat was sold for $160,000, more than £50,000, at the end of 1959.) Once elected, members pay an annual subscription of up to 180 guineas.

Stockbroking firms must have unlimited liability, which means they have to be partnerships or unlimited companies: Bloggs & Co., not Bloggs & Co. Ltd. Brokers and jobbers (like architects and doctors) often combine to form a service company that looks after office management, providing scope for ingenious loopholing by the accountants. For instance, the service company may charge the partnership a high rent for offices; this doesn't really cost the partners as much as might appear, since the money they pay in rent would otherwise be swallowed up in surtax – and with the rent, the company, which of course exists for the benefit of the partners, can supply them with all manner of comforts.

Another sign of strict professionalism is the absence of individual of advertising; no firm may advertise, and circulars may be sent only to clients. The Stock Exchange's *Notes for New Investors* catches the official flavour: 'The traditional way for an intending investor to get in touch with a Stockbroker is by personal introduction through a friend or acquaintance. This method has always seemed appropriate to the relationship between a Broker and his Client, which is essentially one of trust and confidence . . . . However, the Council is anxious that the services of the Stock Exchange should be available to all investors, whether large or small . . .' A list of fifteen firms, it says, is prepared each month. The Council will send it to anyone who asks, without singling out any firms for special mention. The American situation is looked on with a mixture of horror and amusement, with streaks of envy for the stockbroker's freedom to sell himself with this kind of flourish (from the *Wall Street Journal*): 'It's almost impossible for anybody to grade a broker good, better, or best until he's done business with one. Which is exactly what we're suggesting here – that you give us a try. We're willing to stand on the grade you give us.' British stockbrokers have to be content with prestige advertisements that publicize the Stock Exchange as a whole.

Professionally discreet but always in the news, occasionally poor by middle-class standards, usually comfortably off, sometimes rich, the broker or jobber is expected by the public to conform to certain characteristics. He should live in the stockbroker belt, not less than ten and not more than forty miles from Charing Cross: preferably to the west or south of London. 'Stockbroker Tudor' is a recognized style in large detached villas, and stockbroker country is usually and correctly thought of as Surrey. More than one-fifth of all brokers and jobbers live in the well-kept county of Surrey, which has an air of lawn-mowers and fresh paint, with neat fingerposts indicating storybook addresses like Seven Acres and Heather Farm. Ewell, Cheam, Woking, Esher, Guildford, and a dozen other places provide their morning contingents for the fast electric trains that run, from the counties south of London, the best suburban rail service in Europe.

It is further expected of the stockbroker that he shall study the newspapers on his way to the City and have a little private gamble. Again, he often comes up to expectations. It's open to anyone to speculate on the Exchange – as the apologists say, a broker is an agent who does what the public tell him. If there's a sordid scramble for shares, the broker is scrambling on behalf of the public. But although it's true that the retired schoolmaster who buys cheap in January and sells dear in December is a speculator, the opportunity and know-how for sustained speculation belong to a comparatively small circle, which of course includes the broker and jobber. It's true that most of the really big tax-free fortunes made in recent years – tax-free because they are capital gains – have gone to clever gentlemen outside the Exchange, using stock-market speculation as one of the routes to wealth (others have been property-dealing and take-overs). Inside the Exchange the prizes are generally more modest; and as members point out, there are capital losses as well as capital gains, not to mention the tax on short-term capital gains introduced in 1962.

Pure speculation involves a piece of business that remains on paper until the end of the operation, when the marginal difference between amounts in a ledger is translated into cash, and either collected or paid out. The speculator hopes for rising prices, and buys shares he has no intention of paying for; or he hopes for a fall, and sells shares he doesn't possess. In the first case he is a 'bull', in the second he is a 'bear' – the phrases 'bull market' and 'bear market' are extended to cover a rising and a falling market. Various technical devices help him perform this pocket-lining function of free markets everywhere, so natural to its practitioners, so strange and sometimes reprehensible to outsiders. The Exchange calendar is divided into fortnightly accounts, with an occasional one lasting three weeks. Bargains are paid for at the end of each account, so that within it a speculator can juggle about with purchases and sales, hoping that before the time comes to pay for what he has bought, or deliver what he has sold, prices will have moved and so enable him to undo the situation and emerge with a profit. If 1,000 shares are sold at a price of £1 each, and the speculator doesn't own the 1,000 shares, he must sooner or later buy and deliver them. If the price is falling, he may be able to buy them back at 19s. each before the account ends, leaving him with a profit of £50, less the expenses of doing the deals. Strong nerves are needed for large-scale speculation: to be caught 'short' of a share that rises in price instead of falling, or to be 'long' of a share that falls instead of rising, can be expensive and even ruinous. The bear runs more risk than the bull. The bull, who has bought and must pay, will never have to find more than the price of the shares. The bear, who has sold and must obtain shares, may, if he has misjudged the market, find the price soaring. But buy he must, however expensive they become; and the cost of getting even has broken more than one speculator. Jobbers, who continually find themselves in short and long positions – as a result of the system, not necessarily of speculation – need large resources, either in cash or in overdraft facilities with their banks, so that if their book fails to balance they can pay their way out of trouble. Traditionally, jobbers are men of enormous means; but forty years of heavy taxation has bled them. In a rising market, jobbers can hardly fail to make money, since the shares they take on their books are immediately unloaded at a profit; in a falling market they have to be exceedingly cunning to exploit the minor ups and downs within the major slide downward, and often lose heavily.

To aid the *cognoscenti* who find the fortnightly account too small to manoeuvre in, the process of 'contango' can be used. A man has bought shares; the end of the account approaches, but the shares have failed to rise as he hoped – or perhaps they have risen a little, and his natural cupidity restrains him from selling at a small profit when another week might turn it into a large profit. He finds someone, frequently a firm of jobbers, who will 'take in' the shares from the previous owner, paying for them and charging him interest (this is the contango – the origin of the term is obscure) till the end of the next account, when he pays for the shares – and, he hopes, matches this payment with a sale that gives him a profit large enough to offset the contango he has paid to the taker-in. The taker-in is using contango in the opposite direction. He is the bear, the man who has sold shares he doesn't possess, and at the end of the account can't, or prefers not to, buy for delivery. He uses the taken-in shares to tide him over to the end of the next account. When, as usually happens, there are more bulls than bears in search of contango facilities, the bull pays the interest; should bears be more numerous, then the bears have to pay. The rate for contango can rise to more than 10 per cent.

The man who wants cash for speculating may be accommodated by a straight loan from a stockbroker, who in turn is borrowing it from his bank from account to account. Five per cent is the least an ordinary member of the public ever pays a bank on his overdraft, but the broker can get terms which enable him to lend it out below 5 per cent and still make a profit. The bank, needless to say, holds the shares as security.

The best time to be a speculator is during a bull market, when buyers predominate and prices rise steadily. The London bull market of 1959 made many investors feel it was good to be alive. The textile firm of Boardman Marden had the privilege of heading the list, with a 535 per cent rise in its shares, though this was exceptional. Steel shares rose 160 per cent, car shares 100 per cent; newspapers, stores, plastics, and textiles averaged up to 80 per cent. At 9.30 on the October morning after the Labour Party had conceded victory to the Conservatives in the general election, brokers and jobbers were milling round the doors of the Exchange; coats were torn as they surged in, and presently a queue formed from Throgmorton Street leading to the public gallery as word went round that the floor of the House had to be seen to be believed. Brokers crowded jobbers, forcing them on to seats, where they stood, sweating and happy, as orders to sell at a profit and buy for a bigger one flooded in. Steel shares, freed from the fear that the steel industry might be renationalized if Labour won, had £60,000,000 added to their value within an hour. It was pandemonium, and if you had your fingers in the honey it was lovely. A year or two later, when shares slumped badly, fingers were burned and fists were shaken at the unkindness of the gods. And then there was the wickedness of the Government in actually taxing short-term speculation. But this was all in the game – even the waves of selling that hit the market in the Spring of 1962. As long as there's a Stock Exchange, somebody, somewhere is making a nice little profit.

PORTRAIT OF A SPECULATOR

In the autumn of 1959 I got to know a speculator, a pleasant middle-aged industrialist called, let's say, Nicholas Nickleby. Mr Nickleby is broad-shouldered, with a cheerful, open face, an indestructible optimism, and an air of complete concord with his job and his times. Whenever anyone talks about Stock Exchange booms or about 'the role of the speculator in society', I think of Mr Nickleby. Mr Nickleby is not very strong on the role of Mr Nickleby in society. He comes from an indigent middle-class family who launched him with £25, made his first money by opening a small factory during the war and selling his business ten years later for £250,000, and regards himself as a technician, as a 'product man', not a financier. He moves in and out of syndicates, those informal clusters of men with money to spare who each chip in and buy an hotel or a factory, or, more ambitiously, an old and moribund company with old and moribund directors who want to save themselves from surtax (see page 32) and their families from death duties. He moves on the fringe of modest take-overs, of deals and bids and consultations with expensive lawyers, though his name never appears in the papers. He likes making money but has none of the marks of greed, being willing to waste time talking about tax, golf, salesmanship, industry, people, and even, without envy, about the money that some of his more money-conscious associates make by playing the market.

I met him first in his Holborn office as a director of company X. By the last visit he had resigned from company X because it was becoming involved in take-over offers and counter-offers, and he wanted to try his luck elsewhere; but he continued to sit in the same chair behind the same desk because he was a director of company Z, which had a smaller brass plate somewhere between the street and the dark-panelled offices which looked a cross between a cocktail bar and a bank. September sunshine slanted through the branches of a plane tree in the square outside; 1959 in Britain was one of the finest summers of the century, a fact that must have aided the market by making investors that much more cheerful. One or two eccentric speculators are said to exploit the state of the weather, getting in first thing in the morning with buying orders if the day is going to be fine, with selling orders if the rain is pelting down, and so anticipating share movements. Mr Nickleby thought that was a silly idea. This is the Nickleby system – so simple, as he said, a child could use it:

I buy three thousand of this and a couple of thousand of that. When they go up two shillings or something like that, I sell 'em. Certain shares I keep, like British Motor, Tube Investments, Stewart and Lloyds, Shell, B.P.s – they give me dividends and I know in the long run they'll be higher. Sometimes I use my loaf. I was walking down Regent Street and I saw people carrying light suit-cases, going for holidays in all this hot weather, so I hunted round and found the people who make Revelation suit-cases, called W. Wood. By the time I found out, the shares were ten shillings. I watched them and they went to twelve shillings. I bought them and now they're at fourteen shillings. If they go to fifteen shillings I shall sell.

But he said this was small stuff beside a friend of his who played the market for 4 per cents. For two years, said Mr Nickleby, this friend of his worked hard on the end of a telephone, aiming to make 4 per cent on every share every week. His friend made £100,000, mainly on a single share that was rocketing up, which gave him a good start in the take-over business.

Mr Nickleby, Mr Four Per Cent, and some others had chipped in a few years back to buy up a Midlands company managed by an ageing board. It was part of a run-down industry, and the directors had been reluctant to plough money back into the business. They bought Government stock – and because this has been an unhappy market, saw £400,000 worth lose £50,000 in two years. The syndicate bought them out cheap, sold off the machinery and buildings, and started putting a variety of companies, making boots, paper, chemicals, and many other goods, into the empty shell – which had the advantage of an existing Stock Exchange quotation (see page 100), thus avoiding the trouble and expense of applying for a new one.

Mr Nickleby had the pleasure of seeing his personal share-holding in the revitalized master company become more valuable each week – he had a small slice of forty thousand shares. Some valuable companies were brought in by the time-honoured method of finding a private firm that doesn't know what to do with its profits. A private company – one where the shares are held by a handful of directors, probably most of them in one family, instead of dispersed among a large number of shareholders – has trouble with surtax as soon as it makes a profit. If the profit is distributed as a dividend to shareholders, it simply loops through the books and arrives back in the directors' bank accounts, where most of it is swallowed up by the higher and hated form of income tax, surtax. If the profit isn't distributed but left to swell the corpus of the company, the Revenue can direct the company itself to pay surtax, which leaves the directors just as badly off. Such directors are often only too glad to exchange their share-holdings for a lump sum, non-taxable, plus service contracts for a salary at the level of their previous income. One of the companies so absorbed, said Mr Nickleby, was making £200,000 profit a year. 'They wanted to declare £30,000 a year dividend but the Revenue said "No, that's not enough, you must pay another £70,000 in dividends" – and of course it all goes to the proprietors, who are already receiving £4,000 or £5,000 in salary. It means that £50,000 of the extra £70,000 declared in dividends goes in surtax.' When the syndicate bought them out, the directors continued as before – except, added Mr Nickleby, rubbing the side of his nose, that they had gained as a lump sum an income that would have taken them the rest of this life and part of the next to earn. And they all had new Rolls-Royces – the directors had insisted. Mr Nickleby added as an aside that one came to expect the perks of industry. 'When I go to play golf,' he said, 'I make sure the chap who works the boilers comes along and carries my clubs and cleans them afterwards, as part of his duties to the firm. That's a very nice gift from you and the other taxpayers, isn't it? It's a perk.'

Although the syndicate paid more than £500,000 for this particular bargain, it didn't have to produce such a sum – syndicates never do. The bank loaned most of it, against the security of shares in the master company. ('If you're successful in business you can get all the money you want. It's if you're a second-class firm you have a hell of a time.') The taken-over company contained several hundred thousand pounds, in cash and investments, and the difference between these and the price paid was immediately offset when the shares in the master company rose in value, in response to the injection of a new source of steady profits. Shares fluctuate in response to many things, from weather and the state of international politics to interest rates and the economic outlook; the immediate profits and prospects of a company are the largest single element in assessing the value of its shares, and a simple calculation put a new value on the master company's shares. As Mr Nickleby said approvingly, 'The financial people in the City are very quick.' He did a lightning calculation in his head, and explained that when the City realized another company with a £200,000 profit was being added, it was (he assured me) worth their offering 17s. 6d. for a 5s. share.

For nothing in Mr Nickleby's world stands still, and before I met him the master company had been in turn taken over by another group. This group made its offer one afternoon when a director of a small firm of merchant bankers arrived with a letter for the master-company directors, who between them still held a large block of stock. The directors recommended shareholders to sell, and accepted the offer for themselves; two of the directors collected about £300,000 for their shares, and Mr Nickleby came out with more than £20,000. The new group had grown around a 'shell' company – a company with assets but not engaged in trading. It had been part of one of the industries nationalized by Labour after the war, and, equipped with a core of cash provided in compensation, and a Stock Exchange quotation, had gone from strength to strength. On the face of it Mr Nickleby and his friends might have appeared to be still in charge, just as, a few rungs down the ladder, the bought-out and service-contracted directors of component companies might appear to clients to be still in charge. By amalgamating companies and showing good profits, by meeting the public demand for plenty of industrial shares that could yield a good profit if the boom went on, Mr Nickleby's syndicate had laid hands on shares that multiplied in value within a year or two. The new group, whose offer had helped to push up the price of shares, hoped to benefit in the same way – pumping in companies, raising profits, seeing the value of the shares inflate still further. Yet another group, when I was seeing Mr Nickleby, was bidding to take over the group that had taken over the syndicate that had taken over the Midlands company and the rest. It was like an aquarium full of predatory fish. Mr Nickleby spoke guardedly of a couple of offers that were in the air, and the next time I saw him he had resigned his directorship. It was no wonder that a City journalist who rang up while I was there talked at cross-purposes for a few minutes, before realizing that he was one take-over behind the times.

Perhaps 'speculator' is the wrong word to use for Mr Nickleby. He thought it was: under the prevailing prosperous conditions, it was child's play to sit on the end of a telephone that bypassed the office exchange – in case of an indiscreet operator – and do a little successful business, coupling this with the meaty rewards of profiting in shares whose price you yourself helped control. It was like the case of a small piece of property in the West End that another of his syndicates had bought with £8,000 of their own and £30,000 they borrowed from the bank. I said I had always thought banks were reluctant to lend money for speculation. 'Speculation?' said Mr Nickleby with patient contempt. 'Who's talking about speculation? You can always borrow money on property – it's the universal lending unit, and it gets more valuable every year.'

On my last visit to Mr Nickleby we went to have lunch at one of his clubs, and he told me he had just 'done myself for a clot by selling my Stewart and Lloyds too soon': if he had held on to these steel shares for another few weeks, he would have made £1,000 more than he *did* make. 'It's as I told you,' he said, 'I'm a product man, not a financier.' He ate and drank modestly, and we had coffee in the big lounge, with coal fires and heavy leather furniture. A property magnate I had met the previous week, a young Jew, sat in the far corner on a sofa, smoking a cigar that looked too big for him and talking respectfully to an older man. I said I had one final question. I had been to see the managing director of an important firm (it was Sir Frederic Hooper of Schweppes, the soft-drink and jam makers), and he had told me to rid my mind of the idea that industry and commerce were the ruthless activities that the innocent supposed. Sir Frederic had read an article I had written about a B.B.C. documentary programme describing a take-over – I thought it was an outstanding programme, and in reviewing it I talked about 'greed, hate, cunning, and even bloody-mindedness' in industry, which was perhaps laying it on. That view, said Sir Frederic, could only be founded on ignorance of what really happened. He invited me to look around the Schweppes organization, which I did, finding everything impeccable and slightly dull. I put it to Mr Nickleby that *his* picture of British business, while not composed of greed, hate, cunning, and bloody-mindedness, was somewhat different from the other man's. 'Well, naturally,' said Mr Nickleby. 'There are all different sorts. Personally I think it's a jungle and they'll eat you.' He said it without menace or fear. When he wished me good-bye at a quarter past two, after marching back to another of his offices, he looked as if he was bursting with the joy of living.

THE GILT-EDGED MARKET, OR HOW TO BORROW £19,000,000,000

Shares worth £50,833,363,550 were quoted in London at 31 March, 1961. More than half this sum was represented by Ordinary stock ('stock' and 'share' in common usage mean virtually the same thing), and the odd few thousand million pounds were in loan or preference stock, held by investors with a first claim on their companies' profits but drawing a fixed rate of interest instead of a variable dividend. All these were the borrowings of industry. Following at a distance came the borrowings of the Government, which under the heading of 'British

Government and Government-guaranteed stocks' amounted to £14,899,000,000. The humble citizen's traditional dread of debt turns into *annoyance* at debt higher up the social scale, while at the exalted level of Government borrowing there are never any naïve ideas about making ends meet. The £14,899,000,000 is only a part of Government debt. The nominal value of the stock, the face value of £100 per unit at which (within a few per cent) it had been paid for, and at which much of it would have to be ultimately repaid, was £19,213,000,000. And Government borrowing by issues of stock is only one aspect of that strange and apparently limitless burden, the National Debt, which was calculated by the wise men of the Radcliffe Committee to be close on £31,000,000,000 net. Several thousand millions came under Treasury bills, which are short-term I.O.U.s issued weekly (Chapter 3). National Savings added more thousands of millions, and so did notes and coin – representing a debt of the Bank of England – and overseas loans and loans to local authorities; but far the largest item was Government stock – 'gilt-edged' or 'gilts' or 'the Funds'.

The gilt-edged market has an air of special dignity, though quantities of mud have been slung at it in recent years, and some disappointed investors have renamed their sagging stocks guilt-edged. Whether the stock is dated, with a definite date or period when it will be repaid at its face value, or undated, when it represents a perpetual loan, it bears a fixed rate of interest. But since rates of interest are inconstant, varying both nationally and internationally over any period, the constant factor is found in the yield – the relation between the interest on the piece of stock and the price it costs in the market. The interest is fixed, so it's the price that must vary. The higher interest rates of the 1950s, 5 per cent and more, pushed down the value of gilt-edged stock that had been issued when rates were as low as $2\frac{1}{2}$ per cent. Stock worth £100 has fallen in some cases to less than £50. There have been other disappointments in gilt-edged. The machinations of governments, Left and Right, have been loudly damned. 'Swindle', 'daylight robbery', and 'taken for a ride' have become routine invective. Angry or pathetic letters have told of the plight of widows, clergymen, and retired colonels who put their money in the Government. Apologists have pointed out that what the protests are about is inflation, not any act of callous swindling (though the Labour Government's post-war issue of Treasury 2½ per cent stock, the 'infamous Daltons', as part of a deliberate cheap-money policy that involved rigging the market to make the 2½ per cent acceptable, finds few defenders among financial journalists). But whether or not the words 'gilt-edged' have become odious to family solicitors and retired gentle-folk, the market goes ahead at full blast. Once, the Consol market – another of its names, from Consolidated Stock, still in issue – was the one safe receptacle for savings. In recent years insurance companies and other institutions with customers' money to invest have begun to treat high-class Ordinary shares as investments that aren't likely to explode and scorch the unwary. But Government stock remains a basic investment for every bank, insurance company, pension fund, and industrial undertaking. Nowhere else can such large sums be funnelled into the Stock Exchange, or stock be translated back into cash, without clogging the system and causing prices to fluctuate sharply.

In the gilt-edged market a million pounds worth of stock is moved around as casually as a sixpenny bit. One of the gilt-edged jobbers – traditionally among the wealthiest in the Exchange – gave this general view of the market:

Pension funds, insurance companies, and building societies are getting enormous sums in every week, and it's a question of finding an outlet. At the moment people want to buy Ordinary shares, but eventually they get limited – besides, you can't invest a million pounds all at once in Imperial Tobacco, you just can't do it – and if they have enough money to invest they have to come to our market eventually. Then there is your ordinary selling for people who want to buy pro-perty or go into other stocks, and then of course people keep track of the relative positions of all these gilt-edged stocks, and the moment two of them get out of line, the professional buys one and sells another. He'll pop out and back again in a week or two's time and make a profit on it – there's a lot of that goes on. Then there are those people who want to avoid receiving a dividend because of taxation. They sell

one stock cum dividend – that is, whoever buys it buys the right to collect the dividend – and buy back the same amount of another stock
when it's gone ex dividend, as it does some time before the dividend is
due. When it goes ex dividend it drops slightly in price because the
dividend has gone out of it. If the stock was standing at ninety seven and
a half, rather than wait and see the stock down to ninety five, they'll sell
it at ninety seven and a half and buy it back at ninety five. They collect
two and a half per cent tax free instead of two and a half subject to tax.*

I said I grasped the point of the operation, to translate income
into capital gain, but that I didn't see who was going to be kind
enough to buy the stock cum dividend and so attract the tax that
the seller was avoiding. It was easy, said the jobber: sell it to
something like a pension fund that doesn't pay tax on income.
If you paid a lot of tax, he added, it was natural to want cheap
stock with a low rate of interest, redeemable at some not too
distant time. Why should an oil company, say, wish to put money
in Treasury $3\frac{1}{4}\%$ 1977/1980, standing at 77 that morning? It was
because in another twenty years it would collect £23 tax free on
every £77 it invested now; you could, he added, build tankers
like that.

As for the business of popping in and out of Government
stocks, known as switching, he said this was practised on such
a scale that it was maddening to have so many professionals
watching the market. There were two varieties of switching.
One arose as a result of taking a view of the market. You might
consider that interest rates were likely to rise, that Bank Rate
was about to go up; if it did, this would depress the price of
existing stock, and the longer the stock had to run before redemption, the more it would be pushed down. So with this view
of the market a man would switch into bonds – short-dated stock.
The other kind of switching arose when one of two or more
similar stocks, which in theory should be worth the same amount,
rose or fell in price as a result of massive trading. By changing
quickly from one stock to another, the switcher could translate
this ephemeral margin into a profit. In certain cases, when a sale

* 'Bond-washing', which is illegal though so far unstoppable, is more
complicated in practice, but the principle is as described.

of one stock is matched by the purchase of another, no commission need be paid to the stockbroker on the second deal, the one that closes the position. Stockbrokers maintain beautifully kept charts and files, the pride of the back-room analysts, giving the history of gilt-edged stocks in various combinations, so that past performance can be compared and future trends estimated. A fractional deviation brings out the folders and calculating tables, and three minutes later, if the margin is sufficient to cover overheads, firms are racing to be first with the order; half an hour later the stocks are back in step.

The twenty or so firms of gilt-edged jobbers, dealing in such large sums, face the additional complication that, at least in theory, deals in Government stock are for cash. In practice no jobber, now that jobbers' fortunes have dwindled, could run a book of millions of pounds unless he was able to borrow stock when necessary. There are brokers who arrange these facilities, while, as a last resort, operating generally as a buyer of stock, there is always someone to fall back on: the father-figure of the gilt-edged market, in a sense the father-figure of the whole Exchange, the calm, top-hatted City dignitary known as the Government Broker.

The appointment is held by an individual, usually the senior partner at the stockbroking firm of Mullens & Co., with its offices in Moorgate, a few steps from the Bank of England. Mr William John Herbert de Wette Mullens is the present Broker, a large man with an impressive manner and a distinguished war record. The Mullens family has been in the City a long time – a William Mullens was Cashier of the Bank of England from 1795 to 1814. His official title is Broker to the Commissioners for the Reduction of the National Debt, a body which has given up the unequal struggle and calls itself the National Debt Commissioners. For this he receives the modest fee, all things considered, of £2,000 a year. In effect he is broker to the Bank of England, the Government's bank, which conducts its massive buying and selling of gilt-edged through him. He peddles out remaining amounts of recent issues, at the same time buying back stock as it approaches maturity, so as to lessen disturbance when the time comes to pay out. He supports the market by buying for the Bank, if this happens to be Bank policy, and everything from the appearance of a line of stock via one of his dealers to the expression on his face as he enters the Stock Exchange is news. As agent of the Bank in a central position Mr Mullens is probably the most *noticed* individual in the City. But Mr Mullens, though kind to the Press, is appalled at the idea of being quoted. There is a certain regretfulness about him. In the summer of 1961, when the amended Trustee Bill became law, trustees became entitled to invest half their funds in Ordinary shares, instead of being restricted to gilt-edged. Embittered with their experience of gilts, a number of trustees transferred their money into industrials, and pushed share prices up 4½ per cent in a couple of days. It was the sort of thing that must sadden Mr Mullens.

SHADOW OF THE S.E.C.

The first time I heard the American Securities and Exchange Commission mentioned was in the office of a senior stock-jobber who was ridiculing it and saying it would never do for the City. He called it 'the Exchange Control Commission or some such thing' and said that in the matter of new issues of stock, which he was discussing at the time, it would be an awful old nuisance. Once word of an attractive issue leaks out, the price of the old stock is pushed down by the prospect of the new. 'In America,' he said, 'you've got to give chapter and verse and photograph-of-the-chairman sort of thing. Now, we'd regard that as fatal because of keeping it dark.'

The more people I met in the City, the more central this idea of discretion appeared to be – and the more I kept hearing the Securities and Exchange Commission referred to as the last thing the City wanted. What exactly it is that the City wants, or needs, in the way of reform was increasingly discussed as the 1950s brought more small investors within the orbit of the Stock Exchange. The idea of popular investment, whether direct or through unit trusts, began to soak through to the public, to such an extent that early in 1960 the *Daily Mirror*, the largest-selling daily in the country, abandoned its total neglect of the City apart from the occasional wisecrack about port-and-pheasant bankers, and broke new ground with a strip cartoon called *Keeping Up with the Joneses*. This told a moral tale of Joe and Prue, a young married couple waking up to the great world of investments. From regarding his well-heeled friends with innocence ('He's a financial *genius* from upstairs, Uncle, *and makes a mint on the Stock Exchange* – or so he says'), Joe moved through many tribulations until August 1961, by which time the *Daily Mirror* had decided that the public, keen on investment though it might be, wasn't prepared to stomach Joe and Prue indefinitely. On 11 August Joe was going through a bad patch. By 18 August he'd invented the Wedgeclamp scaffold clip. By 23 August he was demanding – and getting – £2,000 for the patent. Next day he was offered a job as 'consultant' with a salary of £1,750. And on 26 August, equipped with bowler and rolled umbrella, he and family were walking off into what was meant to be a sunset, though it looked remarkably like a nuclear explosion. Prue, wheeling a pram, looks proudly at umbrella and bowler, and says: 'The status symbols of the man who's caught up with the Joneses at last!'

Unfortunately most investors fail to stumble on anything as useful as the Wedgeclamp scaffold clip. What the ordinary small investor needs is protection from the wolves and a lot of good advice. This old truth became increasingly apparent with the spate of post-war take-overs, the mushrooming of finance companies with their seductive promise of high interest on deposits, and the crop of get-rich-quick companies, particularly property companies. So no one was particularly surprised when the Jenkins Committee, a committee of inquiry under Lord Jenkins, was set up in 1959 to report on the Companies Act and the Prevention of Fraud (Investments) Act, and to consider the whole field of take-overs, directors' duties, and shareholders' rights. With so much ground to cover, it was June, 1962, before the committee reported; when it did, the City breathed more freely, since for the moment the threat of a British S.E.C. was removed.

The Securities and Exchange Commission was set up by Congress in 1934 as an aftermath of the Wall Street crash of 1929. (And also, it is said, with political motives: the Democrats wanted to keep the Republican Party, with its big-business associations, permanently in the dock.) It operates in nine regional and eight branch offices throughout the United States, administering laws for the protection of investors, and disseminating much sound advice to the public ('WARNING TO INVESTORS!' cries the cover of a pamphlet explaining what the S.E.C. does, listing such dangers as 'strange securities firms', 'high-pressure sales talk', 'promises of spectacular profits', and 'tips and rumours'.) Shares not quoted on a stock exchange but dealt in 'over the counter' – this can't be done in Britain – escape the S.E.C. The Commission is concerned with quoted securities, which are covered by the Securities Exchange Act (1934) and the Securities Act (1933). Solicitation of votes, for instance, must be accompanied by 'all material facts concerning the proposals upon which [shareholders] are asked to vote': enough to drive British take-over bidders to despair.

City resistance to the idea of an S.E.C. is not altogether because individual provisions are disliked. For instance: an important section of the Securities Exchange Act seeks to curb improper use of inside information, by compelling directors of a company with shares listed on a stock exchange, and any others who own more than 10 per cent of the shares, to file monthly reports with the Commission and the stock exchange, detailing their holdings and any change in them. Any profits they obtain from selling-and-buying or buying-and-selling within a six-month period can be recovered by the company. The same people are forbidden to sell their companies' shares short – to sell 'bears' of stock they don't possess. In Britain, the idea of at least forcing owners of shares to declare their interest to the company, and not hide behind registration of shares under nominee names, has been proposed in the past. Disclosure by everyone holding more than *one* per cent of shares was suggested before the 1948 Companies Act was drafted, but the banks and stockbrokers who run the nominee companies ('front' companies, with uninformative titles and no clue as to whom they represent) protested so loudly at the extra work involved that the idea was dropped. When the more manageable American figure of 10 per cent was proposed, it was pointed out that with such a large figure it would be perfectly possible for a modest sized syndicate to by-pass the regulations by allocating 9·9 per cent of the shares to each member. Still, the idea is there, and will no doubt turn into a law one day.

No: the real, sustained objection to a British S.E.C. seems to be a new version of the old fear that officialdom will start meddling. Jobbers say that if transactions are publicized on the American scale, the system will break down. 'What we're afraid of', said one jobber, 'is that we'd have to disclose our positions. If the fact that I'm short of fifty thousand I.C.I. is known, other jobbers dealing in the same stock may be tempted to take advantage. Even the fact that jobbers in general are short of I.C.I. will bring the speculators in to make the agony a little bit worse.' As it is, so little definite information is available in London that even the overall total of transactions is unknown: apart from a few categories, there is no rule making it compulsory to mark bargains on the slips provided. Further, the list shows only one mark at any specific price, however many slips are put in for bargains at that figure. When at busy times 30,000 or more bargains are announced for the previous day, the true figure is thought to be at least 50 per cent higher.

New issues are another area where vague fears exist that bureaucracy might trample on custom. Flotation of a public company is the point where mugs can be most easily relieved of their money, and British regulations are devised to protect the applicant for shares in a new company. But are the regulations sufficiently strong? Opinion is sharply divided. In defence of the present system, no one suggests it bears any resemblance to the shambles of the 1920s, when the Stock Exchange still clung to the notion that its function was to provide a market for securities, not to inquire into their merits. Seen from the Stock Exchange's Share & Loan Department, the rules governing permission to deal are perfectly adequate. A new issue may be handled by an issuing house or by a stockbroker – roughly speaking, major issues are looked after by issuing houses, minor ones by brokers, but there is strong competition for the overlap, and bad feeling often results. Whether or not the company employs an issuing house, a firm of stockbrokers will act as go-between with the Exchange, and a representative goes before a panel of the Quotations Committee. Then (if the issue is a large one and the usual method is employed) a prospectus is drawn up by the lawyers, a report on the company is prepared by the accountants, and the material is sent to the Share & Loan, who may follow up with a request for more details about directors, assets, overdrafts, tax, salaries, profits, dividends and anything else they think germane. The Records Department, which has files on companies and directors available to Exchange members, and a strictly classified rogues' gallery for the eyes of a few officials, comments on the prospectus; so do the Legal and Document departments. If everything is in order, the broker to the issue arranges for the prospectus to appear in two morning papers, forty-eight hours before the Quotation Committee meets to consider the application – this allows time for any newspaper reader to write with unflattering particulars of the company or its directors, though the advertisement doesn't solicit such information. What the prospectus – generally a full page of tiny type – must include is a statement that application has been made for a Stock Exchange quotation; pending the success of the application, all money received from the public must be lodged in a separate bank account, ready to be returned if anything goes wrong. This last requirement is made by the 1948 Companies Act, but the actual vetting of issues is left to the Exchange itself: neither the Board of Trade nor any other Government department intervenes. The Cohen Committee on Company Law Amendment, in a passage proudly quoted by the Share & Loan, said the flexibility of self-regulation by the Stock Exchange 'makes it possible for the rules to be more stringent and to afford the investor a greater measure of security than could be achieved by a statute except at the cost of hampering legitimate business'. The S.E.C., so a former Secretary of the Share & Loan told the Institute of Bankers, is 'a giant bureaucracy, controlling investment from Washington – and if you have had any experience of reading American prospectuses you will, I think, agree with me that though everything is set out there, the length is so inordinate that very few people read and digest the information'. He thought the British method, with its greater flexibility, took 'every possible precaution to see that no known rogue or person with a doubtful reputation has managed to smuggle himself into an issue'. After the quotation has been granted, the Share & Loan keeps watch on the company, having secured guarantees: to be told of changes in directors or nature of business, to see proofs of circulars to shareholders before despatch, to be given all information useful to shareholders, and so on. But none of this is backed by statute, and the system's critics say that flexibility can be a synonym for loopholes.

The standards of the Share & Loan are not as exacting as the standards of leading brokers; and there will always be some brokers content with the bare minimum. 'Fairly often', said a leading new-issue broker, 'we see companies that we've refused to handle being handled by other brokers who don't object. The trouble is that the Stock Exchange Council work by exhortation rather than insistence – and if we aren't careful we shall end up with an S.E.C.' Normally there is no need for an *independent* accountant to report on a company; some brokers insist on it, others don't. The Share & Loan want to know that stocks of goods have been valued on a consistent basis, but some brokers insist, reasonably enough, that it must be made clear whether the goods are readily saleable, or whether they would fetch only knock-down prices. An acceptable accountants' report may conceal tax liabilities. The estimate of future profits may be too optimistic (though under the Companies Act this can lead to gaol). Another broker said: 'The trouble is that very often no brief is given the accountants. *We* won't allow a property company to take account of rents not actually being received, but it's we who must give the direction on the matter. There've been some panic regulations in the past year or so because of all the new property companies, but a lot of it's applied in a half-hearted way.'

Laissez-faire in company regulation generally has been attacked by Ted Leather, a Conservative Member of Parliament: a Canadian by birth, connected with insurance in the City, who knows more about finance than most M.P.s. Leather has advocated a British S.E.C.; one of his complaints is that a situation may arise in a company where the authorities say: 'You're right, this is deplorable, but we can do nothing about it.' This absence of power of adequate censure short of criminal prosecution by the police – a power granted the S.E.C. – is something which strikes all but the most extreme flexibility-men. Leather, who says that 'high finance is no longer a game played by gentlemen who went to the right school and learned the rules', told me: 'The traditional view is that the Stock Exchange Council will say, "We must be satisfied that the information put to us is true. We will go as far as we can to see that this board is made up of honest men, but it would be presumptuous of us to go further than that."' He gave the instance of a company that got into the wrong hands. 'It was wound up in the war, and ended up as a few bits of paper with the articles of association in the vaults of X's bank. Three years ago someone came along and bought it for £1,000, changed the name, pumped in a lot of flats and houses, applied for a quotation, was granted it, and away he went. Knowing the circumstances of the individuals concerned, this seemed to me exactly what I'd been talking about, so I wrote to the Stock Exchange and asked why they approved it. They sent me masses of detail, and said the prospectus was returned several times for more information, studied very carefully, and revised by the Share & Loan Department. They said that to go beyond that and refuse to put their *imprimatur* on the ability of this company to manage property was not their business.' And since then, the company had landed itself in trouble.

People who alleged that a crook could get anything past the Stock Exchange didn't know what they were talking about, concluded Leather. But the Exchange must 'get beyond the stage of saying that all it provides is a market place. It's the traditional concept, and a perfectly honest one for the auctioneer, but circumstances have changed too much. Every year there are thousands of new investors. The new situation carries responsibilities which the Stock Exchange wants to avoid as long as possible – and meanwhile they are making an overwhelming case for an S.E.C.'

Evidence about the S.E.C. was heard by the Jenkins Committee, but in the event there was no question of its recommending an S.E.C. for Britain. In 1959 the City had been having some bad publicity, particularly as a result of the British Aluminium take-over (Chapter 5) and some property scandals. By 1962, the scandal had lost its edge, and the City seemed in for a more respectable phase. An S.E.C. remains a strong possibility one day. In the meantime the Jenkins Report took note of some criticisms. Company reports, it suggested, should be more forthcoming. So should take-over offers to share-holders. And compulsory disclosure of a nominee holding in a company of 10 per cent or more (see pp. 42–43) was proposed. On the whole, the City got off lightly.

THE OUTSIDE BROKERS

Unlike the United States, where there is a large over-the-counter trade in shares not quoted on a stock exchange, security dealing in Britain is almost entirely channelled through the London Stock Exchange and its smaller brethren in the provinces. If business from members of the public doesn't reach the stock-broker direct it will be passed on to him by a bank manager or a solicitor: or by a group of firms with the melancholy nickname of Outside Brokers. These firms are the respectable successors to the bucket-shop days when security dealing was frequently a pastime for the con-man, the spacious era before the Prevention of Fraud (Investments) Act gave the Board of Trade the power to exempt or license (and refuse to exempt or license) dealers who aren't covered by membership of a stock exchange. Exempted dealers include most banks, issuing houses, pension funds, in-surance companies, trustee savings banks, and other concerns which are constantly dealing in securities on their own behalf. Licences are granted, for a year at a time, to about thirty firms, which for a variety of reasons want to be able to deal. None of the exempted dealers, and few of the licensed dealers, act as intermediaries between public and stockbroker – they go to stockbrokers and issuing houses to buy and sell shares for their own account. But the Outside Brokers, officially the Association of Stock and Share Dealers, are in business as middlemen; they use their dealers' rights to buy shares wholesale, then re-sell in small lots to the public. Outside Brokers bring much business to stock exchanges; but mention of them causes some stockbrokers to look distant or irritable, in the manner of doctors being forced to notice osteopaths. This brings a certain sadness into the Outside Brokers' life.

The association has a general council and the excellent address of 11 Ironmonger Lane, in the City, which is the address of Peat, Marwick, Mitchell & Co., the accountants. Since members are allowed to advertise, and generally use circular letters to contact clients, great care must be taken if no one is to accuse them of the heinous sin of share-pushing, which means, when carried to criminal lengths, that reckless statements are made about a share in order to gull the public. Between a reckless statement that would bring in the Fraud Squad, and the neutral purveying of shares, are perfectly legal recommendations of the snap-this-up-now variety which cause a pursing of lips and writing of letters by association officials. Outside Brokers will do business as agents for clients, instructing stockbrokers and passing on the stockbrokers' commission charges (often concealed in the net price of the shares); but split commissions aren't allowed, and this work is generally unprofitable. The real money is to be made by acting as principal: buying a cheap line of stock from a stockbroker, or if it's a new share from an issuing house, recommending it in a mild sort of way in a circular, and hoping that sufficient orders will come in. The first essential is to have a large amount of stock at a price below the market level, so that it can be supplied reasonably to clients; and jobbers with stock on their books are sometimes glad to be able to ring up an Outside Broker and offer it. Since jobbers are forbidden to deal with the public, the Outside Broker, if he wants the stock, replaces his receiver and waits patiently till an excited stockbroker, who *can* deal with the public, rings up ten minutes later to say he has just purchased a line from a jobber, and would the outside man happen, by some coincidence, to be interested?

To see the chairman of the association I went to Upper Grosvenor Street, in Mayfair, where Mr Philip G. Smith, referred to around the office as 'the Major', is managing director of the long-established firm of George Brodie & Co. Ltd. Thirty (of fifty) member firms are in London, and several, like this one, are in the West End and not the City. Mr Smith, a handsome and agreeable man in black coat and striped trousers, said regretfully that Outside Brokers were sometimes dismissed in the City as 'all those damned bucket-shops'. This was very unfair, though to take money from the public was admittedly a business demanding caution: 'Put a foot wrong and you've had it.' The licence to issue circulars placed a powerful weapon in their hands. 'We here are incredibly careful,' he said. 'No one in the firm is allowed to buy a share that we recommend, at the time we recommend it – not that this would be illegal, but we mustn't damage relations with the market or the public.' Circulars, he said, were worded with extreme care. He pushed five samples over the desk: foolscap sheets, cyclostyled in blue off an electric typewriter. Only two contained phrases that gave any specific suggestion of wanting actually to *sell* the shares. The one-shilling Ordinary shares in Godfrey's, Ltd, 'the well known motor engineers and car distributors operating mainly on the outskirts of London', were recommended with the whispered suggestion that 'It is our belief that a buyer of the shares today will be given little cause for disappointment.' As for the two and sixpenny Ordinaries in the XYZ Manufacturing Co.: 'We consider that the comparatively high yield obtainable . . . make them an attractive investment for income purposes.'

Mr Smith said he had bought 100,210 shares in XYZ at 5s. 6d. a share, plus 1½d. a share commission. This was well below the market price of the shares as they were being retailed by the jobbers, who were quoting 5s. 10½d./6s. 1½d. in the Exchange, but were willing (through a stockbroker, of course) to quote lower prices for such a substantial sale. On the strength of his circular, Mr Smith sold the entire line at 6s. 1½d. net, in lots of an average size of £75. With a profit of sixpence per share, George Brodie & Co.'s turn on this transaction came to £2,505 5s., and I asked why it was that more people didn't turn their hand to this kind of thing. Mr Smith said that a good deal of capital was needed and it was hard to get started: though once you did start, dealing as a principal could be immensely profitable. He said he wouldn't let customers invest less than £50 a time and preferred them not to invest more than £100. Companies liked the Outside Brokers because they did more than inside brokers to distribute shares among small investors, and so avoid a concentration of power in the hands of a few stockholders. Circulars go off by second-class mail on Thursdays so as to arrive on Saturday morning in nice time for a weekend of study; Mr Smith also advises investors who can't afford a *Financial Times* every day to buy it on Saturdays, when the week in the markets is summarized.

He admitted that at times he was a little dismayed by the behaviour of members who, by the association's standards, went too far in pressing shares on the public. One firm had been telling people that the price of a certain share was rising, 'so phone us at once'. 'The wording's all wrong,' said Mr Smith. 'I wrote to them and they wrote back to say they *didn't understand why I was appalled!*' Another firm's phrase he didn't care for was: 'This week's nap selection.'

At this point one of Mr Smith's two co-directors, who turned out to be the Marquis of Milford Haven, pressed a lever on a comptometer-like machine on his desk across the room. Earlier he had been having several protracted end-of-the-day telephone conversations in which the Ritz, Whites, a game of cards, and a trip to the Continent had been mentioned. As he touched the machine it whirred loudly and Mr Smith started and said: 'David!' Lord Milford Haven said 'Sorry', and as it was getting on for six p.m. everyone got up to go. Mr Smith took me to a club along the road, where some business men he knew (none of them Outside Brokers) were up at the bar, drinking very large gins. One of them became philosophic and self-critical. 'If we were dealing in sweets on the Stock Exchange,' he said, 'we'd all have a hell of a lot of toffees in our pockets which we'd taken from the pot. We may be gentlemen, but when you get into the money world you find there's a certain amount of greed and avarice comes to the surface.' Everyone laughed at this, except Mr Smith, who said that when option dealing was reintroduced by the Stock Exchange earlier in the year, it was promptly banned for George Brodie clients. An option is the right to buy or sell shares at some definite time in the future, usually not more than three months ahead, at a price fixed when the option is taken out. Investors use options to limit the extent of any possible loss, speculators use them to gamble on price movements; a particular share-affecting event like a general election brings out the optioneers in force, and as the election had just taken place Mr Smith was asked why on earth he had banned this popular sport. 'Because we deal with the public,' he said firmly. 'And we will not encourage the public to speculate in any form whatsoever.'

A man with a dark face swayed forward and said: 'I'm very interested in oils at the moment. If only there were six-month options I'd be even more interested in them than I am in three. I want to put my money on the B.P. horse for six or preferably nine months.'

'It's the chap on the Stock Exchange who's going to win,' said the philosophic gentleman.

The dark man said: 'Oh, nonsense! I can't believe that a great company like that is going to be affected by the machinations of chaps on the Stock Exchange.'

'The oil market', Mr Smith began to explain to me, 'is a highly speculative market –'

'Good gracious!' said the dark man, swept along on some half-submerged current of thought. 'What other market are you possibly looking for nowadays? I bought steel shares immediately before the general election and sold them immediately after. Could you have a more speculative market than steel? I was staying in Glasgow on the night of the election where I had a suite in the hotel, and I sat up all night watching television. It was wonderful seeing us winning, and if the Stock Exchange had been open I'd have been buying and buying the entire night.'

I left soon after this. A few weeks later I was reading an informed article in the *Stock Exchange Gazette*, on the question of whether stockbrokers should be allowed to advertise, and found a sharp criticism of 'stock and share dealers who are not members of the stock exchanges. They may well set out chapter and verse recommending a share to their clients, but I am by no means uncertain that they do not buy up a large parcel of shares before their recommendation goes out, and make a useful turn by selling to clients.' I blinked at this, since it seemed to be exactly what the Outside Brokers did, as explained in detail by Mr Smith. Sure enough, two months later the journal carried an article by Mr Smith. 'Of course this is exactly what they do do,' he wrote. 'And I cannot imagine why anyone should think that they did anything else.' He refuted the first article neatly; but I expect he felt a little sad at the need to refute it at all.

IN THE CRYSTAL BALL

No impression of the Stock Exchange and its environs would be complete without a brief look at the wonderful art or science of investment advice. The *Stock Exchange Gazette* (which is not an official journal) often prints entertaining letters which ram home their point like this: 'Only in a momentary flash of honesty will a broker declare that, just like the investors, he himself is living in a misty, nebulous world, and that he is unable to advise you to come or go, because he himself doesn't know whether he is coming or going.' To this letter the editor appended a pertinent quote from the writings of Bernard Baruch, the American financier: 'Both my failure in whisky and my success in copper emphasized one thing – the importance of getting the facts of a situation free from tips, inside dope or wishful thinking. In the search for facts I learned that one had to be as unimpassioned as a surgeon. And if one had the facts right one could stand with confidence against the will or whims of those who were supposed to know best.' Mr Baruch was in great demand – the following week a firm called Investment Research of Cambridge was taking advertising space to quote another passage from the old master. This read: 'What of the man or woman with modest savings who is simply looking for a fair return on his or her savings and who cannot give full time to a study of investments? My advice to such persons is to seek out some trusted investment counsellor. The emergence of this new profession of disinterested and careful investment analysts, who have no allegiances or alliances and whose only job is to judge a security on its merits, is one of the more constructive and healthy developments of the last half century.'

Mr Baruch was thinking of the American scene; however, investment advisers have been appearing in Britain for some years, and a few can be said to have a national business. Investment Research are among these, describing themselves as 'Security Consultants and Portfolio Supervisors. They do NOT in any circumstances act as agents or principals for the purchase or sale of subscribers' securities.' I wrote to the owner of the firm, Mr A. G. Ellinger, who invited me to spend the day in Cambridge and sent me a packet of literature. Mr Ellinger's services were multitudinous. The Monthly Investment Letter, with a general indication of policy rather than a selection of hot tips, had sub-sections headed *Outlook & Strategy* and *Distribution & Tactics*. Notes for Subscribers, an irregular service of sixty or seventy papers a year, went into more detail. There was a Monthly Kaffir Service (Kaffirs are South African mining shares). There was the Weekly Index Service and the Monthly Index Service, and various classes of Personal Service. These included work on retainer for City institutions, opinions on individual shares at 25s. a time, a Revision and Supervision service for an investor's portfolio of shares, and supplies of photostat charts from the I.R. library. Professional chartists flourish in America, but are rare in Britain, where Mr Ellinger is one of the few professionals providing a regular service – he has more than 1,000 varieties of chart, from individual shares here and on American stock exchanges to weekly and daily indices covering specific industries and an assortment of other information, from gilt-edged activity to the price of Bradford Wool Tops. His charts have a horizontal time scale, 1/20th of an inch to the week, and a vertical price scale so constructed that the distance between 1 and 2 is the same as the distance between 2 and 4, and so on in proportion. This produces a rectangular effect, with the rectangles growing stubbier as you go up the page. It is 'single cycle semi-logarithmic', and Mr Ellinger writes that 'this scale represents a market reality, in that the profit on an investment of £100 is the same in a share that rises from 20s. to 25s. and one that rises from 40s. to 50s. On this scale the intervals between 20 and 25 and 40 and 50 are the same size.' Pure chartism ignores everything but the patterns on the paper, on the assumption that everything the investor hears is already history, and that the chart informs on what other investors, the people who actually move the shares, are doing now or were doing twenty-four hours ago. The fanatical chartist doesn't bother with the name of the company till he rings up his stockbroker with an order. But before I got to Cambridge I could tell that Mr Ellinger wasn't going to be a pure and perhaps comical chartist locked away in a bare room with no access to company reports, market slips, and City columnists. Enough of him came through the pamphlets to suggest the better type of English academic: dry, precise, perpetually amused, and unlikely to put his faith in one solution.

When I arrived he was about to dictate a letter to *The Times* into a tape recorder: certainly an academic figure, with thin, greying hair and heavy-lensed spectacles, sitting facing the green lawns of a college. 'Sir, comma, you suggest that British stock-brokers should think again about advertising, full stop. This is an excellent idea and as an investment adviser I would certainly not wish to oppose it, full stop. But certain points must be carefully considered, full stop. First let us take the attitude of the Press, full stop. While I have had no difficulty elsewhere in my fourteen years of activities, comma, it has taken me twelve years to find any form of advertisement that will be welcome to your columns. . . .'

When the letter was finished, Ellinger said his relations with the Press were odd. 'They're odd and we're odd,' he said. He had done some journalism himself, beginning with the time he bought a copy of the *Investment Review*, which contained an article about textiles that didn't come up to his expectations. He wrote and said he knew more about textiles than they did, and could he have his sixpence back; they replied that he couldn't have the sixpence but would he write the article?

Ellinger seemed to have prepared himself, in a resigned way, to run through his life story. 'I was born in Manchester in 1904. My father was a partner in a firm of shippers sending cotton to the Far East, a good enough business to pay for Rugby and Oriel. The business folded up in 1930, two years after I went into it' – he laughed loudly – 'and I went to an uncle in London who was an arbitrage broker. You might say I was a confidential office boy.

'In the war I was five and a half years in the R.A.S.C., from which I emerged with two important conclusions. One, never be ordered about; two, never live in a large town because it's so unhealthy. Having decided there was room for an investment consultant, there was the problem of finding where to go. It had to be south of a line from the Wash to the Bristol Channel because north of this they had early editions of the morning papers, without the Wall Street closing prices.

'It seemed to me there were only two eligible and humane cities where one could settle: Oxford and Cambridge. I felt Oxford had an unbearable climate, and in any case "Investment Research, Oxford" sounds a lost cause, whereas "Investment Research, Cambridge" sounds up and coming. I came here and started plotting share charts in a room downstairs, where we stayed until 1953. Then we started to expand.'

He handed over a folder of his accounts, from the first year, when there was a loss of £454 9s. 7d., to the present, when there was a substantial profit. The phone rang. Ellinger talked at length. 'No, no,' he finished up, 'I see everything at the moment in terms of a fuel crisis. There's too much coal, there's too much oil, everybody wants atomic power.' He put down the phone and said: 'That was a don from Corpus. I don't generally give verbal advice like that.' A few minutes later a pottery manufacturer was calling from the Black Country. 'Ah,' said Ellinger, 'I'll tell you what I think about Colvilles. Colvilles are going to be the great steel share of the next bull market – not this one, unless this one goes on for a long time.'

By now it was time for lunch. Ellinger introduced me to members of his staff, most of whom seemed to be Oxford or Cambridge graduates; he said the trouble was that in boom times he couldn't pay enough to compete with the City. One of his bright young men had left at the start of the year for a job with Warburgs, the merchant bankers. A young woman, an economics graduate, came with us for lunch. 'I take a holiday every year, and always an hour for lunch,' said Ellinger. 'It may be a meal, or it may be simply an apple and a piece of blue Wensleydale.' We stopped to drink sherry at a wine bar. For lunch there was roast wood pigeon and a bottle of burgundy. Ellinger talked quickly and overwhelmingly. One word would set him off. *Colleges.* Several Cambridge colleges took his published services, and one retained him as investment adviser. *Fieldwork.* 'We ought to do more of it. I wrote to one firm and I was summoned to appear before the directors. It was great fun.' *Company reports.* 'The quality has greatly improved. In 1950 B.S.A. right in the middle of their company report with a spade dug a large hole and buried £350,000 profit.' Even at speed the language had a curiously formal quality. *Charts.* Could one, I asked, successfully use charts as a sole guide to investment? 'There is a difference between "Can one?" and "Can you?" *I* can't. But I've found them of enormous assistance.'

The Ellinger approach to charts is crisp and unhesitating, but like all chartism has to cope with a certain amount of jargon. The short basic movements of the graph are 'tertiaries', building up into larger 'secondaries' lasting from three weeks to a year, in turn forming part of 'primaries'. What appears to the ignorant as a chart with a line going up-down, up-down over short periods, but steadily up over the months, reads like this to the chartist (as described by Ellinger in *Using Share Charts*, which doesn't refer to I.R.'s actual practice):

Clearly the buyers are dominant – they push the price up till their thrust is exhausted, then sellers push the price down, then buyers come in and impart a new upthrust to a higher level. When the upthrust is exhausted, the sellers force the price down; but before the previous low point is reached the buyers come in again and up the share goes to a new high. As long as this pattern persists, buyers are dominant and the share goes up; they may tell you that the chairman is under the thumb of the managing director's sister, that the managing director drinks like a fish, that the buildings are falling down, the plant is obsolete, the pro- duct is useless and the men are all on strike. Don't let them make you sell the shares, because the chart shows you there are more buyers than sellers. The buyers know something you are not being told, and you won't be told till it's good for you to know – that is, when you have sold your shares at too low a price to somebody who knows better. Just the same, if each tertiary decline outruns the preceding tertiary rise and the secondary movement is downwards, although the company had dis- covered the elixir of life and the philosopher's stone, the share is dom- inated by sellers and the price goes down till that domination comes to an end.

Mr Ellinger's tongue may have been some way in his cheek; still, he has the entire chartist mystique at his fingertips. There are the reversal patterns of supreme importance: perhaps a Head-and-Shoulders at the top, a Reversed Head-and-Shoulders at the bottom. The Head-and-Shoulders pattern may signify the end of a long rise, and is said to be common at the great turning points of the market. A share falls back a little, leaving a small peak: the left shoulder. A rush of new buyers carries it higher again; they fade away, leaving the head. A third rise appears as a few buyers come in to take advantage of the fall in prices, but the movement is weak. If the share now falls away from the right- hand shoulder, below a neckline drawn between the shoulders at what Ellinger calls the collar bones, 'the pattern has been resolved and you must expect a further decline from the neckline at least equal to the vertical distance from head to neckline'. Gaps, Triangles, Trendlines, Rounding Bottoms, Double Tops, and Wedges are among the other signs in the sky; Ellinger's enthusiasm gives the whole business authority, but the incidence of neurosis and despair among amateurs must be high.

Seen from such an outpost in academic territory, the stock markets seemed more a form of entertainment than the sinews of finance and the engrossing passion of thousands. Even without the abstractions of chartism, it was hard to relate the Cambridge atmosphere of bicycle bells and windblown gowns to the busy ants of Throgmorton Street. An elderly physicist had come into the restaurant, recognized Ellinger's pretty assistant, paused to talk, and gone into a corner with three colleagues, where their conversation buzzed gently into the afternoon. One phrase came over: 'If you put it in a test tube . . .' Ellinger told how once he demolished a foolish detective who came prowling with questions about a circular: 'I took him round to the police station and made him read the Prevention of Fraud Act.' There was the matter of the wine: should we finish it now, or have some more bread after the pudding and drink it then? We passed to the question of how long the bull market would last, and when it would become the inevitable bear market, with the secondaries sliding away down the charts. Ellinger made no prophecies. We went back to the office, and soon everyone was working at high pressure.

'What about House of Fraser? Has he got any Gestetner? . . . Parkinson and Cowan? Not his cup of tea at all, I'd have thought.'

'It started making bottoms along this line here. I said to my-self, I believe it's going to go through. And it went through.'

'I enclose a copy of our Monthly Investment Letter and with it our prospectus, semi-colon; Revision and Supervision may be what you want, full stop.'

A day with Ellinger provided an academic, uncoloured view, like football seen through pools coupons. It was about the nearest one could get to seeing the Stock Exchange as that 'national institution, standing apart from political controversy', that the publicity men dream of.

3

THE BILL BROKER'S CAREER

EVERY morning at ten a body of seventy-five men in dark suits and black toecapless shoes, aged from twenty to eighty, step briskly through the front doors of a dozen offices and set off to call on the banks of London. In sun, rain, or high wind their heads are crowned with solemn black top hats, and their uniform appearance, which marks the daily burgeoning of the London discount market, is so formal and precise that one is tempted to make it sound even neater than the truth. The time varies: the exact number and age-limit aren't officially recorded, and one of the participants wears a trilby (he is known throughout the market for his iconoclastic view of its traditions). What is certain is that every day except Sunday a tourist who lost his way while looking for the Tower of London and came to the Bank instead would be unlikely to traverse the V of Lombard Street and Cornhill between ten a.m. and noon without encountering an impressive or absurd top hat — opinions vary. It might belong to the senior partner of a firm of stockbrokers, or a jobber in the gilt-edged market, but the probable wearer would be a director of a discount house: one of the select company of bill brokers.

Their function is mechanical and orderly but performed with spirit. The discount houses, themselves a species of bank, have grown up on the civilized principle of borrowing from those who have it and lending to those who need it, creating a margin of profit for themselves in the difference between the rates of interest they pay and charge for loans. The margin is small but the profit can be large because of the quantities dealt in. The discount market is the reservoir of national cash. Banks use it as a convenient means of disposing of daily surpluses, and the discount houses re-lend the money to the Government against Treasury bills, and to private traders, merchants, and hire-purchase firms against commercial bills of exchange. The twelve houses of the London Discount Market Association dispose of £800,000,000 of which £200,000,000 may turn over daily. What the bill brokers are doing, as bill brokers were doing a hundred years ago with rather less respectability, is going from bank to bank in search of large cheques. They work a six-hour day, and as a career for gentlemen the discount house has much to recommend it. Working directors, often distinguished from part-time colleagues by the title 'managing director', might draw fees of £4,000 or £5,000 a year, and have a lucrative shareholding in the firm. Among smaller houses one-third of those employed may be directors: five managing directors, born into the business or into a family with strong banking connexions, and a staff, better paid than at a clearing bank, made up of cashier, accountant, company secretary and assistant, two managers, two clerks, two typists, and a telephonist. To ring up even a medium-sized house can be frustrating unless the caller wishes to talk about money. Either the telephonist says the directors are all out, or the call goes straight through to a director who wants the line clear so that he can talk to a bank, or the cleaner answers and says everyone went home at a quarter to four. Some of the smaller houses run to no more than a couple of rooms for working in – one still called the partners' room, though taxation has now driven the last of the discount partnerships to become a public company, the other a general office with holiday postcards under the calendar. There will also be a room for receiving visitors, decorated with framed bank-notes or one of the inevitable City prints, like *A Prospect of the City of London after that Dreadfull Fire of 1666*, containing dark cupboards and leathery, comfortable armchairs; someone may apologize for them and say how shabby everything is, but this is polite deprecation, not to be taken seriously.

Her Majesty's Stationery Office, in what must be its most discouraging piece of advice to school-leavers, says in a booklet on commercial careers that 'Advancement depends upon personality and a flair for the business, but as the total staff employed by all the discount houses together does not exceed 200 it is obvious that opportunities in this sphere are restricted'. Though the true figure is nearer 400, anyone who fancied a career in banking with the chance of a seat on the board at forty-five would certainly be better advised to try a clearing bank, or emigrate: he would be wasting his time at all but one or two of the largest discount houses, since practically every board is the preserve of a few families and their nominees. An enemy of capitalism who wanted to lambaste the system with an unconventional cudgel might do worse than try the London discount market: it not only has anachronisms, it knows about them, and a little of its confidence has leaked away.

The market grew fat in the nineteenth century by purchasing commercial bills of exchange. Bills, the staple means of financing trade until this century, and still widely used, are *not* the most exciting subject. Essentially they are promises to pay a stated amount of cash to a specific person at a specific time – usually three months ahead. In the favourite example of the textbooks, the wool exporter wants his money as soon as the wool is aboard the ship, but instead receives a bill of exchange from the importer, who is unable or unwilling to pay until he has received the wool and turned it into socks. To make the bill a saleable document, a bank, often a merchant bank, 'accepts' it, writing or stamping the word *accepted* across its face for a fee of one or two per cent of its value, thereby guaranteeing to honour the bill if the importer fails to do so three months later. Once accepted, the bill can be sold to the bill brokers, who discount it – they buy it but pay less than its face value, since they expect to be compensated, at current rates of interest, for providing the money involved for whatever length of time the bill has to run. The discount houses will also pay less for a bill if they have doubts about its safety – and the City long ago brought calculation of infinitesimal gradations of risk to a fine art. The discount houses developed with, and were part of, London's commercial sovereignty, providing a simple means of turning bills into cash that attracted not only the business to be financed, but overseas banks which found the market the most profitable channel for lending out money a day at a time. Bills were first scrutinized and accepted by the merchant banks, but the discount houses were the second line of defence, and early on the bill broker became a legend, credited with legendary powers. The bill broker could smell a bad bill. The bill broker's brains were in his feet. The bill broker was said to be blessed with a cunning, penetrative mind that was even more formidable than the merchant banker's. Unfortunately his reign as international financier was short. The business in commercial bills has fallen away: merchandise travels faster, money can be transferred by cable, it has become easier to verify the standing of creditors. A straight bank overdraft is generally the most convenient means of financing trade. But at several of the houses they still talk as if they were the old kind of bill broker, living in the paradise where nothing worked so well as the bill on London; and only when pressed will they admit reluctantly that commercial bills now form a minor part of their business. The credit-squeeze conditions of the 1950s, when clearing banks were unable to lend money freely, sent industries and traders scurrying to the discount market as an alternative means of raising credit; but this didn't last.

Nostalgia isn't allowed to interfere with work, and as the commercial bill has declined, the State's growing appetite for short-term credit has been turned into profitable if unromantic business by the massive purchasing of Treasury bills – three-monthly Government I.O.U.s, of which some £5,000,000,000 worth are always outstanding. Dealing in short-dated gilt-edged stock is another, and the newest, method of employing borrowed cash, and the shrinking of Stock Exchange jobbers' resources has opened the way for discount houses to become large-scale dealers in Government bonds. The profit is there: what they hate having lost is the satisfaction of being indispensable to the carriage of thousands of specific cargoes – timber, coffee, cotton, wool, oil-seeds, ores, tobacco, and the rest – and the vicarious excitements of worldwide trade seen through the crinkly bills of exchange. Most of the houses have ringing titles worthy of spacious days: King & Shaxson; Allen Harvey & Ross; Jessel, Toynbee; Smith St Aubyn; Seccombe Marshall & Campion; Gerrard & Reid;

though the least euphonious, Union Discount – a company with a clearing-bank-like string of 'assistant managers' instead of 'managing directors' – handles one-third of the market's business.

Tradition in the market is hotly defended; some directors, often the young ones, insist that tradition and practicality are the same thing. The morning visit to the banks, the standard target for critics, is defended without a blush. At one modest-sized house behind a small green garden, reached through an archway across the road from the Bank of England, they talked with pride of their six rounds, which take in more than 100 banks of the 120 or so to be visited in London. Every kind is included: the domestic institutions like Midland and Barclays – these, with six Scottish banks, have about £400,000,000 in the market; then the merchant banks, and all the overseas banks who have offices in London, with the other £400,000,000 between them. No one at this house writes anything down: this is a rule. Bank No. 1 may call £250,000 of the money which has been loaned overnight at $4\frac{1}{2}$ per cent. Bank No. 2 may have £100,000 in commercial bills that it wants discounted, and a discount rate of $6\frac{3}{4}$ per cent could be agreed – the bank receives the face value of the bill, less interest at the agreed rate, calculated over the number of months the bill has to go before it matures. Bank No. 3 may want to buy Treasury bills maturing at a specific date. A young man of suitable background is pitchforked into these negotiations and left to learn by himself, meeting tough professional bank officials who are not past pulling a fast one, in the market slang 'hotting' him; returning to the office by noon with his head full of figures. 'An individual may make mistakes,' said a director, 'but we look at it like this. A mistake of $\frac{1}{32}$nd in bills for £100,000 with the full three months to run only comes to seven guineas. Normally he'll only be dealing to the extent of £500,000, so the most he can lose is £35 and we think it's worth that much for experience.'

But why do the banks have to be visited in person? It seems a pre-telephone ritual, and in any case the morning visit is followed by intensive work from the office – a few people make a second round, but the general rule is that after the first visit has given an idea of what cash and bills are available, the real business is done by phone. However, the top-hatters don't see it like that: nothing, they say, is a substitute for personal contact. This phrase is magic. 'We all offer the same thing at more or less the same price,' said a director, 'so the only way we can take business from our neighbours is by personal appeal. Also you get a picture of what the City is thinking by going round and seeing the banks. They're seeing stockbrokers and so are you, so you get to know whether a crisis is likely to happen, which is very important because of our bill rates. When we tender for Treasury bills we have to think what'll be happening in three months' time, when they mature. Then there's the man's face, his expression as he's talking. Over the telephone you may never know if the man you're talking to is good at his job. He may be a liar or a fool and not give it away on the telephone, but when you see him you get at the truth.'

Top-hatters seem to enjoy visiting in an archaic manner. They can be seen queueing at a bank, four or five in a row on a hard bench, striped trousers tugged up to show uniformly dark socks, polished pointed shoes neatly side by side on the cold tiled floor. Time passes. A *Times* is exchanged for a *Telegraph*. There is an absence of documents, a bland assurance that events are being coped with – as indeed they are, since between them the discount houses are smoothing out the surpluses and shortages of the banking system, which means that not only 'British' money, left with banks by the public, is being passed backwards and forwards, but quantities of foreign funds. The London office of an American bank may have credits on behalf of clients lying idle for a few days. Idleness being an unforgivable condition for capital, the bank may shovel it into the market and collect 3 or 4 per cent, knowing that the money can be 'called' at an hour's notice. About two-fifths of the funds lent in the market will be 'good' money, left there more or less permanently and 'called' only in emergency; the rest is overnight money, renewed or withdrawn each morning.

The top-hatters are coping; but the morning is drifting by. When his turn comes the bill broker steps into the office of what-ever official the bank employs to deal with the market, says

'Good morning,' pulls up a chair, and begins to talk about cricket or last night's television. This is hearsay: it would be unthinkable to let an outsider accompany a bill broker on his rounds, and the broker's account may unconsciously over-emphasize what he likes to think will be described as the 'typically English' part of the business. But all the versions agree: sport, weather, a little politics are usually touched upon, and there may be some innocuous banter, before either reaches the naked word 'money'. The official who looks at his watch and sticks grimly to business will be the exception; he will also be unpopular. Ideally the relationship between the two is of equals who show an equal amount of respect. If anything the bill broker is inclined to be more deferential. He lives by the good will of the banks. He's the one who does the asking, and even though he may not receive the compliment in return, he's likely to call the bank official 'sir' at some point in the conversation, probably the beginning. 'Sir', of course, has two meanings in Britain. To many it smacks of servility, but to the middle-class Englishman who has been to a public school it is a recognition signal, flown on a hundred occasions (though in occupations like advertising and journalism it would be quietly dropped). It means: 'I am an Englishman. I hope you are too. Let us get together. You are probably as good as me. I am definitely as good as you.' The City's attitude to 'sir' was put by a middle-aged director of a discount house in one of those comfortable and faintly shabby waiting rooms. Heavy curtains were drawn against the sound of passers-by hurrying through a lane, a short cut between banks, in the late afternoon. Behind the curtains a telephone clicked now and then – as in merchant banks, telephones click and flash but seldom ring bells.

'I don't say "sir" to everybody,' he said, 'because I know most of them are called Charlie or something. But the banks are our customers and they are ours, so when they ring me up they always call me "sir". The City manager of a bank would call you "sir". The best bankers are the politest, in fact. It's one of those curious things, that manners are part of the business of exchange.

'This business of How-do-you-do? – does it mean anything? Of course it does. You are saying in effect: "We accept the normal rules of society, and we can now start exchanging ideas." If you see people trying to make bargains who aren't steeped a bit in the etiquette, in the manners of the thing, they end up making clumsy asses of themselves. Go to any market – go to Mincing Lane, go to the Baltic, go to the Stock Exchange – you'll find they have a language of their own.

'Then there's top hats. If you go to a bank with a top hat they say "Oh, it's one of the brokers", and you walk right in. If you went in in a homburg there'd be an awful business of "Good gracious me, Mr —, where's your hat this morning?" There'd be a *thing*, which of course you want to avoid at all costs.'

The rounds are finished; the brokers are back in their offices. On a normal day millions of pounds will already have been moved without a single paper contract. Later in the day cheques for the amounts will be handed over, and bundles of bills will be sent round to the banks as security. The division between matters where one's word is enough, and matters where there must be strong formal guarantees, is obvious to businessmen but not always to outsiders. A verbal promise is sufficient guarantee that money is going to be loaned, but when the cheque arrives in the afternoon the bank must have security from the discount house to cover the loan; so round go bundles made up of Treasury bills, Government bonds, and commercial bills. A certain amount of unsecured borrowing did take place in 1957 and 1958, when a jump in interest rates withered the assets of discount houses and left some of them technically bust, but that was a crisis operation. When Bank Rate rises – Chapter 6 goes into detail – it pushes down the price of gilt-edged stock, so that houses with large amounts in bonds were unable to cover their borrowing. Normally a bundle of collateral is not calculated to give exact cover for the loan – it will err on the plus side. But in 1958 some houses had to keep revaluing the collateral (which, as the bills and stock composing it advanced towards maturity, would grow more valuable each day), replacing it with the precise minimum required. Directors had to transfer money from their own bank accounts; they are still described as 'those wretched chaps'. Banks helped – at a price, since no one in business would expect a helping hand to be also a free hand. As a bill broker said: 'You think to yourself, what do we do now? He wants to continue in business, and on the whole I want him to continue in business. He serves a purpose and we gain something out of him. We'll see that he doesn't go out of business, but we'll squeeze him. Now, if you squeeze him too hard, charge him ten per cent or something, he may go out of business. So you charge him half per cent more than usual, and he pays up and looks happy.'

Normal procedure when borrowing is to cover every loan with the securities which earlier loans have been used to purchase, so that it becomes a gigantic juggling operation – borrow money, buy a bond, pledge bond against fresh loan, buy a bill, pledge bill against loan, and so on with a greater or lesser margin of profit. Lunch is taken quickly. Most houses have a luncheon room where phone calls can be put through; or a sandwich and glass of brandy in a bar round the corner will suffice. In the hour that follows, from 1.30 to 2.30, the atmosphere swings towards tension, though by most commercial standards it remains decorous. At the end of the day the book must balance; money returned to whoever called it must be replaced by new money, and the rate will rise or fall one-sixteenth or one-eighth of 1 per cent at a time in response to supply and demand. Before work started the market will have had an idea what conditions to expect. The nationalized industries, the Health Service, and the income-tax authorities all provide predictable movements of money through the banks. As *The Times* will report in the esoteric down-column regions of its City page: 'Erratic money conditions were experienced in Lombard Street yesterday. Substantial withdrawals of funds were balanced by Government disbursements being made on behalf of the Ministry of Health' – or it might be the Milk Marketing Board, handing over money for farmers, or the Ministry of Education, with teachers' salaries. The banks, presented with large credits of this nature, promptly lend them out again to the market until such time as they're needed.

By early afternoon the houses know how easy or difficult a

balance is likely to be. Each house makes and receives several hundred phone calls within an hour or two, and red and green bulbs on individual switchboards built into the dealing table flash like a boy's electric-train outfit as directors and dealers – the larger the house the smaller the proportion of directors – work their way down lists of banks, dialling two or three in a minute and talking loudly:

'Could I have money, please? Ah, X's here – any windfalls?'

'X's are *the* house, you know. Yes, sir. One quarter we pay for that [5¼ per cent]. Ah now, that's a friendly gesture.'

'How's the money? One hundred for us? [£100,000]. We always say it's our charming personality gets the money.'

A pause comes. A voice says to the room: 'Can we have a policy conference?' The man at the head of the table says: 'Tell them the rate is coming down. We're paying an eighth.'

A new wave of calls comes in; and money flows from the banks. Should it fail to do so, the market still has to raise the wind. No cash has changed hands, no suitcases of lovely green money have been passed across the counters; but the cheques shuttling between offices are as real as blocks of gold, representing wealth that must be accounted for by the end of the day. To help him balance his book the bill broker can take 'privilege money', drawing on his bankers to an agreed amount: a short-term overdraft which had its origin around 1925, when many American bills, particularly to finance cotton exports, were coming on the London market. Because London time was several hours ahead of New York, the number of cotton bills that needed discounting was unknown till well into the afternoon. Some form of last-minute help was needed, and privilege money was the answer. It can go up to above £1,000,000; but still more help may be needed. At this point the system becomes a trifle mystic. What has happened is that the banking system has lost blood. Money has vanished – perhaps tax payments have been passed on to the Government by banks; perhaps money has been withdrawn by foreign banks, whose clients want to sell their sterling on the foreign exchange market; perhaps the public has been withdrawing more cash. Money is short. 'MONEY SHORT AGAIN:

LARGE AMOUNT OF HELP' will be down the page in *The Times* next morning. There is only one place where this help can be found, only one source of fresh credit for the economy: and that's the State.

The standard financial euphemism is 'the Authorities'. In some situations 'the Authorities' may embrace Treasury and Bank of England, but in the discount market it means the Bank. If money is short, the Bank will intervene. There are limits to the intervention, or there would be no end to the supply of money: at every shortage the Bank would pump in some more. So the Bank divides its help into two kinds: there is the straight-forward injection of money into the market, but there is also the loan of money at an unpleasant rate of interest – Bank Rate – which will induce the discount houses to repay it quickly. (It is in theory the rate at which the Bank will discount bills for houses, though the usual practice nowadays is for the Bank to make a straight loan against the security of bills.) Through the market the Authorities keep a finger on the economy. They never refuse to provide money, so the system can chug along safe in the knowledge that the central bank is behind it; all the Authorities will do is vary the means of assistance. This is where Englishmen and money together begin to produce curious results. It's a curious system, and the fact that no other country has one exactly like it – many are said to envy it – must have some effect on hardening the brokers' determination to keep what they have unchanged. But the mystery which surrounds this feeding in of money belongs to another age altogether.

In private some brokers call it mumbo-jumbo. A discount house which finds itself short of money must present itself, in person, to the discount office of the Bank of England by 2.30 p.m. By leaving it to the last minute a house can continue combing the banks for money till twenty past two, leaving a man ten minutes in which to take his top hat off the peg, cross a couple of streets, and hurry past the pink-coated attendants into the lofty precincts of the oldest, slyest, stuffiest central bank in the world. A framed notice announces in ancient display type: 'No Alteration in the Rate of Discount This Day.' Through tall

windows the mulberry trees can be seen flourishing in the inner
courtyard, and above them, on the first floor, a long row of
chandeliers illuminates the courtroom. Below the courtroom are
the parlours, where the Governor works, and near it on the
ground floor is the discount office. With a minute to spare the bill
broker turns a couple of corners and joins a small queue outside
the principal's room. It doesn't take long; the principal asks how
much, the broker tells him, and the interview is over. The market,
or part of it, has been forced 'in the Bank', and has had to go
like a naughty boy and ask Grandma to help. All that remains is
to arrange for collateral to be sent round to the Bank, generally as
Treasury bills or bonds; best-quality commercial bills, 'fine bank
bills', are also accepted. Though 2.30 is the deadline, banks don't
close for another half-hour, during which money may become
available to ease the situation. It sometimes happens that a bill
broker is stopped at the last minute by a phone call to the
Bank of England, telling him that the £500,000 has been found
elsewhere. To use the loan account and borrow at Bank Rate is
expensive: the loan must be for a minimum of seven days, so
assuming a Bank Rate of 5 per cent, to borrow £1,000,000 for
a week costs nearly £1,000. It would be more convenient if the
Bank kept its discount office open till three o'clock – but the
Bank of England likes its little mysteries. It likes to keep the
market guessing. Once a week two representatives of the Discount Market Association visit the Governor in his parlours:
the preliminary to the weekly application, every Friday, for
the three-monthly Treasury bills, when the houses bid as a
syndicate, offering, say, £98 13s. 1d. for every £100 worth of
bills, which works out at an annual discount of about 5⅔ per cent.
They have to look ahead and try to gear the discount they
obtain to interest rates over the next three months: if a house has
to pay a bank 6 per cent for money, Treasury bills which show a
return of 5⅔ are unprofitable. The tender is a complicated matter,
full of unknowns, and the meeting with the Governor is not
intended to make all things clear. There is another of those
famous general discussions. The Governor doesn't say the
Treasury bill rate is running too high or too low. He hints. No

one asks for the hints to be amplified. 'He is', said one broker, 'very much the Delphic Oracle on these occasions, and everybody reads into his remarks what they can. Sometimes we read right and sometimes we don't. Then the Bank shows its displeasure by forcing the market into the Bank – forcing us to borrow at the penal rate.'

This uncertainty pervades the market, and is thanks largely to the Bank of England. The Bank likes the dark. It loathes publicity – it often refuses to disclose the most elementary facts about its methods, and never leaves anyone in doubt about its lofty status as the grandmother of central banks. Founded in 1694 to raise money for the impecunious Whig administration of King William III, its services to the State were rewarded by such privileges as becoming banker to the Government and the right to issue paper money; by slow stages it grew to be a reserve bank behind the monetary system. It has been pre-eminent in the City for so long that one gets the impression that if capitalism lasted a thousand years, the Bank would never acknowledge the need to explain itself to anyone. The first thing to be nationalized when the Labour Party came to power in 1945, it has continued as before. Northcliffe bought *The Times* but absolute control of it eluded him; the State took over the Bank, but to this day it goes its own way, issuing a weekly bank return which is of no monetary significance, and (a concession to nationalization) an annual report of which, according to Radcliffe, 'the meagreness has become a byword'. The head of the intelligence department at a clearing bank indignantly produced for me a 160-page report of the U.S. Federal Reserve System, and one of 118 pages from the West German Deutsche Bundesbank. 'We find it difficult to believe,' said Radcliffe, in a passage that delighted the City's enemies, 'that the Bank of England is so differently placed from the central banks of other countries that there should be such a wide disparity in the volume of printed comment for which they make themselves responsible. It seems to us also that this apparent reticence does harm to the standing of the Bank as a national institution . . .' The twenty-odd pages of the annual report, containing facts and tables that are public knowledge anyway, give no clue to what the Bank thinks about foreign exchange rates, interest rates, the National Debt, or economic trends generally (though the Governor has now said in public that he 'sees much force' in the argument for fuller information).

Its attitude to the visiting journalist is tinged with pain and horror. There is a Bank official whose job it is to see the Press. He has no ascertainable title, and when asked directly he says that this is a Bank matter. His writing paper says *Bank of England* in one corner but doesn't give the phone number. Talking to him about the discount market I mentioned a certificate used by houses when they have bought gilt-edged stock but before they have taken delivery. The certificate is accepted by the Bank as collateral, in lieu of the stock itself. I asked what it was called and his face grew solemn. He shook his head. 'It's a name that's not generally known outside. It's one we wouldn't wish to make public.' I pressed him, to see what would happen. 'I couldn't possibly,' he said. (Later that morning I asked a bill broker. He said it was called a Z certificate.) The Bank official was an elegant man, with a crisp, professional manner. When I asked if he could arrange an interview with the principal in charge of the discount office, he hedged for a while and then said No, it was out of the question. He leaned a little closer over his desk. 'We are here,' he said, 'to protect Bank officials from the likes of you, if you don't mind my saying so.' That was that – it was annoying at the time, though there must be plenty of officials in Vickers and Unilever and I.C.I. who wish they could be so effectively shielded from the irritations of journalists. One can see why the Bank makes a mystery of itself to the Press, since it's always more convenient not to have to keep explaining yourself; what is less understandable is why the Bank goes on making a mystery of itself to the discount market – except that the very fact of mystery and mumbo-jumbo probably strengthens its hold on the houses.

Even the penalty of forcing houses to borrow at the penal rate is more a hint than a practical measure. 'You see,' said a broker, 'the Bank never like to think they give direct advice. They flatter themselves it's an absolutely free market, that they merely give *indications*. Borrowing at the penal rate is always over-emphasized by the Press. All it means is that one construes that the Bank wants interest rates raised. I feel life would be a lot easier if the Bank had a board outside saying "We are buyers of x number of bills at such-and-such a price", but they prefer to work discreetly.' This daily purchase and sale of bills by the Bank is its other method of intervention, and may operate so as to feed the market with money or to take it away – to 'mop up'. In the same broker's words: 'It's rather like finding how much a child can eat by stuffing it, then going round and mopping up.' The instrument of this two-way traffic is called the special buyer, alias the 'hidden hand', and its dealings are known, ironically enough, as 'open market operations'. The special buyer holds his appointment as an individual – at the time of writing Mr Campion of Seccombe Marshall & Campion, who thus have a dual existence: as a small discount house, and as the Bank's agent in the market. If the Bank wants to inject money into the market, it will buy bills from the houses (direct assistance) or from the banks (indirect assistance). If it wants to mop up, it reverses the process and sells bills. The special buyer, linked to all houses and his master, the Bank, by direct lines, has the confidence of everyone: and works in secret. Mr Campion asked to be excused and I saw someone else. I asked for a few details. He shook his head. 'I'm not going to talk to you about our business. We don't even disclose to other members of the market how our business is done.' Sitting in a narrow room, off a tiny hallway like the entrance to a small hotel, with revolving doors and frosted glass, I felt I had committed an indiscretion. As I was going he mentioned an article on the market that 'appeared in the *Morning Post* the other day'. The *Morning Post* was merged with the *Daily Telegraph* more than twenty years ago, and its title lost. I asked if he meant the *Telegraph*. 'Yes,' he said, 'that's what they call it now.' The discount market often has this air of insularity; but unlike the Bank of England, which seems impervious to everything, the market is frequently sensitive to what outsiders think. The Radcliffe Report was awaited anxiously, especially for what it would say about the Treasury bill tender. Every week the syndicate buys several hundred million pounds worth, meeting beforehand, usually at the offices of Union Discount, to decide what price to offer before filling in the pale green forms obtainable at the Bank of England, addressed to 'The Lords Commissioners of Her Majesty's Treasury', with space provided to show how many bills are required at their face value of £5,000, £10,000, £25,000, £50,000, and £100,000; a footnote reminds applicants that 'Each tender must be for not less than £50,000'. The houses are always willing to take up all bills on offer, to 'cover the tender', but never get all they apply for. Applications arrive at the Bank around lunchtime on Friday, and details of how many bills have been allotted are pinned up on the notice board an hour or two later. Anyone can tender for Treasury bills, and foreign banks and industrial organizations often do so – there's nothing to stop a British bank tendering, but the custom since before the war has been to leave it to the discount houses and repurchase bills from them, selecting them so that they mature on dates when the bank knows it will need cash.

The syndicated bid is technically a restrictive practice. Radcliffe pointed out that it could 'theoretically be exploited by the discount houses to enrich themselves', but added the comforting thought that 'in fact the clearing banks keep a lively eye on the market's profit margins on bills, and are quick to squeeze the discount market by altering the terms on which they lend money to the market'. As far as Treasury bills are concerned, said the Report, the houses weren't indispensable but provided a 'highly efficient market'. It was the same with the short-dated Government stock, in which the discount houses help to keep an active market. There were a number of pats on the back from Radcliffe; but the conclusion wasn't effusive. 'It is no service to claim', it said, 'that the discount market is indispensable to the functioning of the monetary system.' However, it smoothed out ebbs and flows, and simplified the work of banks. 'It would not be beyond human ingenuity to replace the work of the discount houses; but they are there, they are doing the work effectively, and they are doing it at a trifling cost in terms of labour and other real resources.'

This, said a bill broker, was bloody patronizing: where would the City be without a market to look after surplus funds, discount trade bills, and provide the Government with its cheapest form of borrowing? Others thought it was fair enough. (One firm of stockbrokers thought parts of it were fair enough. They quoted Radcliffe on the cover of an investors' booklet about discount houses, but left out the bit about it not being beyond human ingenuity to replace them.) Perhaps no one in the City is as confident as he was; and the discount market, whose function is to be sensitive to what others are doing, realizes how times have changed. It's no longer an international market in the old sense; bills no longer roll in from the world's merchants. What it still does is provide a smooth money-market, and incidentally encourage overseas banks to settle in London: the British clearing houses, resentful at the number of foreign banks in the City, would never provide them with such facilities. Its brokers remain impressive – like the elderly gentleman who said testily that he couldn't understand why the market's wide knowledge of foreign trade wasn't used by the banks as it should be, that 'the managers of those clearing banks think they know everything'. The clearing banks, with their hard, professional air, must seem alien at times. Still more impressive than the old bill broker was the very young one who said that though it was difficult to believe, bank officials really did like to see you every morning, and would hate you to use the telephone all the time. His top hat made his cheeks look pinker and rounder. He was impeccably groomed, impeccably connected, and full of enthusiasm for the way the market works and the traditions that decorate it. A couple of the people he visited each morning were amateur painters, he said. So he often talked about painting. 'And a lot of them want to talk about cricket, of course, or why the Lions lost the Rugby Test match in New Zealand. There have even been times when I've completely forgotten about money and just walked out, having had a long conversation about cricket or something.'

The Bank of England, if it ever feels the need for public relations in keeping with the 1960s, will have to work hard to project a favourable image. It should be easier for the discount houses. A bill broker was once introduced to the producer of the television programme *What's my Line?* as a possible candidate. The broker was willing to appear, but the producer turned him down. 'Viewers wouldn't understand what you did,' he said. 'And if they did they wouldn't believe it.' But it shouldn't be difficult for a man to gain the public's confidence by explaining that he begins the day with a chat about sport: then becomes so engrossed, he forgets to talk about work.

4

MERCHANT BANKS OF OLDE ENGLAND

THE London telephone directory shows that of the seventeen firms who enjoy membership of the Accepting Houses Committee, and so form the core of merchant banking, only five describe themselves as 'merchant bankers'. Three are 'merchants and bankers', four are 'bankers', one has the word 'bank' in the title, two are 'merchants', and two consider themselves so important that they don't bother to qualify the name of the firm. They are a heterogeneous group, and no one ever knows quite what to make of them. They include the names that come to mind when anyone speaks of 'the great bankers of London', but exactly what they do is a mystery, except that they deal in their names rather than in deposits. They have a lingering reputation for holding strings of power, for knowing the right people, for being mixed up in political intrigue and empire building and enormous profits, and owning country mansions of remarkable ugliness within a few miles of a railway line and express trains to London. The merchant banks are Dickensian. They belong in tales of fog-coated streets and hansom cabs, with tea clippers coming softly up the Thames – the gas lamps are burning in the banking parlour where all the partners sit together, a rich foreign banker has just been sent away with a flea in his ear, an emissary from a distant king waits by the bright coal fire in the outer hall, a pigeon is arriving on the roof with a despatch from Dover, and the carriage that is pulling up outside contains the senior partner's beautiful young wife, who is closely related to four Cabinet Ministers and the Archbishop of Canterbury.

For a hundred years the merchant banks were a living exaggeration. When London was the centre to which all countries looked for credit and the guarantee of credit, the merchant bankers were the most sought-after private traders who had ever been, perhaps who ever will be. Most began as merchants on the Continent of Europe who found it more profitable to deal in credit than in goods. They would guarantee a transaction, generally by 'accepting' the bill of exchange; if anything went wrong they would pay the seller themselves, but usually it was simply a case of signing a bill and collecting 2 per cent commission. They became great contact men – they had to be, to know which risks were safe – and although they operated from London they were in touch with the world. They always knew what was going on. Not only merchants but governments came to depend on them. The money they raised by gigantic loans, or sometimes found themselves, paid for armies and diamond mines and railways, not to mention such odds and ends as £400,000 for the City of Boston in 1872, or £1,750,000 for the New York Telephone Co. in $4\frac{1}{2}\%$ First and General Mortgage Bonds in 1912 – these last figures are from the files of Baring Bros., where the list ends abruptly just before the first war brought down the curtain, signalling the start of the process by which credit stopped pouring out of London and began to flow in the other direction. London still gives credit; but not in the old way.

The most famous name of all was Rothschild, and the family is still to be found at New Court, under the sign of the Five Arrows. There were five Rothschild brothers. One stayed at home, which was Frankfurt, in Germany; the others went to Naples, Vienna, Paris, and London, and became bankers with varying degrees of success. Nathan Mayer was the one who came to London; he died in 1836, and it was under his heir, Lionel Rothschild, that New Court, originally the family house, became the best address in finance. There's still an important Paris house, but the other Rothschilds are all out of business – the Naples house as long ago as 1861, Frankfurt in 1901, and Vienna in 1937, when Hitler invaded Austria. Like many merchant bankers they're Jews, with a predilection for doing business with other Jews – there is an important distinction between merchant banks of Jewish origin which have shed their past, and merchant banks that continue as Jews. Offence can be given by getting this wrong:

not, as far as I know, to the Jewish house that is mistaken for non-Jewish, but the other way round.

Many books have been written about the Rothschilds, but without their blessing. No one, however refined his motives, has ever been allowed to potter round in their vaults and go through the ledgers and boxes of letters. They look on themselves as a part of history, not to be spied upon. They did monumental things, like raising £20,000,000 to compensate British slave-owners when slavery was abolished in 1833, and finding £4,000,000 at short notice when Disraeli wanted to buy control of the Suez Canal from under the noses of the French in 1875. Under Lionel's reign they brought out eighteen Government loans for a total of £1,600,000,000. They followed a policy of inter-marriage – someone calculated that in the nineteenth century, of the fifty-eight marriages contracted by the descendants of Mayer Amschel Rothschild, the German ancestor of them all, exactly half were between first cousins. This was an effective way of keeping dowries and marriage settlements in the family, and may have something to do with the present state of N. M. Rothschild & Son, which remains that almost extinct creature in British high finance, a partnership, with no 'Ltd' on the end as a reminder that taxation, death duties, and sometimes the need to go to the public for money have conspired to make every accepting house but Rothschilds either a private or a public limited company.

A managing director often refers to 'the partners', then corrects himself with a shrug and explains how taxation makes a partnership intolerable since the earnings of good and bad years can't be averaged out, as they can with a limited company. He isn't apologizing or even complaining: rather, he sounds contemptuous of a system that doesn't recognize the advantages of partnerships. 'Partnership' is an honoured word. The tradition at merchant banks is still 'the Parlour', where the managing-directors-who-wish-they-were-partners all sit, one or two to a desk in a large ornate room with a grate and a thick carpet, looking over one another's shoulders and making (in theory, anyway) snap decisions. 'Even merchant bankers have their

Achilles' heels,' said one merchant banker. 'But when you've got four chaps with their own money at stake, all with different contacts, all with different ideas, you know that everybody's contributed all he's got, and you know where you are.'

New Court is in St Swithin's Lane, a short cut between Lombard Street and Cannon Street Station. Just past a window-ledge stall where *U.S. Glamour* and *Strip Lingerie* are on sale is the sign of the Five Arrows, above an archway with heavy wooden doors folded back, leading to a courtyard with buildings on two sides – rather like a large Victorian house, with a solid-fronted provincial bank at right angles. Couriers sit in a row of wooden stalls along the third side, waiting to run errands – not to carry despatches around Europe, as they once did. Even the view is by permission. The large man in dark overcoat, gloves, and bowler hat standing under the Five Arrows turns out to be a guard, posted all day until the wooden doors are closed, to intercept rubbernecks and cranks. There is what one might call Rothschild Syndrome: anyone who goes a little mad, and whose madness takes the common shape of being convinced that there's a fortune lying in a vault for him somewhere, thinks immediately of Rothschilds. Letters arrive with curt instructions to transfer so many million pounds, representing £100 deposited by some ancestor plus compound interest over the years, to the writer's account at the Midland Bank forthwith. The attempt by a crazy Jewish student to shoot a partner as he was arriving at New Court fifty years ago is remembered, like so much else, as if it was yesterday (the student missed, and the guard got the bullet in the neck).

Inside N. M. Rothschilds are leather and dark furniture, strips of carpet on pale wooden floors, and the general look of a house converted into an office for gentlemen. The partners' room is panelled and lined with portraits and old accounts; one doesn't see the partners, only their names and extension numbers on the card by the telephone: 56, Mr Edmund; 47, Mr Leopold; 59, Mr Evelyn. David Colville, a Scots investment trust expert, was the first non-Rothschild to become a partner. (The head of the family, Lord Rothschild, is a scientist at Cambridge, though he occasionally looks in at New Court.) They employ two hundred and fifty people. 'A small, unique business,' says the man detailed to act as buffer. 'Accepting bullion, foreign exchange, issuing loans, unit-trust management.' You mention the consortium formed to develop the resources of Newfoundland. What part, exactly, do Rothschilds have in this? There is a long silence. Then: 'A business like this is vast, very vast. I'd rather not tell you anything. You see, people come here asking to see our archives, but when you have acted for practically every government in Europe, what can you do but maintain absolute discretion?' Rothschilds were among the first to see the possibilities – not to mention the necessities – for bankers, when the European Common Market became a reality; and they were soon making plans to join with merchant banks on the Continent to exploit the European market. But here, again, they prefer to act, not talk to strangers.

Without exception the merchant banks share a distaste for publicity. Their reputation is what counts, they say – and that, they argue, involves the exercise of absolute discretion. To have their name in the paper is agreeable only if it appears in a small, discreet paragraph dealing with a new issue or a consortium to raise funds for South American enterprises. Many houses refuse to advertise – like the house of Lazards, who describe themselves as 'merchants', and whose five-storied building faces the street with a coat of arms and two night buttons, one for the porter and one for the caretaker: it doesn't *say* 'Lazards'. The worst thing in the world happened to Lazards in the autumn of 1957 when they found themselves heavily involved in the Bank Rate inquiry (Chapter 7), which exposed them to painfully detailed scrutiny: it was not that anything unseemly came to light, simply that questions were asked which should not have been asked.

Merchant banking is, needless to say, an occupation for gentlemen, chiefly English gentlemen. Occasionally, as a result of the strong foreign connexions of most of the houses, a trace of a European accent can be heard at the top levels; but as a rule the managing directors sound at least as upper-English as their colleagues (who may be their sons and nephews) in the discount houses. The Baring family, which owns Baring Brothers, second only to Rothschilds in traditional glory, has five separate lines of peers, including Cromer, Ashburton, Revelstoke, and North-brook. Byron (writing on what must have been an off day) put Barings in Canto XII of *Don Juan* in 1823:

> Who hold the balance of the World? Who reign
> O'er congress, whether royalist or liberal?
> Who rouse the shirtless patriots of Spain?
> (That make old Europe's journal 'squeak and gibber' all)
> Who keep the World, both old and new in pain
> Or pleasure? Who makes politics run glibber all?
> The shade of Buonoparte's noble daring? –
> Jew Rothschild and his fellow-Christian, Baring.

Barings, founded in the early eighteenth century by a German emigrant from Bremen who settled first in the West Country, at Exeter, became the leading 'American house' in London. From the 1820s there was always an American citizen among the partners, helping direct European capital to the New World. Nothing could be more revealing than the list of loans raised by Barings in those years. ('Every loan', added Byron, warming to the subject, 'Is not a merely speculative hit, But seats a Nation or upsets a Throne.') Between 1860 and 1892, more than £40,000,000 and $500,000,000 raised for U.S. and Canadian Government loans. Between 1868 and 1913 more than £80,000,000 for U.S. and Canadian railways. Between 1888 and 1912 more than $100,000,000 for American commercial and industrial loans. At the same time Barings were finding the money for Russia to build the Trans-Caucasian Railway, for the Chinese Imperial Government, for developments in South America, in France, Germany, Belgium, Austria, Hungary, India, Iraq, Egypt, Italy, Japan, Portugal, South Africa, and Turkey. After the first war there is scarcely anything. One of the rare post-war foreign loans brought Barings into the news in 1959 when for no apparent reason the Czech Government defaulted on interest payments for three successive loans that had been negotiated by Barings in the early 1920s. First Barings wrote letters; then they sent teleprinter messages. The Czechs took no notice. So a director, Sir Edward James Reid, second baronet and a godson of King Edward VII, flew out to Prague. For days he went from department to department, like a man in a Kafka novel, and had to fly back to London without getting any sense out of them. Barings refused to discuss the matter, though one of the directors went so far as to commit himself by saying: 'What a pity it all is.'

Barings have been a limited liability company since the 1890s, when they got themselves into deep water and nearly crashed. The immediate cause was a crisis in the Argentine, where money had been pouring in through the eighties, and where the economy had overreached itself with among other things a surfeit of railways. Barings were left with a large amount of unmarketable stock on their hands; the first Baron Revelstoke seems to have overreached himself generally, and Barings were about to suspend payments when the City came to the rescue. Barings were saved before news could get out and cause a panic, but for a few days it was touch and go. At another of the senior merchant banks, three minutes' walk from Barings, they have some elaborate mahogany in their lavatories. The reason for this is solemnly sworn to date from the Baring Crisis, when Lord Revelstoke was wandering the City in a desperate search for money. At his neighbours' he saw one of the senior partners, but they couldn't find a private room to talk in. The best they could do was go into a lavatory, where Revelstoke revealed his grave news. Meanwhile the partner was so ashamed at the humble state of the fittings that he had immediate improvements put in hand.

Schroders, the third in the traditional triumvirate of Rothschilds, Barings, and Schroders, while not as successful as Rothschilds at resisting change, hasn't done badly. It turned itself into a public company and offered its shares to the public in 1959 – the idea being to prepare for the inevitable blow of death duties by having ready shares quoted on the Stock Exchange. Schroders, who began as emigrant merchants from Hamburg in 1804, had had only four heads of the firm between then and 1959, all Schroders; the present one is Helmut William Bruno Schroder, a gentle-faced man who turned over 15 per cent of the privately held shares, worth nearly £1,200,000, to the public. More profitable than the London end of the business is the New York subsidiary, the J. Henry Schroder Banking Corporation, which

Barings helped establish in 1923, and in which they had, when the prospectus of the Schroder issue was published in September 1959, a stake of more than $500,000 at the shares' nominal value. This prospectus gives a rare glimpse of who owns what in a merchant bank – though 'glimpse' is the operative word. By far the largest stake in the new holding company of Schroders Ltd was acquired from an odd collection of companies with such names as Flavida, Winley, Horos, and the Veritas Trust – companies used by the Schroder family to hold shares. Of a total of 5,000,000 new £1 shares, 3,376,762 were left with the Flavidas and Winleys, and ultimately with a new family company called J. H. S. Holdings. These shares were believed to represent the holding of H. W. B. Schroder himself and his sisters – Helene Dorothee Eveline Emma Baroness Schroder and Marga Marie Hilda Schroder. A block of 291,033 shares was held mainly by directors and managing directors in London; 33,000 shares was the normal holding of a working director. The Tiarks family hold an important interest: apart from 33,000 shares as a director, Henry Frederic Tiarks held another 135,922, and two other members of his family shared 126,136. Baring Bros held 320,147, which left just 750,000 £1 shares available, at 32s. 6d. each, that the public could and did apply for. The public now have a stake in Schroders Ltd; but the Schroders remain firmly in charge. To have it otherwise would be unthinkable for a merchant banker whose walls are decorated with this kind of inscription – the script is Persian, with a translation beneath which reads:

Having regard to the concord happily existing between the two countries of England and Persia and in consideration of the High Imperial favours entertained towards the Honble John Henry William Schroder, this year sent in an epistle a decoration of the order of SHARE KHOORSHEED – the Lion and the Sun – of the First Class is given him, and we hereby order him to wear that said decoration and boast and pride himself in it, so that this graceful ornament, while it fixed its own honour on the breast, may be held high and exalted. Dated this month of Rejab 1808. Equivalent to from 10 February to 9 March 1891. The Seal of the Ameen-ul-Sultan, Grand Vizier, is affixed on the back of the ornament.

But however impressive they look in tableau, merchant banks can be properly appreciated only in motion. They get their most frequent mentions in connexion with take-overs, share issues, and the affairs of British companies generally, since they have become increasingly important in this field with the decline in their overseas business. They, rather than the clearing banks who do the straightforward banking business, are the ultimate advisers to a growing slice of industry – a fact that clearing banks often resent in private, though they admit that they aren't so well equipped to nurse a company and have no wish to be involved in the actual trading side by, for instance, taking a prior charge on goods, as a merchant bank will do. A clearing bank official said: 'It isn't good enough to ask us to provide £50 worth of silver on a Friday for pay packets, and then go and see your merchant banker on Monday morning.' But in public at any rate everyone is discreet about this and talks of 'complementary services' and 'all pulling together'. An industrialist feels he's buying something special by going to a merchant bank. By 1960, with the economy in better shape than it was through most of the forties and fifties, clearing banks, freed from restrictions, were doing what they could to make themselves attractive; but the merchant bankers, who were able to fall back on their unique knowledge of the bill of exchange as a means of giving credit, have remained more flexible all along. There is something superior about the way they refer to the 'joint-stockers', though any one of the leading joint-stockers could buy out half the merchant bankers on the spot. And industrialists continue to be attracted by the mixture of expertise, glamour, confidence, and *élan* that the merchant banks provide.

One of the houses they have been attracted to in large numbers is the new and humming business of Siegmund George Warburg, which, founded in London in 1946, has stolen a march on some of the hoarier houses when it comes to industry-nursing. Warburgs is the newest member but one of the Accepting Houses Committee, and one of the two that leave their names unqualified in the phone book (the other one is Barings). Warburgs have been known on the Continent since the time of the French

Revolution, and in Britain it hasn't taken them long to enter the select inner circle. To be in the first rank, a City merchant bank has to satisfy the Bank of England: specifically, the bills of exchange which it accepts must rank at the Bank as first-class security in the event of a discount house, or anyone else, wishing to deposit the bills as security for a loan. Such a bill is, in the jargon, 'eligible paper'. It is a 'fine bank bill'. Along with Treasury bills and short-dated bonds it represents the next best thing to cash. The committee has no written rules, going one step further than the Discount Market Association, which has rules but says it finds difficulty in understanding them. It's more of a gentlemen's agreement than a formal committee, but it has snubbed more than one bank that would have liked to get in. To have one's acceptances taken at the Bank of England is the first requisite for membership. Members regularly send parcels of accepted bills to Threadneedle Street for the Bank to see there are no dubious ones among them. They must never have more than three times their capital resources under acceptance. In a sense they are at the mercy of the Bank, though since accepting now forms a comparatively small part of their business they are more independent than they were. Probably the prestige is the really important part of being on the committee. Four of the Bank's sixteen part-time directors are from the accepting houses – none from the big clearing banks, an anachronism from the days when merchant banks were the only ones that mattered. There is a parallel organization, the *Issuing* Houses Committee. Seventeen of the eighteen accepting houses belong to it, but so do more than forty other firms; it's nothing like so exclusive.

Warburgs became members of the Accepting Houses Committee soon after they merged with a merchant bank that was already there, Seligman Brothers. Technically the member is one of the Seligman family; as with many City organizations, an·individual nominated by the firm, not the firm itself, is the member. Founded in Hamburg in 1798, Warburgs were merchants and bankers in Germany, but not in Britain till 1946, when the present house was started by S. G. Warburg, who had been a partner in Hamburg till he had to leave Germany in the

1930s: the Warburgs are Jews, though Gentiles now outnumber them on the board. S. G. Warburg has a square, sensitive face, a thick accent, a sharp wit; he likes pictures and music, has dispensed with the formality of the banking parlour, and established a reputation for shrewdness and determination. Most types of business have one special character like Warburg – an individualist, a person of whom all those inside that business and plenty outside it have heard, a source of small legends even in his early days, a successful man of action who insists that he doesn't want publicity, but can never hope to avoid it.

The hand of the house of Warburg has been seen in, among other places, commercial television in Britain, where it advised and helped finance one of the major contractors, Associated Television, in its early days; more dramatically, Warburgs were in the thick of the Great Aluminium War of 1958, a City episode that gave the best opportunity for a long time (always excepting the Bank Rate tribunal) to see the merchant banks in motion and full Technicolor. American take-overs of British interests are always regarded with suspicion by Britons. When American Ford bid more than $300,000,000 for British Ford in the winter of 1960, there was a public outcry, though the fact was that control had never shifted from Detroit, which already held 54 per cent of the shares when the bid was made. The Mayor of Dagenham went to see the Chancellor; M.P.s made angry speeches; but the offer, handled by the banking house of Lazards, was bowed through by the Treasury (which had to approve the transfer of shares to the United States).

However, the Ford take-over roused few City passions in the manner of the Aluminium War. This began when two American leaders of the aluminium industry decided the time was ripe to obtain a foothold in Britain and have access to the large potential markets there. The British Aluminium Co., making one third of all aluminium products in the U.K., was the tasty morsel that they coveted simultaneously. B.A.'s output of aluminium, supplied chiefly from its refineries in Scotland and Canada, was only 3 per cent of the world total: small stuff by American standards. But a new reduction plant that B.A. had just completed in Canada made it particularly attractive to the American Reynolds Metals. Alcoa, the Aluminium Company of America, was the other bidder. It was one of those well-publicized take-overs in which banks and chairmen grope around interminably, never wholly in view, like giants in heavy armour performing slowly on the skyline. The merchant banks fell into two camps, one of them stiffly supporting Alcoa (which was B.A.'s own choice), the other, the Warburg camp, supporting Reynolds. Before the affair was over, questions were being asked in Parliament, tempers were flaming in the banking parlours, appeals to British patriotism were being made in public and in private, and some of the Old Guard in the City had suffered a painful slap in the eye. The Press came out with such headlines as *This Has Gone Far Enough*. It was, said the *Financial Times*, 'building up grudges which should not exist between the leading institutions of the City itself', adding that to Reynolds and Alcoa, who were making the running, it was probably no more than 'a fight between two vast empires for a distant province – almost like Russia and Austro-Hungary fighting in the Balkans in the old days.' It was (though the *F.T.* didn't say so) another reminder that the City, for all its domestic power and glory, nowadays often finds itself a spectator on the fringe of the crowd.

When Reynolds Metals decided to go after British Aluminium, they took the advice of the New York investment bankers, Kuhn, Loeb, to cooperate with a British firm and so make the take-over more acceptable in Britain. They went into partnership with Tube Investments, a leading British metals firm, under a contract signed in September 1957. Meanwhile Reynolds, and later Tube Investments, were acquiring British Aluminium shares through the market and under cover of nominee buyers. Warburgs were organizing these purchases – S. G. Warburg has been a partner in Kuhn, Loeb since 1951, and the London house is an associate company. The buying went on slowly, month by month. British Aluminium had the makings of a take-over bidder's target. Its shares stood around thirty-seven shillings, after being in the eighties in 1956. It needed money to expand. The chairman, Lord Portal, and his directors, knew someone was after them, and in November 1958 cards were laid on the table and a meeting held at British Aluminium headquarters. S. G. Warburg was there as adviser to Reynolds and Tube Investments. Advising the other side were men from two of the most impressive and long-established houses – Lazards, with several peers on the board, and Hambros, the biggest merchant bank of all.

The potential purchasers were flatly rejected. Less than a month later B.A. were announcing a deal with Alcoa. Either way, it was now inevitable that at least partial control of B.A. would pass out of Britain. But the B.A./Hambros/Lazards axis insisted that the Alcoa deal meant American collaboration, while the Reynolds deal meant American domination. If the Reynolds bid succeeded, the B.A. stock would be vested in the new Reynolds-T.I. company, which was 49 per cent American and 51 per cent British. This left control in British hands; but, said the B.A. camp, aluminium was a new field for Tube Investments – it was Reynolds who had all the experience. The Alcoa deal meant that only one third of the B.A. stock would pass to an American company.

However, the financial Press was quick to point out that a one-third holding was normally enough to give whoever owned it absolute control, when the other two-thirds were spread among shareholders; besides, if Alcoa won and the Reynolds-T.I. camp sold out their holding of B.A. stock (they had acquired about 10 per cent so far), Alcoa might end up with more than 40 per cent. The financial Press also came out with sharp criticism of the B.A. board for doing the deal with Alcoa – it involved selling 4,500,000 unissued B.A. shares, a third of the equity – at a time when B.A. had already received approaches from T.I.-Reynolds. The truth about these early approaches was soon obscured by the dust of general disagreement over what was best and what was proper for City men to do. Few merchant bankers are now willing to talk about the details. Hambros won't. Lazards won't. S. G. Warburg won't. But mixed up with purely commercial considerations were strong personal feelings, a sense of animosity that coloured the open struggle for shares and support through November and December 1958. The climax came on New

Year's Eve, when, with neither side's offer having attracted
sufficient acceptances from shareholders, an anti-Reynolds consortium of bankers, a strange galaxy of fourteen accepting houses,
issuing houses, and investment trusts, made an offer, apparently
off its own bat and not on behalf of British Aluminium, to buy
B.A. stock. The letter to shareholders, signed by the then chairman of Hambros, R. Olaf Hambro, and the chairman of Lazards,
Lord Kindersley, declared that the Reynolds offer must be
resisted in the national interest. The City had spoken. After all,
the consortium had a backbone of the stiffest kind in the shape
of seven accepting houses: besides Lazards and Hambros were
Brown, Shipley; Guinness, Mahon; Samuel Montagu; Morgan
Grenfell (who are very friendly with Lazards; they're associated
with Morgan Guaranty Trust Co. of New York); and M.
Samuel. Rightly or wrongly, the impression got around that here
was the Old Guard of the City closing its ranks, setting its face
against newcomers – for even the important Tube Investments
was a Midlands firm that had risen quickly in the world, with its
head office in Birmingham.

After this all restraint was abandoned; the consortium did
more harm than good. Reynolds and Tube Investments stopped
treading carefully, went into the market, and bought every share
they could lay hands on. Insurance companies and other institutions, not to mention the Church of England, which held large
blocks of B.A. stock, annoyed by the consortium's heavy-
handedness, avoided accepting either offer but instead sold on
the Stock Exchange, where the Reynolds-T.I. stockbrokers were
buying furiously. Within nine days they held 80 per cent of the
shares, and the consortium had suffered a dismal defeat. Two
months later Lord Portal got the golden handshake – £30,000
tax free – as did the B.A. managing director, the Honourable
Geoffrey Cunliffe, who collected £58,000 tax free as a parting gift.
(Substantial, but a long way from the record. Sir Charles Colston
got £83,575* when he left Hoovers, the domestic-appliance
makers, in 1954. Sir Frank Spriggs got £75,000 when he left

* Sir Charles looks like keeping the record for ever. The Chancellors'
1960 Budget Speech ended the golden handshake.

Hawker Siddeley, the aircraft manufacturers.) Alcoa, still without a foothold in the U.K., had to wait another eighteen months; then they joined forces with Imperial Chemical Industries to form a new British company, Imperial Aluminium – I.C.I. keeping 51 per cent of the shares. Alcan, the Aluminium Company of Canada, already had U.K. outlets. Only Kaiser Aluminium and Chemical Corp., among the American giants, were left odd men out, and this was remedied in January 1960 when Kaiser acquired a half interest in James Booth Aluminium. Whether the City liked it or not, the Americans had moved in in a big way on British aluminium: not just British Aluminium.

In the weeks after B.A. fell to the Reynolds camp, tempers cooled slowly in the City. In a letter to *The Times*, R. Olaf Hambro put the losers' disappointment on permanent record when he wrote that it was 'very unclear why the majority of the City editors of the Press seemed to be against City opinion and openly wrote in favour of the take-over bid'. Not surprisingly this got Hambro a bad press. However much anonymous support there had been for the consortium, as he suggested, no one could help noticing the absence of any outward sign from such senior banks as Rothschilds and Barings. Schroders had been on the same side as Warburgs, advising Tube Investments; so had Helbert, Wagg, one of the prime issuing houses. As Hambro said, these two banks had inevitably to back their clients. But I know of at least one senior merchant bank that was asked to join the save-B.A. brigade, and refused point-blank. Hambros, it was suggested, would do better to forget the whole business as quickly as possible.

Making contact with the outside world is not, naturally enough, the merchant bankers' strongest point. If all publicity is felt to be abhorrent, what happens when there is need of favourable publicity? Hambros Bank found their own solution not long after the Great Aluminium War, when it became known that the remarkable public-relations firm of Patrick Dolan, an American who settled in London after 1945, had begun to handle the bank's publicity. The contrast in styles is total: the venerable banking house in gear with the brash young agency. As much as anything, it was a sign of changing times in the City.

5

HOW THEY DO IT AT HAMBROS

A BRIEF account of how Patrick Dolan, proprietor of Dolan, Ducker, Whitcombe & Stewart Ltd, advertising agents, and Patrick Dolan and Associates Ltd, public relations consultants (both merged, in 1960, with the third biggest U.S. advertising agency of Batten, Barton, Durstine, and Osborn) got to know Hambros Bank Ltd, founded in London in 1839, is instructive. Dolan was in U.S. Intelligence during the war; at one time he had been a newspaperman, but he crossed the line into advertising and after the war worked with the London office of an American advertising agency. He was due to go back to New York to be an executive vice-president of the agency when a quarrel blew up and Dolan walked out. That was in 1950, a year when, strange as it seems, organized public relations had yet to arrive in Britain. Dolan decided to fill the gap. He had returned from a trip to America and was surveying the territory when he met a banker called Jocelyn Hambro. It was a casual social meeting. Hambro was a charming, handsome Englishman of thirty-one, who talked about horses and jazz, and seemed interested, in a vague way that could be attributed to good breeding, when Dolan mentioned the P.R. agency.

Next day he rang Dolan and invited him to Bishopsgate, a street where four of the accepting houses live, for lunch. Hambros is at 41, a solid building that couldn't be anything but a bank. It was the first time Dolan had been behind the counter in a British bank, and he didn't know what to expect. Away from the public departments on the ground floor, where the atmosphere resembles a clearing bank except that fewer customers are in sight, is an upper region of carpets and silence. It doesn't have the look of an executive suite rigged out for the purpose, no doubt because it embodies the best executive-suite style of a century ago, though the building dates only from 1926. Instead of looking like a group of rooms which have been quaintly furnished, it's the remainder of the building which seems out of place, as though stripped of its rightful elegance. A merchant bank is good material for a P.R. man since it has an impressive ready-made persona waiting to be projected. Many people have a built-in distaste for the world of striped pants and deferential manservants, but I have yet to meet anyone who isn't impressed by it in the raw, as distinct from being scornful of it in theory. The Hambros butler in morning coat is all you expect of a butler: large, firm, precise, and stern. One feels an overwhelming obligation to whisper. The cabinet of the teleprinter in the hall must have had pounds of polish rubbed into it over the years; beside it, long strips of teletyped messages from the Reuter City Service dangle exactly parallel down the wall. An old raincoat is lifted from you like a precious garment, braced on a coat-hanger, put carefully away in a cupboard; are they trying to make you uneasy? The waiting room, which is also where the bill brokers are received every morning, provides light relief with its sheet of fake books covering the wall on the left of the entrance. From the far end the bust of a Hambro above the heavy fireplace stares at ranks of beautiful old volumes with such titles as *Paley's Works* and *Public General Statistics*, carefully torn here and there, leaning a fraction to left or right, engineered as cunningly as expensive false teeth. Hambros is a big bank, a fine bank, a knowledgeable bank, a powerful bank with many ramifications; but like other City institutions, it's a shade too aware of its dignity.

When Dolan, a heavily built man with a slow heavy voice, called at the bank, he was given an excellent office lunch in the painted Hambro dining room, ending up with port and fruit cake. Other managing directors were there as well as Jocelyn Hambro, but no one mentioned money – they preferred to discuss American politics, and it was only when he and Jocelyn Hambro were walking downstairs after the meal that Hambro put his arm on his shoulder and led him into a small, dark, private room. They sat on high-backed chairs and the banker probably said he had mentioned Dolan's idea around the bank that morning, and everyone had agreed it was very good. Why didn't he go ahead, and Hambros would finance him?

Dolan would say he didn't need financing. The banker would tell him not to be so silly: everyone needed financing. Well, Dolan didn't know how much money he needed. That was easy: the bank would give him a substantial line of credit. At this point no doubt Dolan began to wonder where the catch was, and what he was going to have to sign. But that turned out to be the end of the negotiations. Neither then nor at any time since was he asked to sign a guarantee or produce a piece of collateral. Unsecured borrowing sounds like the business man's dream and the banker's nightmare, and even with the freer credit of the last few years – let alone the stringent conditions of 1950 – few clearing bankers would behave like the Hambros. 'Merchant bankers always know a good credit risk' is one of the axioms – their favourite half-joke is that they can tell a man's suitability for credit by the colour of his socks, and I have even heard a merchant banker give a specific instance of weighing a client's elegant manner against the cut of his clothes, and deciding not to help him ('and you might be interested to learn that that gentleman was in deep water a year later'). It's a good idea to meet men socially and watch them unfold; it's also a good idea to have contacts, the stock-in-trade of merchant bankers – it might be relevant that one of the Hambro directors, who held a high wartime post in British Intelligence, knew Mr Dolan's wartime boss, the famous Major-General 'Wild Bill' Donovan, of O.S.S., the Office of Strategic Services.

It's the thing they are most proud of at merchant banks: the personal touch, the circle of friends, the secret-sharing. They like the elaborate pretence, which isn't altogether pretence, that they are still small family firms where decisions are taken over a cigarette or a brandy, and taken so naturally and easily that they don't appear to be decisions at all, merely coordination by a set of limbs. When I began to ask questions about one of their clients, with the idea of pinpointing a detail of Hambros at work, there was a pause for breath while the client was approached to see if he was willing to allow such an unorthodox inquiry, and then, when he agreed, it turned out there were several versions of how they began doing business with him. It was at a cocktail party – no it wasn't, he walked into the office one afternoon – no he didn't, he had an introduction. It was like asking an individual, rather than an organization, what he was doing a year last Saturday.

Four Hambros are on the board, and though it's a public company, they hold sufficient shares to give the family absolute control. The chairman, Sir Charles Hambro, is also a part-time director of the Bank of England; with him on the board are Jack, Jocelyn, and C. E. A. Hambro. In 1961 the bank's accounts showed deposits of more than £79,000,000 and liability for bills of exchange to a total of £29,000,000. Profits are very comfortable at Hambros. There is, for instance, the Hambro Automotive Corporation, handling all exports of British Motor Corporation cars to the United States, which may be worth anything from £20,000,000 to £30,000,000 in a year. H. A. C. had a curious beginning, as Jocelyn Hambro assured me one afternoon when I had called at 41 Bishopsgate, and saw him in the waiting room. He talks with bursts of energy, not very clearly; with a slightly pedantic, very English use of the full phrase – 'motor car', 'motor bicycle', 'Continent of Europe' – but at the same time a throwaway manner, as if the story really concerned someone else. It was about money, deals, rogues, and hard selling, but it didn't seem to have the weight of those things behind it: it was merely a funny story about enthusiastic young men wandering round the United States, having a rather amusing time.

It began after the war, when the Governor of the Bank of England sent (among others) for the accepting houses and said the duty of all good City men was to earn dollars for Britain. 'To earn dollars' became a ritual phrase after 1945, more significant even than such bits of the post-war vocabulary as 'squander bug', 'Mr Rising Price', and 'inflationary spiral'. The United States was the universal provider; either it lent you the money, or you painfully persuaded it to take your imports, and so built up a credit balance for yourself. There were those who didn't take the dollar-drive seriously. 'Spivs' and 'black market' were other key words of the time. In the City there were characters who felt that they and their wives or mistresses needed a holiday in the New World, and went off on bogus sales trips with official dollars in their pockets. Other characters ploughed ahead and did their duty.

What Hambros did was to form a little company in Dallas, Texas – it wasn't clear why they picked on Dallas, except it was felt that the Mid-West was an easier market than the East Coast – and, with an advance of $10,000 from the Bank of England, start exporting any kind of English manufactures that Americans were likely to be interested in. I mentioned to Jocelyn Hambro a remark I had heard elsewhere, that the merchant banks had long since passed from the adventuring stage into senescence. 'If I told you the story of the Hambro Trading Corporation,' he said, 'I bet you'd say we were adventurers.' They exported women's skirts, pottery, glass, and two-stroke motor bikes. Thinking hopefully that there was a virgin market for English honey, they shipped a large quantity to New York, where several thousand pounds were lying in a warehouse when fermentation got the better of it and the containers blew up. They tried Scottish kippers, found they were exporting the wrong size for the American market, had to deal with quaysides covered in rotting fish, became involved in delicate negotiations with the Scottish Herring Board, and for many months supplied the American market with deep-frozen kippers.

For a year everything went out on a credit basis. There were no books, no precedents, scarcely any record of business except in people's head. Organization in New York was *ad hoc*; there were the perils of starting a business in a strange, tough city where instead of decent whisky they drank dangerous things like martini; in Europe the financial crises rumbled along nose to tail; and when it became apparent that Hambros were losing dollars instead of earning them, the Bank of England, which was in any case more interested in supporting manufacturers, grew cool towards the venture. Only the motor bikes were selling well –

and, after a while, M.G. sports cars. But someone managed to persuade the British Motor Corporation, the largest car makers in Britain, to send out a couple of M.G.s. When they arrived in Dallas a man remarked that it was the first time he'd seen a malted milk machine with wheels on; but it was a new toy, and it became the smart thing to have one.

Jocelyn Hambro and other bright young men from the bank roamed the States looking for dealers who would take the M.G.s – many car dealers weren't allowed to handle imported vehicles – and when they found them, setting them up with new cars on credit. In Dallas it was the local juke-box distributor. In California it was the Philco radio distributor. They would call at a bank and say: 'Who's the nicest chap you know in the neighbourhood?' The snag was that many banks they visited in the Middle West had never heard of Hambros; it wasn't like being in Europe. 'And how do you suppose we could tell a good American from a bad one?' said Hambro. 'It's always harder to distinguish between foreigners than your own nationality, but it's worse with Americans because there's a tendency to think they're more like us. The average Englishman at that time was convinced he knew America and the Americans because they spoke the same language – but that was purely coincidental.'

So sometimes they lost money. 'We had a distributor in Chicago. When he'd got about forty thousand pounds' worth of our motor cars he bought a house for his wife in Florida and went bankrupt himself. We never got it back, and what's more we never looked like getting it back. You could tell from the judge's face in the court – he was damned if any limey was going to get the money out of him. Even the Press reports made it seem we were absolute ogres, trying to screw money out of this poor fellow.' They lost money in Atlanta. They had trouble with the Customs. They were sued for $2,000,000 by an unsatisfactory dealer who said he'd been slandered, and had to settle for a large sum. And all this time they were trying to persuade distributors to take honey, skirts, and kippers as well. In 1950, when a few more dollars were available, the Hambro House of Design was set up on New York's 54th Street. As game as ever, Hambros offered everything from Swedish glass and the ubiquitous pottery to English custard and the products of Fortnum & Mason. High-powered, high-salaried men worked there, under a high-salaried American. There was a linen division; you could buy hand-kerchiefs with your initials, special tiny handkerchiefs, special trimmed handkerchiefs for funerals. It was no good. The Hambro House of Design lost money, and the bank pulled out, losing more money in the process. Jocelyn Hambro says now that he thinks bankers shouldn't trade, not as a rule. 'We don't know how to trade – we know about financing trade, not about selling goods. The popular idea that we're still merchants isn't true. Every time we've tried we've come unstuck, with one or two exceptions, notably cars.'

The car exports prospered, and B.M.C. handed over all their U.S. business to Hambro Automotive Corp. Each month perhaps £2,000,000 or £3,000,000 worth of cars are paid for by Hambros Bank, who send the cheque as soon as the bill of lading reaches them from the docks at Liverpool or wherever the cars are being shipped. A small team works at the London end, paying the cheques to B.M.C. and sending the documents to New York, where H.A.C. has a staff of nearly five hundred. It was an exception worth waiting for.

Hambros pop up all over the place, though their strongest associations are traditionally with Scandinavia, financing general trade and shipbuilding. They are, like the rest of the merchant banks, in on post-war expansion generally. There is Patrick Dolan's group of agencies. There is Gomme's furniture, a com-pany which woke up to the antiquated condition of the furniture industry and started selling branded furniture in the 1950s – an innovation at the time. One of the Hambro managing directors became chairman of the Gomme board at the end of 1959. There is Farley's Infant Food, Ltd, who make a famous rusk; they were floated as a public company early in 1960, and deep in the small print it says that fees of £7,000, less certain expenses, will be payable to Hambros Bank. There is Kenneth Maynard Wood, a rising manufacturer who began a few years ago with electric toasters and egg-poachers, came into the money with a mixing machine, and is prospering like, and to some extent because of, the bankers.

K. M. Wood was the client who had to be consulted before anyone could tell me about him. In a sense one could say 'the bankers moved in' on Wood, except that the phrase might suggest there was something wrong. In the end the bankers move in everywhere. Few firms can hope to keep expanding out of profits. Industry lives on an overdraft, and between lending money and suggesting how best to persuade others to lend it, the banks make themselves indispensable. When a merchant bank moves in, it's unlikely to be by advancing its own money. K. M. Wood's mixers and refrigerators, the ones that go to the docks for export, are paid for by a revolving acceptance credit. At any time the firm can draw bills up to a specified amount, send them to Hambros, and collect cash for them – the bills then being sold by Hambros in the discount market, the ultimate owner of the bills being reimbursed by Wood's company, Kenwood, when the bills reach maturity in three months' time.

For a steady exporter with a permanent gap between making goods and getting the money for them, this type of credit can still be more useful than a straight overdraft from a clearing bank. There's less red tape, fewer formalities. The Kenwood factory is at Old Woking, twenty miles outside London. To deal with a clearing bank means dealing with the nearest branch, so that any matter involving head office has to go through the branch manager, who pushes it up the line to London, who pass the answer back to the branch – that was the impression they had at Kenwood. Another advantage of being with Hambros was that advice was ready when the company decided to push the boat out and expand.

This happened in 1958 and 1959: a routine operation from the outside, worth the occasional paragraph in the financial Press, but rather different from the inside, where files were opened, deals made, counsel briefed, ingenuity stretched, nails bitten, bills run up, and many hundreds of clerk and management hours expended. The point of the operation was to turn Kenwood into a public company. Before the war Wood made radio sets. After it he had a hunch that domestic appliances were the thing; he was looking for a factory one day in 1947 when he changed trains at Woking, found time to call on an estate agent, and got what he wanted. He now has a new factory, with a plaque to say it was opened by the local Member of Parliament, and striped upholstery in his office; Dale Carnegie's *How to Stop Worrying and Start Living* was in his bookcase when I called, though you couldn't honestly say he looked as if he needed it.

But a private limited company is no use to the expanding man who wants to make the most of the system. A public company can issue shares and raise money: that's one reason for going public. Another is, of course, surtax, which begins to nibble high incomes on a scale that rises to seventeen, eighteen, and at one time more than nineteen shillings in the pound. People pay surtax: companies don't. At one time a privately owned company could plough its profits back into the business, which would gain in value accordingly, without its owners having to pay surtax. But this pleasant loophole was stopped up long ago, and in the case of a private company the Revenue can treat the income of the company as the income of the members – and start charging surtax. Going public puts an end to that.

There are various ways of becoming a public company, and the Kenwood/Hambro method was to obtain someone else's quotation. This meant a saving of several thousand pounds: when a company goes public and applies for a Stock Exchange quotation, full-page advertisements have to be placed in two newspapers, giving a mass of detail in tiny print. These, and the attendant preparations, can be expensive and troublesome. Fortunately there was a company to hand that suited Kenwood's purpose, a concern called Peerless & Ericsson that had been going downhill and had lost money to the extent of £242,907. Peerless & Ericsson made canteen equipment, so it was suitably similar to Kenwood. It had a Stock Exchange quotation. And it had that convenient loss of nearly a quarter of a million pounds.

Taxation, so the accountants are fond of saying, isn't a matter of equity or common sense. Britain's is said to be better than most countries', but no one could say that tax law amounts to much more than a lumber of jargon and precedent, nicely riddled with loopholes: not the *same* loopholes all the time, of course, since the Revenue and the public's taxation advisers are in a constant state of war. However, the tax-loss company is no loop-hole. It has the status of a principle – should a man think it sounds curious, it means he lacks business acumen. To the non-business-man a company that has lost money is the last thing you want to buy. To the businessman a loss can be a valuable thing, worth paying a price for. Because if you combine your business with a business that has lost £100, you are buying the right to set that loss against profits: you can make a profit of £100 and instead of paying tax on it, set it against the loss, whereupon the two cancel out. The Revenue's attitude is that the money *has* been lost by someone in the first place; there is a genuine loss, and if the company that has sustained it cares to set a price on the loss, and another company cares to pay for it, that's legitimate. Having heard the explanation it still sounds a little crazy. Finance has a very special air of cloud-cuckoo-land, of a State within a State; it has its own standards, laws, and cast of thought, so that once a man is absorbed into this realm he can see nothing odd about it. Perhaps this lack of introspection is less common than it was. The City has been needled so often in recent years that they can scent a criticism before it leaves the tongue. As I once heard someone say: 'There's nothing wrong with tax-loss com-panies, but people don't need to stress that side of it, do they?'

It was decided that a merger with Peerless & Ericsson was the thing to arrange. They had to be careful, because though Ken-wood was really making the running, P. & E. were the company with the Stock Exchange quotation. Should P. & E. be ex-tinguished by some miscalculation, the quotation would dis-appear and the operation would collapse. As a Kenwood director put it: 'We're the company with profits but no quotation, they're the company with quotation but no profits. What we have to do is put ourselves into their shell.' In such cases a third party is called for: someone or something to stand out in front and ostensibly do the work, while behind the scenes the organizers do the organizing. This would allow both Kenwood and P. & E. to deal with a theoretical neutral and so lend verisimilitude to the idea that P. & E. were taking over Kenwood instead of the other way round, as was really the case. 'Inverted take-over' is the phrase they use.

The third party was a company bought for the purpose in a shop just outside the City, at the eastern end of the Strand. Knowing where to go for the right company would hardly count as one of Hambros' important services, since anyone who knows anything in the City knows about buying little companies to do odd jobs. But the idea of a shop that sells companies for spot cash, ready-made for collection, is an eye-opener for innocents.

Nothing could be easier than to form a private company in Britain. Formalities are down to a minimum, so that all one has to do is prepare a couple of documents establishing what the company is and what its function will be, and fill in a handful of forms; law stationers sell the necessary paper. A lawyer will do it and charge anything from £50 to £100; at the shop in the Strand a company can be bought, ready-made to suit any purpose, for £25 or so.

Mr Thomas Arthur Herbert, Bachelor of Laws (Honours), of the Middle Temple, Barrister-at-Law, is the man who offers this remarkable service. On the front page of *The Times*, where English eccentricity condenses into print in the form of small-ads (a woman once wanted to contact anyone who had been friendly with a toad) the Herbert ads are by contrast cold, clear, and precise:

A Bargain £25. – For Sale, English and Scottish Co. Regns. (Seal, Statutory Books.) Guaranteed no trading, ready now, state trade wanted. – BUSINESS ECONOMY (T/SP), 156 Strand, London, WC2 (Tem 8377/2294); also at 19 Walker Street, Edinburgh, 3 (Cal. 1167). Seven-day incorporation service in England and Scotland. Get copy – 'ADVANTAGES of TRADING as a LIMITED COMPANY', 3s. post free.

I arrived at 156 Strand one summer's afternoon. Across the road men in neat suits were returning from lunch to the official Companies Registration Office at Bush House – this is where City

journalists anxious to find who owns a company pay the shilling
search fee and look up the list of shareholders (as often as not the
shares will be held in the name of a nominee company, so they're
none the wiser). Outside the shop three or four men were looking
in the window with the sad absorption of tourists outside strip
clubs in Soho. Their eyes followed the words on a set of revolving
cards:

Q. When can I start trading as a limited company?
A. Now! Today! At once!
Q. Does it matter if delay occurs in starting to trade with the
   limited company?
A. No!

The window was solid with information written on cards,
pasted up from newspaper cuttings, and chalked in colour on
blackboard. 'Company annual return forms 6A. 4d. each only
(including purchase tax), 4s. per dozen minimum order.' 'Our
limited companies give unlimited borrowing opportunities to
directors.' 'Aliens can be sole directors of British limited companies. Company's registered office must be here.' Inside the
entrance was a staircase going straight ahead, and a door on
the left. I tried the door. There was an office with a couple of
girls, a smell of tea and gas, and a typewriter with the word
Torpedo on the back of the carriage. A grey-haired man came
down to see me and said he was very busy; they were all very
busy. He said he was a bacteriologist by profession. The person
I needed to see was Mr Herbert, but he was at the Scottish
office – Scottish law being different in many ways from English,
and so requiring special services. I asked if he could confirm that
a company called Smaden Investments had been bought here in
connexion with Hambros, the famous merchant bank, and Kenwood, the well-known manufacturers. He thought a minute, then
said: 'Yes, I believe Smaden was coined in the fertile brain of
Mr Herbert. Come back and see him next week.'

The following week I climbed the narrow stairs to Mr Herbert's
office, pausing on the way to read the battery of signs on the
first-floor landing. These began:

Please Walk In. Herbert's Commercial Register, Ltd.
When door is locked please call at third floor. Please shut the door.
  Thank you.
Business Economy Products, Ltd.
Business Economy Company Registrations, Ltd.
Herbert's Commercial Register.
Anglo-French Press Agency, Ltd.
North London Passenger Protection Association, Ltd.
Brownia Investments, Ltd.
Cranbridge Trading Co., Ltd.

– and so on for another twenty-seven names. Mr Herbert's room
was large, with a desk deep in paper and full filing baskets. Plush
dining chairs and steel tubular ones stood about; there was a
gas fire and ferns. Herbert, an engaging man with a grizzled face
and untidy grey hair, sat behind the desk and explained how he
came to be a specialist in company sales. He had gradu-
ated at Liverpool University, been a journalist, and worked in
solicitors' offices as everything from office boy to chief clerk. He
had practised at the bar. In 1947, with the Labour Party in power,
austerity and rationing in force, and a feeling among many
businessmen that private enterprise would never be the same
again, Herbert went calmly ahead and started his over-the-
counter sales of companies. The previous year, 1946, had seen a
flood of company formation as conditions adjusted themselves
after the war – 24,170 companies in twelve months. It might be a
few years before there was another season like that, but in the
meantime, in spite of nationalization, fuel crises, and bread
rationing, companies would continue to be born as surely as
babies. Herbert had twelve years to wait, till 1959, before there
was another record year, with 28,150 companies registered –
followed in 1960 by another 34,312, giving a total of 390,000 in
Britain. All but 15,000 of this remarkable number were private
companies, formed for practically every purpose known to man
that could be made to appear legitimate. Hundreds of little
investment companies, formed by property dealers to expedite
their operations, have helped swell the total; and since Herbert's
share is a fair cross-section, some of the anagram-like titles of the

property boom have come to be thought up at 156 Strand. The use to which people put their companies is not, of course, any more to do with Herbert than with the Companies Registration Office. His companies are seeds that could grow into anything. Each has an authorized capital of £100, which means that stamp duty and Government fees have been paid entitling the company to issue shares up to £100. The minimum number of shares that must be paid for is two, and Herbert's ready-made companies have two apiece, subscribed for by himself and his wife, which are transferred to whoever buys the company – Herbert is a member of the Association of Stock and Share Dealers, the Outside Brokers, and so can arrange these transfers.

Company titles need careful thought. If Herbert is forming a company to order, the client, deluded with grandeur, may light on the British National Limousine Corporation for his second-hand car lot off the North Circular. It won't do, though it would have once, as many pre-1948 titles go to prove. In 1948 the Companies Act empowered the Board of Trade to reject titles that displease it. The Board is displeased, on the whole, with the overtones suggested by 'Royal', 'King', 'Queen', 'Princess', 'Crown', 'Imperial', 'Commonwealth', 'International', 'Corporation', 'Bank', 'Banking' (but you can tack on the word 'Bankers' and get away with it), 'British', 'National', or anything suggesting some subtle link with a Government department or a town council, let alone anything that flatters a humble company by suggesting it's worldwide or record-breaking or about to make millions. A man's name and initials, followed by the name of the town or district in brackets, seems to be the Board of Trade's ideal. When Mr Herbert is forming companies and stockpiling them for readymade sales he has no idea who'll buy them; he has to avoid all the pitfalls, including the risk that it will sound like an existing company; and this accounts for the anonymous sound of 'Smaden'.

Mr Herbert and I never quite came together with our questions and answers, chiefly because the more I learned about the trade in companies the more extraordinary it all seemed, and my attention wandered. Among the papers he pushed across the desk was an extract from his Company Sales Register, cyclostyled on a foolscap sheet. A typical entry read:

TOURING AGENCY. COACH CRUISES. Incorporated 1954. Authorized Capital and Issued Capital £2,000. Directors' Loans Transferable £8,164. Excellent name. Agreed Income Tax Loss £10,513 + £500. Price 20% of Tax Loss.

This meant that Mr Herbert also acted as a broker in tax-loss companies. But I didn't understand what directors' loans were, and when I tried to ask, he was on the phone to another part of the building. 'Let me have a word with Joan. Joan? I tell you what, I've got a gentleman here who's writing a book about the City, and he wants some information with regard to ready-made companies and ordinary companies. Bring him up the forms he'd have to sign – I want a property company, a property-dealing company, and an investment company, and I want a yellow form and I want the green forms . . .'

While we waited for the forms we got on to the subject of his house. There was a double garden, with pools and goldfish that ate from the hand, and a waterfall: once upon a time in (I supposed) some halcyon days when everything was nicer, there had been four boys who were so devoted to their childhood nanny that when they grew up they each made her an allowance so that she wouldn't have to work. She saved the money and left it back to them in her will, and the men, faced with this touching product of reciprocal love, ploughed it back into the property; this was the reason for the two gardens around the house that Herbert now occupied. 'And this happened many, many years ago,' he said. 'We've got two garages – and if you look outside the window you'll see my Jaguar, and we've got a Daimler automatic as well.' He said he had to travel a good deal. I couldn't see the street from where I was sitting, but I could hear a street musician playing, on an accordion, what sounded like a hymn.

'Directors' loans –' I began; but the forms had arrived. 'I don't want to sell you a company that is no good to you,' said Mr Herbert. 'There's no high-pressure salesmanship. It says there, as you see, that this particular company's for investment and you must not traffic in lands. You'll only be able to claim management expenses for that. Now then, you fill in R.M.C.1 – that's Ready Made Companies One. You see here it says . . .'

The system had been brought to a fine art, and it seemed almost a pity not to buy a company for luck. (I later heard of a barrister specializing in company matters who was given a £25 company as a wedding present.) Herbert finished abruptly, looked at his watch, and decided it was time he left for an appointment at Pinewood Film Studios, outside London, where a technician earning £4,000 a year intended to form himself into a limited company (common practice with, among others, film stars and successful journalists: income can be spread more evenly over the years, and expenses charged more easily). There was just time, between the desk and the stairs, to learn about directors' loans. He gave me an instance:

There was a rich woman who had decided that she would provide the money for her daughter and son-in-law to run a company exporting to Nigeria. Nigeria is known to be the worst market you could ever have for getting your money. Everybody avoids Nigeria. This export company could get heaps of business provided they gave credit. So they gave credit – twelve thousand pounds worth.

Now, they'd formed a £100 company and she'd been feeding it. It was her baby. One day she got fed up with putting money into it and seeing it being lost, and she said: 'I'm stopping.' So another firm that was exporting similar goods said: 'We'll take over this company and leave you as director. We'll give you four bob in the £ for your shares, and we'll make it a success.'

The rich woman, I saw, was getting four shillings in the £ from her speculative venture; but what were the purchasers getting?

'Don't you see?' said Mr Herbert. 'It's simple – the directors could collect the debt back from the company surtax free. If they were debt collectors they wouldn't get it. But provided they're a trading company, that's all right. The directors bought her debt. She's loaned the company £12,000 and so the new directors could draw out the money to repay the debt without paying tax on it.'

It was all so easy. A few doors down the Strand the contents bills of a magazine were advertising 'Highly Paid Executive

Posts Vacant', and you knew there was a catch in it. On the bus going back into the City was a long strip of advertisement for or by the Tramcar and Omnibus Scripture Text Mission, displaying a gaudily printed Biblical text, and again it seemed probable that there was more in the words than met the eye. But those directors' loans weren't dreams or hopes: they were a cast-iron piece of, comparatively speaking, something for nothing.

Back at Hambros I heard details of the offer by the bank, acting on behalf of Smaden Investments, acting (except that this wasn't publicized at the time) for Mr Wood, for the Pre-ference and Ordinary shares of Peerless & Ericsson. By now, the autumn of 1959, it was already a year old. The money for the offer came from Hambros, who lent it, not direct to Smaden – this would have been a most elementary mistake – but to Mr Wood, who was then able to lend it interest-free to Smaden Investments, while claiming surtax relief on the interest he paid Hambros for the loan. The offer was only partly successful. Instead of being plain sailing, there was the awkward matter of a minority of shareholders who wouldn't sell. They may have included some late buyers who invested in P. & E. when market gossip was pushing the price up, and who wanted a still better price than Hambros/Smaden/Mr Wood were offering. Between 70 and 80 per cent of shareholders accepted; the rest hung on. Wood and his co-directors were able to move in on the Peerless board and start reorganizing – they did this so efficiently that Hambros were a little worried that things had taken a turn for the better so quickly. But Mr Wood, though he controlled 72½ per cent of the £300,000 5½ per cent Cumulative Preference stock and 77 per cent of the £126,000 Ordinary stock, couldn't go ahead with his plans as he would have done if the whole of the stock had come into his possession.

The prelude to the inverted take-over was to reorganize the capital structure of Peerless. In effect, this meant taking into consideration the money that had been lost. The 504,000 five-shilling Ordinary shares would become 504,000 one-shilling shares, which is what they were thought to be worth. But the total authorized capital of the company – the amount that could be raised by issues of shares – would stay the same; it simply meant that a higher proportion of the shares would now be un-issued. There would be 5,596,000 unissued shares of one shilling each, ready for future contingencies: which would include an exchange of shares with Kenwood when the time came for the merger. With the capital reorganized, a simple swap of Ordinary shares – one in Kenwood for every four in Peerless – would be rubber-stamped by the Peerless board, which was to all intents and purposes the same as the Kenwood board. In this way Peer-less would have bought Kenwood, and all Peerless would need to do would be change its name to Kenwood, so ending the dream-sequence with the reminder that Kenwood, not Peerless, was where the whole masterly design originated.

Unfortunately, among the minority of shareholders who held out was a group that didn't like the capital-reorganization scheme. As well as the Ordinary shares there was the block of 300,000 $5\frac{1}{2}$ per cent Cumulative Preference; and a small group of these shareholders refused to accept the scheme without concessions. New-style 6 per cent Redeemable Preference shares were to be created in place of the old – the company would have the right to pay off the shareholders at the par value of £1 per unit, but no date was fixed. The objectors asked for a definite redemption date. They suggested, in the nicest possible way, having a rate of interest higher than 6 per cent and a bonus of some sort to compensate for the $46\frac{3}{4}$ per cent of arrears in which the Peerless Preference payments now found themselves. Politely, they pointed out that the increase in interest from $5\frac{1}{2}$ to 6 per cent would mean ninety-three and a half years of regular payment before the arrears disappeared.

This was a sad prospect, and even sadder for the Hambro planners was the prospect of sustained objection by this small thorny group. The High Court's approval is needed for a scheme of arrangement between a company and its shareholders – the idea, not always realized, being to safeguard the interests of shareholders. The protesters might take their protest to court. It was a black thought, but the whole scheme, without which Kenwood would never find itself cosily tucked away within the

Peerless shell, might be put back for months – and all because the holders of 9,000 Preference shares refused to accept terms.

I knew nothing about this for some time. No one seemed very interested in the meetings of shareholders to be held on 16 September 1959, under the aegis of the High Court, since they would be formalities. Mr Wood and his friends held an overwhelming majority of votes, so nothing could halt their resolutions. But never having attended a shareholders' meeting, I thought I'd drop in. Preference shareholders were to meet at 12 noon, Ordinary shareholders at five past. The venue was the Abercorn Rooms in the Great Eastern Hotel, a large railway hotel beside Liverpool Street station which does good business in City meetings and lunches. When the day came I arrived late, having lost my way between dining rooms where waiters were standing about waiting for customers to appear, and reached Abercorn just as a man at the front in a plain brown suit was saying that Ordinary shareholders were making no sacrifice under the scheme. The new Preference shares, he said, were described as redeemable, but when would the board redeem them? Why not set a date for redemption, say fifteen years hence?

It seemed a fine speech, full of reason, and all the more impressive for being delivered at such short range to the imposing row of eight men, sitting at the long raised table, who made up the Peerless board. Mr Wood was there, to the right of centre, with a flowing blue tie, no waistcoat, and a ring on the small finger of his left hand. He looked ruddy and healthy, even in the artificial light – heavy red curtains were drawn across the windows – without having the hot, near-bursting look of some managing directors. But he didn't appear moved by the Preference shareholder's speech. Neither did the chairman of the meeting who was also the chairman of Peerless and the chairman of Kenwood, a cheerful accountant called Mr Senior. 'Ah,' said Mr Senior presently, 'it's so easy to produce a different scheme! If you think you can get sufficient support to stop it, go ahead, but I don't think you can.'

He sounded absolutely confident, but the objector said briskly: 'Then I must vote against it.'

'Oh yes, vote against it by all means,' said Mr Senior encouragingly.

A card vote was passed by a heavy majority. The Ordinary shareholders' meeting followed and went off smoothly, as did the extraordinary general meeting, at which overall approval was sought for the scheme of arrangement. Wood kept standing up shyly to second, or letting Mr Brooking, one of his colleagues, have a turn. It was all over by 12.30, and as the doors were opened and a strong smell of food came down the corridor, a man who had been standing at the back went up to Wood, who was all smiles, and said: 'Easy, wasn't it?'

Still, there remained that minority of Preference shareholders. An air of dampness and frustration settled on faces when I asked what was happening about P. & E. It all depended on the court. The scheme, everyone said at Hambros, was very fair to the Preference people, but you could never tell what the court would think. On the Monday fixed for the hearing I went to the Royal Courts of Justice, a little to the east of the Business Economy offices, only to find, after hanging about in a stone corridor for twenty minutes with a crowd of barristers in wigs and solicitors in hard black hats, all smoking furiously under large NO SMOKING PLEASE notices, that the case had been put off for a week. I went down to the canteen with a man from a solicitor's office who said the law was a very wearing profession. Lord Goddard, when he was Lord Chief Justice, had tried to speed things up, but nothing could speed the wheels of British justice. You waited in corridors and you wasted time. Look at them, he said – the canteen was full of solicitors' clerks wasting their time. The Peerless thing was depressing, but an agreement might be reached among the parties; that was why there had been a postponement.

Sure enough, a week later the Peerless party in the corridor contained some of the top brass, and everyone was smiling. The Peerless hearing was well down the list at Mr Justice Roxburgh's Chancery Court 2, coming under a list of applications by creditors to wind up failing companies – the court was having one of its 'company days', and all the business was commercial. The court itself was a room, not very big, filled with pew-like rows of benches, cases of books behind wired-in glass, and the judge's dais. Several rows had sheets of paper at the end with 'Counsel Only' in crayon, and fifteen or sixteen bewigged barristers, all appearing for the petitioning creditors, sat there, each with an inkwell, a bundle of papers, and his gown rumpled up against the next man. Mr Justice Roxburgh, seated in his large elevated chair, gave the usual judicial impression of a man who might not be listening but who turns out to be listening very hard indeed. No one appeared for the companies to oppose the petitions, and in a few minutes a string of firms with solid title-words like 'General' and 'Sales' and even 'Reliable' and 'Empire' had been hurried along towards their last resting place, some companion volume to the *Register of Defunct and Other Companies*, where 500 pages of small print embalm such corpses as Last Chance Consolidated Silver Mining Co., Blackpool Gigantic Wheel Co., Childe Harold Gold Mining Co., and Land's Puncture Proof Tyre and Automatic Valve Co. Occasionally the tempo changed when some technicality had to be argued – one counsel insisted on contradicting the judge, who promptly relegated the case to later in the morning, when all the knotty ones would be heard together. A solicitor's clerk who came in shortly afterwards, pushing through the crush inside the doors, whispered in my ear: 'Second time round for that one?' I told him it was. 'There's a bastard!' he said, and went back to the canteen for more coffee. Constant traffic jammed the narrow aisles as barristers, clerks, and interested parties came and went. The business of the court flowed on like background music, as if the whispering and head-nodding in the well of the court was the real heart of the proceedings. A barrister snapped his fingers at a boy with a crew-cut and sent him off to his chambers to find a law book – 'It might be on the mantelpiece, if not it's under the table.' Down the end of the room the judge was saying: 'I said *exiguous*, not *ungrammatical*.' There was a little dry coughing and smiling.

Finally, getting on for noon, they came to the matter of Peerless & Ericsson. The court was emptier now, with the Peerless group near the front, the Preference opposition – two men – near the back, and a few barristers between. The counsel for Peerless half stood, leaning on the pew behind, and explained to the judge that the scheme of arrangement as drawn up and printed had met with opposition, but that agreement had now been reached on a modified scheme. The judge was on it like a flash. He was not, he said, prepared to sanction a secret agreement. What he was being asked to approve was neither the scheme as it stood nor a completely revised one that had been passed by a new batch of shareholders' meetings. 'If a scheme is unopposed, that's all right,' said the judge. 'People are more expert than I am. But if these Preference shareholders have punched a hole in it . . .'

It looked as if the whole thing was going to collapse. Counsel had explained that most of the Peerless shares were held by Hambros Nominees – Smaden Investments, its duty done, had been liquidated by now. The beneficial owners (the real as distinct from the technical owners) of the shares were Messrs Senior, Wood, and Brooking, who were also directors of a company with which it was proposed to enter into an agreement (the word 'Kenwood' wasn't mentioned). 'There are commercial reasons', said counsel for the Preference side, 'for approving the scheme quickly.'

The atmosphere was a trifle tense, but eased by continual good humour. Counsel were cannier than the argumentative barrister earlier in the morning who had quibbled with the judge and ended up going second time round. They appreciated, they said, how unusual the case was – in an ideal world, they seemed to be implying, the whole affair would be started again, with a new scheme of arrangement and new shareholders' meetings; but things being what they were, they simply had to ask the judge to approve this concession of making the Preference shares redeemable in 1970, as the opposition desired. All at once, difficulties melted away. The judge consulted the clerk. New meetings, he said, would have to be held under the jurisdiction of the court, but there would be no need to devise a new scheme of arrangement. The wheels could turn quickly, and the men from Peerless and Kenwood walked out into the November rain beating down on the lunchtime crowds, reasonably sure that by Christmas they would see Kenwood hop safely into the Peerless shell. It all worked out. On December 17 Peerless & Ericsson, controlled by Mr Wood, signed a contract with Mr Wood, major shareholder in Kenwood Manufacturing Co, in which he 'agreed to sell or procure the sale of' the whole of the issued Ordinary stock of Kenwood – 960,000 one-shilling shares. For this consideration Peerless handed over 3,840,000 of its newly created one-shilling Ordinary shares – the exchange of four for one. By the end of January 1960 an extraordinary general meeting of Peerless & Ericsson was approving the change of name to Kenwood Manufacturing Co., and at the same time Kenwood Manufacturing Co. was changing its name to Kenwood Manufacturing (Woking) Ltd. Kenneth Maynard Wood – 'dedicated', Mr Senior told shareholders, 'to the battle of the kitchens' – was in the United States negotiating a two-way deal with the Norge division of Borg-Warner International of Chicago, whereby Kenwood would make small refrigerators for export to the U.S., where they would come in useful in the office, and import large refrigerators for British homes. Everything was under control.

For Hambros it had been a routine operation: there were complications, but without the complications of the system there would be no demand for merchant bankers. One might have read the newspaper paragraphs without suspecting that Hambros had anything to do with it – merchant banks are used to keeping far more newsworthy things under their hats. While the Peerless affair was dragging along in the autumn, the King of Sweden visited Hambros one morning, and the directors entertained him to lunch. But not a word got out to the society columnists. The P.R. man from Patrick Dolan and Associates looked quite frustrated.

6

STERLING CRISIS

In 1957, as in 1955, 1952, 1949, and various other years since the war, the pound sterling was in trouble. The origin of international currency crises is a matter for the economists, who rarely agree anyway; it was the visible, reportable signs of the 1957 crisis in London, among the bankers and brokers and foreign exchange dealers, that interested me. As crises go it wasn't the biggest or nastiest or the one that came nearest to destroying sterling. But it had its points. It marked the end, for the moment at least, of the string of post-war blights that settled on the pound. (Though four years later, in 1961, sterling was once again in deep water, and had to be rescued by massive support from the International Monetary Fund.) It led the Government to raise the Bank Rate sharply, which led to some vicious gossip in the City, which led to the Bank Rate tribunal, which provided half a million words of inside information. It was full of emotions and hunches, a crisis of confidence rather than a crisis of actual insolvency.

The men in the middle, who see currency crises pass through their hands, are the dealers in foreign exchange – the most obscure craftsmen of the City. They live by decimals and fractions – multiples of one-sixty-fourth, since foreign exchange doesn't recognize thirds or sevenths or fifteenths. A dealer will do a lot for a sixteenth or a thirty-second. Dealers are obsessed by the relativity of time and money – heaven, for the foreign dealer, would be a dealing table, the only one of its kind in existence, showing the price of every currency in terms of every other currency in every financial centre in the world, at that particular moment, together with a telephone switchboard that could connect him to any one of those centres in ten seconds flat.

Yet this living by exact margins is done in the most abstract terms. If an American pays a domestic bill by cheque, there is 'real' money, paper money, behind the transaction, and ultimately there are vaults of gold behind the paper currency. Britain abandoned gold as an internal reserve many years ago, but has any amount of nice crinkly paper money that no one except the occasional eccentric would dream of doubting. Internationally, both the American's dollar bills and the Briton's pound notes are useless. When Hambros Bank sells a car in the United States for 5,000 dollars, all it gets is a piece of paper acknowledging a debt of that amount. This debt by an American buyer is a credit when looked at the other way, and as such is valuable to an English importer who wants to buy 5,000 dollars worth of American goods. The foreign-exchange dealer re-arranges the debts and credits to his customers' convenience, translating one currency into another at a rate which fluctuates with supply and demand but is legally tied to within a few cents of $2.80 to the £. Hambros end up with £1,800. The English importer ends up with the right to buy 5,000 dollars worth of American goods. The dealer ends up with a profit.

One-syllable examples never mean much beside the real thing, and in foreign exchange are ludicrous. Translating guilders, francs, yen, pounds, and dollars into one another at speed may be only a matter, as the textbooks say, of simple arithmetic; but it doesn't *look* simple. Advised to try Evitt's *Manual of Foreign Exchange* as a lucid introduction, I found it as lucid as any book can be that deals with these cheerless abstractions. 'At what rate', asks Evitt, using the figure that obtained before the £ was devalued in 1949, 'would you purchase from a customer a ninety days' documentary draft in dollars on San Francisco, if the Telegraphic Transfer rate London on New York is $4.85 7/8 – 4.86 per £, if the time of mailing from London to New York is ten days, from New York to San Francisco five days, and the return journey the same, if market discount rates for commercial paper are 3 per cent in London, and 4 per cent per annum in New York, if the stamp duty in the U.S.A. is $\frac{1}{2}$ per mille [thousand] *ad valorem*, if your agent makes a charge for collecting

documentary drafts of ½ per mille *ad valorem*, and if you require
a profit of 1/32 c. in the rate? (U.S.A. takes 360 days to the year).'
The answer comes out at $4.9245725 per £, or $4.92 29/64 nearest;
I didn't stay long with Evitt.

Further complications arise because on top of the straightforward trade reasons for buying and selling currencies, there's
the speculation motive. As far as possible governments intervene
to shield their currencies from too many pressures. In London
the Bank of England has operated since the 1930s through the
Exchange Equalisation Account, which acts as a reservoir into
which all foreign currencies must be placed, and which will use
these currencies to intervene and buy up surplus sterling if there
is no demand for it. The Account also holds the country's stocks
of gold which are, ultimately, the one form of currency that is
internationally acceptable; gold moves from country to country
if trading results in a deficit that can't be settled in any other way
(and London is the main centre for channelling gold from the
mines into the hands of governments, smugglers, and suspicious
individuals who want something they can stroke with their
fingers. The gold market is described in Chapter 8. As one of
London's leading bullion dealers said in passing: 'The whole
story of gold is ludicrous.') When the gold and dollar reserves
(now called the gold and convertible-currency reserves) were
announced, as so often after the war, to have taken a turn for the
worse, it was the seven or eight hundred million pounds worth
held by the Exchange Equalisation Account that was being
drained away. There are other and greater assets – the total
amount of British investment overseas, money earned there and
left in foreign securities, is at least two or three times greater (no
one knows the exact figure). But the Account represents the
country's immediate assets. If sterling isn't wanted by other
countries, then the price begins to fall, and the Account must
intervene to stop the currency depreciating; to do this it spends
foreign currency and perhaps, in the end, gold.

For years after the war a sterling crisis meant a 'Balance of
Payments' crisis; the Sterling Area, comprising most of the
Commonwealth apart from Canada, was buying more from the

dollar area than it sold there, and the headlines screamed 'Dollar Gap' till it was familiar enough for the gagmen to write jokes about and get good audience-response. By 1957 this type of crisis was over, and instead everyone seems to have been seized with an almost mystical conviction that something dreadful was about to happen to sterling. People, including some people in the City, lost confidence in the pound. Inflation had raised prices in Britain; output had lagged; it appeared to many overseas bankers and economists that Britain might do what she had done eight years before, and devalue the pound – make exports cheaper and imports dearer by altering the limits within which the pound could be traded against other currencies. Against the dollar, the pound was pegged to a couple of points either side of 2.80 – the Bank of England always intervening to keep it within those limits. It might have been devalued to a couple of points either side of 2.20. If that happened, any overseas holder of pounds would find they were worth about 20 per cent less than the day before; conversely, anyone outside the Sterling Area who had been able to postpone changing his foreign currency into pounds would find he was getting 20 per cent more.

The object of much complicated manoeuvring on the foreign exchanges in the summer of 1957 was to get out of sterling as quickly as possible, and stay in a strong currency like German marks or U.S. dollars as long as possible. This produces the effect known as 'leads and lags'. The lags, the delaying of payment, hurt most. The way to delay payment is to get credit – and this, as the very service on which the City has built its reputation, was obtainable as usual in 1957. Everyone who could get credit did. When the Bank of England banned sterling credits for trade between non-residents of the U.K., the kind of merchant-bank financing still quoted in the textbooks as one of the City's central functions, a number of sharp operators from overseas opened City offices with the express purpose of providing a 'London end' to the business, so that they could have an excuse for raising finance here (for some reason the Japanese were very good at this). In 1957 there were some pure speculators against the pound: banks, acting for individuals or themselves, who went through complicated manoeuvres, selling sterling 'short' – that is, sterling they didn't have at the moment, for delivery in the future, by which time they hoped the pound would have been devalued. But most of the speculation was probably associated with genuine commercial transactions. The pound was unpopular. Those who earned sterling took it away from London. More and more credit was squeezed out of the City. Countries like India and Pakistan, holding large sterling credits in London, were spending them fast. Where the Exchange Control regulations could be avoided, money was taken out of Britain and invested overseas, preferably in dollar countries – this was where the famous Kuwait gap, and the equally useful though less publicized Hong Kong gap, came in, making it possible for a man in London to change his pounds into dollars and invest them on a foreign stock exchange, in violation of the Government's idea of what was good for the economy. Kuwait with its oil, Hong Kong with its extensive general trading, impose few currency controls. For a price, any currency can be traded there, and no British Government would be likely to try and stop it; both places are too valuable. As the British Treasury describes it, a resident of Kuwait could buy dollars on the free market, use these dollars to buy American or Canadian stocks, and, since Kuwait and Britain are within the same currency area, sell the stocks to an Englishman. According to Middle Eastern bankers, 'Kuwait' gap was a misnomer. The Kuwaiti only lent his name to the transaction. It should have been the Beirut gap, since that was where the money was remitted and where the real transactions were done. Millions of pounds poured through the gaps, till the Treasury plugged them on 6 July 1957, making the last step in the process – the Englishman's purchase – illegal. There was a last-minute stampede of sterling into North American securities in the first few days of July, as the City got wind of what was going to happen. (For five days $2,000,000 a day went through the gap. It was every man for himself. But when the Radcliffe Committee's transcript of evidence was published in March 1960, bankers were on record as saying that the Kuwait/Beirut gap was never effectively closed.) On top of this was the Sterling

Area's seasonal bad patch, the third-quarter months of July to September when exports from Britain fall off, and sales of Sterling Area commodities – Australian wool, West African cocoa, and the rest – are at their lowest. Altogether it was a rotten summer for sterling – and a busy one for the foreign-exchange dealers.

The market has no geographical site in London, as in some centres. It consists of the foreign-exchange departments of about 120 banks, dealing sometimes direct with one another and with banks throughout the world, sometimes through one of eight or nine firms of brokers. Telephones, teleprinters, and calculating machines are the important equipment. Many of the dealers at British banks, as well as at foreign branches, are from the Continent – Swiss, French, Germans, Austrians, Poles, Russians, often naturalized but as a rule retaining accents and slight mannerisms that mark them off from the natives. It may be the choice of an unusual dish at lunch, and the napkin tucked high in a soft collar. Some of the older dealers look jolly where the City man would look distant. The suit may be lighter, the tie brighter. You hear direct rudeness now and then, which is rare between Englishmen in the City (oblique rudeness is another matter). 'I treat my dealers like dirt when they're new,' said one head dealer of foreign extraction. 'I'm not going to miss my lunch for one of them, I'm not going to be messed about by their mistakes. "Do that again," I tell them, "and you're *out*." What I won't put up with is mental laziness. I can honestly say that I'm ruder to my staff than anyone's been to them since their prep school, yet they seem to love it. On the other hand, if they're in the middle of something and I come in and start dealing, I do what my third dealer tells me if necessary.' In another dealing room, at a merchant bank, I watched a young Swiss dealer with short hair bristling all over his scalp carrying on two conversations at once, one with a Paris bank on his telephone, the other with an elegant young Englishman, a newcomer to the staff, who was sitting in a cubbyhole outside, talking to an Italian bank by teleprinter. The Swiss was advising the Englishman through a loudspeaker what he should say. '*Vous n'avez rien?*' he said down the telephone. Out of the loudspeaker came the dismal tones of the Englishman: 'I say, anything in forward Swiss?' 'Very sorry,' said the dealer. 'Tell him we are a lender of Swiss francs against dollars.' More French went into the telephone, and the dealer began pressing the keys of a small calculating machine on the desk. The loudspeaker crackled. 'I say . . .' 'Tell him we buy the spot at four-thirteen and we sell you the forward dollars at four-thirty-three,' snapped the Swiss – and then, to the room: 'How *much* does one have to tell?'

Why are the Continentals so good? 'We have learned by hard experience,' said a senior dealer at Warburgs. 'Wasn't Austria the first country to have devaluation after the first war, followed by Germany? In our firm I handle the Bank of England's Exchange Control regulations, and I find I can do so almost without studying them – I can always guess how they're to be interpreted.' Most Continentals agree that the English themselves make good dealers. 'They like to have a gamble,' said a dealer of Russian extraction. 'Even if it doesn't look too good they will say: "To hell, I'll make a price." The Americans, now, they are poor at foreign exchange. They think in dollars. They say to you, "What is it worth in money?" – meaning dollars. They don't think in other people's currencies. You understand, the difference between "good" and "bad" is very small. There is no real margin of profit in foreign exchange. The pound against the dollar, there is usually a very small difference – say, two point eight one and three thirty-seconds to two point eight one and one eighth. If you are going through a broker there is brokerage either way, so that eliminates your profit. This is why many dealers now do what they would never have done before the war and cut out the broker, so as to make a profit.'

There are no long-standing traditions in foreign exchange because until the 1920s it was a small, leisurely business of top hats and twice-weekly meetings at the Royal Exchange, a different tradition altogether from the one imposed by the aftermath of the first war. Then there was a general loss of confidence between countries; the bill of exchange was in decline, the direct transfer of money by cable was easier and safer – and the currency upheavals in Europe gave endless scope for speculation, encouraging the market to expand rapidly. All through the second war, and for years after it, there was no foreign-exchange dealing in London: prices were rigid, done through the Bank of England, where a number of the dealers went to work. In the early fifties limited dealing began again, and the dealers drifted back.

Among most dealers a disembodied cameraderie exists, and calculated flattery is sent across the wires, the theory being that one of the prime reasons for having a foreign exchange department, particularly if you're a small bank, is to keep up good relations with clients for other kinds of business. A dealer who used to be at Lazards said that he always had a schedule of calls to Scandinavia, doing unprofitable scraps of business that caused amusement in the office until one day a director, Lord Brand, went there for a holiday and found that he and Lazards were known in the most obscure corners of countries. 'It was costing, let's say, seven and sixpence for the telephone call and fourpence ha'penny for the confirmation letter. The profit on the deal would be three and six, so we were losing a little over four shillings each time. But it was money well spent.'

Speaking the other man's language, even badly, is looked on as another professional asset for the London dealer, since it removes any idea that he might be putting on an insular-Englishman act. A Swiss head dealer at a merchant bank said his Italian was bad, but he always made a show of speaking it; this, and being a good fellow generally, worked wonders. 'If a dealer is a bad loser he might as well leave. He must have a sense of humour. He must be patient. If another dealer makes a glaring mistake which is obviously due to nervousness or ignorance of the actual facts, he must never take advantage of it. Some of the inquiries you get will drive you up the wall at times. You get some little bank in the hinterland of Germany – we had one this morning – asking the most asinine questions. A smart alec would give a snappy answer but the knowledgeable fellow keeps a tight rein on himself. You see, we consider we are members of the same craft. We are here to help each other, not hurt each other, though

I must admit that that idea dies very hard in Switzerland, where they have what you might call the super speculators.'

It was the super speculators of Switzerland, with the Germans close behind them, who sold sterling relentlessly through summer, 1957. The popular British image of the foreign speculator, sitting hard-faced with a telephone in a Zurich bank, must have been realized in at least a few instances: though speculation, as the dealers are quick to say, is often romanticized and made to seem a craft in itself, rather than the application of ordinary business principles. To put off buying a car until the price comes down would hardly be thought of as speculation, but when a bank or a business man postpones a purchase of sterling, there is a strong tendency to see something improper in this. As an English dealer pointed out: 'We have a tendency to deplore speculation against the pound, but we're very good at speculating against the French franc. We call that financial skill. If you speculate *against* the pound, you speculate *in favour* of another currency. When the Chancellor talks about the pound being strong, all he means is that other currencies are weakening and he hopes to see them on their knees.'

In 1957 the French franc was weak and there was a partial devaluation; the pound looked like following. That July the Prime Minister, Mr Macmillan, made a speech at Bedford in which he said that general economic prospects were good and the balance of payments prospects favourable, adding the famous words that became a slogan both for and against the Tories: 'Indeed, let us be frank about it – most of our people have never had it so good.' In Frankfurt, Amsterdam, Zurich, and New York, the foreign-exchange markets didn't share his confidence. Men were prepared to gamble hard in favour of the pound being devalued. When they 'sold sterling short' – the phrase has a perfidious, political ring in Britain – they were entering into a 'forward' contract, a contract to deliver pounds in, say, three months, at a rate arranged in the present. When the 'forward' rate was down to $2.72, it meant that the seller would get this amount in dollars for every pound, no matter what had happened in the meantime. The seller, in order to deliver his pounds, had to buy them somewhere. If there had been no devaluation they would cost him at least $2.78 – the legal minimum for 'spot' transactions. But if there had been a 20 per cent devaluation, he would be able to buy them at around $2.20. 'Either he was losing six cents,' said a dealer, 'or he was making fifty-two. A man who did this with £100,000 stood to lose six thousand dollars if he was wrong, or gain fifty-two thousand if he was right. A man must be damned certain before he'll risk that six thousand, and don't forget the people who were doing this were largely professionals. They weren't old ladies playing canasta, they were chaps who were risking a professional reputation.'

In such conditions the artful dodgers flourished. When the Bank of England clamped down on overnight lending, one foreign bank in the City wriggled past the regulations for days on end by telling hard-luck stories to dealers of how 'we've got a foolish boy in the cable department and he sent a cable to the wrong place, otherwise we'd have been covered. Can you possibly see us through till tomorrow?' Next day the overdraft would be transferred to another bank and the same yarn brought out; meanwhile the credit was available for speculation. Saturdays were always busy, since the usual time for devaluation is on a Saturday afternoon or a Sunday, when exchanges are shut and there are fewer contracts to be upset in mid air. Great dollops of sterling were flung on the market on Saturday mornings, and banks were sometimes able to make a profit by exploiting the fact that many continental exchanges are closed all day Saturday – thus creating a margin that the banker who described it didn't understand himself, but assured me was exploitable because one dealer went too far, came to the notice of the Bank of England, and was fired on the spot, the bank not wishing to run the risk of incurring Grandma's displeasure.

As the reserves crumbled away, the bad news travelled fast along the circuit from the Treasury, in the west of London, to the Bank of England and thence to the whole City, in the east. At the beginning of August the reserves, in terms of U.S. dollars, stood at a little over $2,360,000,000. That month they fell by $225,000,000. In September the drain accelerated to the rate of

$100,000,000 a week, which meant that in another five months the reserves would have vanished and Britain, at least temporarily and theoretically, would have been broke. It was in the middle of September that the Government moved – many economists said they left it too long. Internal spending, announced the Government, would be cut. Credit would be more difficult and expensive to obtain. And the whole operation was crystallized and symbolized by an increase in Bank Rate from 5 to 7 per cent, the biggest in peacetime for one hundred years.

Bank Rate is very much a City symbol. As the rate at which the discount market can borrow from the Bank, it controls the rate at which the market will lend money – either to the Government on Treasury bills, or to private interests on commercial bills of exchange. But an increase in the Bank Rate is a signal from the Bank of England and the Government that is immediately recognized as an instruction to raise all interest rates. Money becomes dearer, and the ripples spread to every corner of business and finance. They also reach overseas. Higher rates of interest attract anyone with surplus cash to lend, so that money withdrawn from London may be expected to return. The opposite happens with borrowing, which becomes more expensive – a bill of exchange on London is going to cost 2 per cent per year more. There is the effect on confidence. When the Bank Rate went up in the third week of September it was obvious that the British Government was digging in its heels, without going so far as to devalue the pound. There is, besides, some mystical quality about raising interest rates above 5 per cent. For a long time in Britain 5 per cent was the maximum allowed under the usury laws. It's the usual rate paid by bank customers for overdrafts. Anything above 5 per cent is looked on, in Britain at least, as 'high', so that a rise from five to seven is a large red flag. As the Radcliffe report says: 'When interest rates change, the main effects that are brought about through a change of people's attitudes – the psychological effects, as they are often called – can be produced only by this kind of breakthrough.'

Radcliffe went into Bank Rate closely, and decided that, as any stranger to high finance might have guessed, the precise effects of a shake-up like this were impossible to isolate. 'With the best will in the world,' it said, 'witnesses found it extremely difficult to give us firm help. Many circumstances relevant to business decisions are simultaneously in a state of flux, and a decision turns on the whole complex of factors, usually without any conscious attempt to assess the relevance of any particular factor. Attempts months or years later to say how much influence any one factor had, or indeed whether it was of real force at all, can have only limited success.' In other words, your guess is as good as ours.

The cool thoughts of Radcliffe in 1959 may have been matched by the cool thoughts of Treasury and Bank of England officials in 1957: but one man who played a significant part in that crisis gave a glimpse of the high-temperature way some minds worked when he talked, positively not for attribution, about the way a weak government – this was before Mr Macmillan came to full flower as 'Mr MacWonder' – coupled with a national, perhaps international, conviction that Britain was on the skids, had undermined the economy. The previous year had ended with the Suez fiasco, and according to X: 'The average man in England, whatever class he belongs to, regards the Egyptian as something that lives in a tree, so when people saw we were beaten at Suez it destroyed their morale. The survival of this country after the war was treated as a continuing miracle by many people abroad, beginning with Abadan [when the Persians nationalized our oil interests]. The economic processes were a long way behind the psychological ones. One important reason for survival was that the young men weren't killed off in the second war as they were in the first – there was no slaughter of the innocents, so the generations of leaders still exist, and there isn't a gap as there is with the first-war men. But the fact that we survived defeat by the Egyptians – *that's* looked on as the greatest miracle of all.'

The emotional residue of Suez was probably an element in the 1957 crisis, even though it may not be true that the entire population of Britain shares X's contemptuous view of Egyptians. Had Suez been the start of a crack-up that economic ruin would complete twelve months later? Those who had gambled on it, or at least been compelled to take it into account, found they had backed a loser. The Bank Rate rise and the general tightening-up did what was expected of them. Confidence came back; funds returned to London; sterling ceased to be an undesirable currency, and as foreign banks, anxious now to meet their long-delayed commitments, began entering the market as buyers of pounds, the price of sterling steadied, and started climbing. It had been a memorable crisis; and then, as if the City hadn't had enough to put up with, it endured a bout of violent publicity in the most un-English tradition because of a couple of unlucky coincidences within the City itself.

It was the fault of Bank Rate. When interest rates rise, share prices tend to fall, especially the prices of fixed-interest securities. People immediately expect a higher rate of interest on their investments. Since the interest on existing gilt-edged stocks is fixed, they then expect what amounts to the same thing, to pay slightly less for the stock, so that the relationship between price and interest-rate, the 'yield', will reflect the change. As soon as Bank Rate goes up, the gilt-edged jobbers mark their prices down. Thus anyone who had sold gilt-edged stock just before would either have made what amounted to a profit, by getting more for his holding than he would have got the next day; or he could show an actual money-in-the-bank profit, by buying his way back into the same or a similar stock at the lowered price.

This was what happened in September 1957: gilt-edged was sold, as it's being sold all the time, on Monday, Tuesday, and Wednesday, and Bank Rate went up on a Thursday morning, the traditional time for this to happen. Some people had guessed right, and timed their selling perfectly. Good guessing happens every day. But on this occasion there was a difference. Rumours began to fill the City and get into the papers that some of the selling had been the result of a leak. Newspaper references crept towards the libel mark. Hints, smears, and dark allegations were made in Parliament, and finally, after much denial that anything was wrong, the Government was forced to hold a public inquiry to clear the names of public figures. It lasted twelve days in December and probed deep, concerning itself with holidays and

train timetables, examining cables in code and private correspondence. cross-questioning a slice of London, from top bankers
and journalists to unsuspecting investors and clerks, dissecting a
cocktail party, peeling back the roof of one of the proudest
merchant banks – and finding in the end that no one had talked,
no one had cheated, no one had behaved with anything but total
propriety. But for the outsider it was a window and a shaft of
daylight into the City.

7

THE BANKERS' TRIBUNAL

FOUR of the five men who were unlucky enough to find themselves at the centre of the Bank Rate affair were, and are, figures of note and unblemished reputation in the City; the fifth, a politician of equally unblemished reputation, was the Chancellor of the Exchequer, Mr Peter Thorneycroft. It was Mr Thorneycroft who, the day before the Bank Rate rose, interviewed a number of people among whom was Mr Oliver Brian Sanderson Poole, now Lord Poole, at the time deputy chairman of the Conservative Party; Mr Poole and Mr Thorneycroft were involved because Lazards, the merchant bank of which Mr Poole was a director, sold gilt-edged stock to a nominal value of £1,500,000; there was also the fact that Mr Thorneycroft had spoken, in the course of discreetly outlining the Government's economic plans, to journalists. Then there were the Keswick brothers, both directors of a banking and merchanting house called Mathesons, which, acting on behalf of its parent firm in Hong Kong, sold £1,025,453, nominal value; they were involved because the elder brother, William Keswick, was a part-time director of the Bank of England. Finally there was Lord Kindersley. Besides being chairman of Lazards, Lord Kindersley was senior governor of Royal Exchange Assurance, which sold gilt-edged worth more than £1,000,000 the day before the Bank Rate went up. Lord Kindersley, the second baron, was and is, like Mr Keswick, one of the twelve part-time directors of the Bank of England (there are four whole-time, plus the Governor and his Deputy).

The Bank Rate Tribunal had to find if there was any truth in 'allegations that information about the raising of Bank Rate was improperly disclosed'. Lord Justice Parker, a distinguished judge, later Lord Chief Justice of England, sat as chairman at Church House, Westminster, with Mr (later Sir) Edward Milner Holland, Q.C., and Mr Geoffrey de Paiva Veale, Q.C., Recorder of Leeds. A hundred and thirty-two witnesses gave evidence on oath. A team of law officers, headed by the Attorney-General, Sir Reginald Manningham-Buller, Q.C. and M.P., questioned them, often fiercely. The tribunal found no truth in the allegations. The public was left with solid proof of the power of rumour, and a view of a sterling crisis from some elegant standpoints.

There was the long-established house of Matheson & Co., the London correspondents and subsidiary of the extraordinary Hong Kong group of Jardine, Matheson. Jardines, the 'Princely Hong', is one of the great names of the East, a rambling but tightly-controlled empire that has grown out of the opium trade with China a century ago, surviving world wars, communism, and nationalism, adapting itself to every decade with good manners, artifice, and frightening efficiency. Two Scotsmen, William Jardine and James Matheson, went into partnership as opium smugglers in 1828 – 'the early pioneering days', as the Jardine advertisements call them. The group has grown up with the British Crown Colony of Hong Kong, which was ceded by China (she had no option, being confronted with the British Navy) in 1842; the stock joke, which perhaps isn't entirely a joke, says that power in Hong Kong belongs to Jardines, the Jockey Club, and the Hongkong & Shanghai Bank, with Her Majesty's Government coming a bad fourth. Hong Kong, within a few miles of Communist China, has plenty of servants, natural beauty, golf, racing, and girls. Taxation is pleasantly light, and private enterprise flourishes. Jardines nowadays seems a microcosm of what commercial Britain might have been if there had been no world wars, communism, or United States of America, and the nineteenth century had been miraculously prolonged. It covers most of the preoccupations of business – finance, insurance, shipping, aviation, trade, and industry. It extends into Borneo and Malaya and Siam and Japan. Pushed off the Chinese mainland when the communists took over, Jardines' reputation for hard-headed smartness credits them with having cut their losses to the bare value of the buildings when they had to get out. Since the war Jardine money has gone into Japan (financing cameras, among other things), Africa, and Australia. The group holds trading agencies for scores of concerns, from whisky and medicine to machinery and chemicals. It owns and operates factories, ships, and aircraft. A lot of money runs through its hands, and some of it comes to London, to be invested in gilt-edged stock.

In August 1957 the gilt-edged market was in an unhappy condition. If sterling was going down the drain, was it good sense to invest in the British Government? For more than a year the managing director of Jardine, Matheson, Mr Hugh David MacEwen Barton, had been thinking of getting out of gilt-edged. He had sought advice from the obvious quarter, Mathesons in London, where he was a personal friend of the chairman, William Johnston Keswick, and the chairman's younger brother and co-director, John Henry Keswick, who between them held 7 per cent of the shares in Jardine, Matheson. At the tribunal W. J. Keswick said of Barton: 'He has always had a dread, I fear, of sterling and he has always wanted to get out of gilts. He equally knows my views in the past, which have been that it is a British colony, and if we possibly can we should support British bonds and British currency.'

This thread of conscience ran through much of the evidence. It was an awkward decision to have to make, and finally, in mid August, Mr Barton decided on a compromise. His immediate concern was for two insurance companies in the group, Lombard Insurance and Hong Kong Fire Insurance. He had sought advice from Samuel Montagu – one of the foremost bullion dealers and merchant banks, founded in mid nineteenth century – who had given Barton some mid-twentieth-century advice. If Jardines had followed Montagu's recommendations it would have meant increasing these companies' North American holdings from 15·8 per cent of their portfolio to 40 per cent. What Barton and his colleagues in Hong Kong decided to do was increase their dollar stockholding to 26·2 per cent; and as a first step, a telegram followed by a letter went to W. J. Keswick, with instructions to make a start by selling sufficient Savings Bonds to produce £100,000. 'With this money', wrote Barton, 'we shall buy U.S. dollar and Canadian dollar fixed-interest stocks immediately.' The bonds were sold. On 22 August W. J. Keswick wrote to say he thought the middle course sensible, and two days later he left for a holiday in Scotland – where, to the indiscriminate glee of Left-wing politicians when the evidence emerged, he was going to shoot at Lagopus Scoticus, the red grouse of the heather moors.

It was the holiday season, and that weekend – the 24th was a Saturday – saw some interesting comings and goings in London. The Governor of the Bank of England, Mr Cameron Fromanteel Cobbold, left for a holiday abroad, two days after the Court of Directors had met at the Bank of England, and Mr Cobbold had proposed no change in the Bank Rate; he was out of the country for three weeks. Back in Britain that Saturday, having cut short a North American work-and-holiday trip by three days, was Lord Kindersley, worried by the attitude of Canadian bankers to sterling. On 2 September the Deputy Governor, Mr Humphrey Charles Baskerville Mynors, a one-time tutor at Cambridge, now temporarily in charge at the Bank, asked Kindersley to call, since he was just back from Canada; Kindersley told him he was 'shocked' at the situation, and that he thought Bank Rate would have to be raised. Mynors said Bank Rate was under review.

Next day Mynors wrote to three directors who were out of London, and so not in touch with the growing crisis. One of them was W. J. Keswick. The letter, hand-written, referred to the August exchange figures, said possible measures were being discussed – the favourite phrase – and that one of them might be a higher Bank Rate, and asked that the letter be destroyed. This was on 4 September. W. J. Keswick read it and burned it, and went on with his holiday.

Sadly if understandably, Keswick declined to see me; he said gracefully that he had had enough publicity as it was. The reference books show a conventional City background – Winchester and Trinity College, Cambridge; member of Whites, perhaps the most exclusive London club, and Boodle's, not far behind. But his evidence had a tough-minded ring; he once sat on the Royal Commission on Taxation of Profits and Income, and on paper at least he sounds a bit of a City intellectual. Aged fifty-four, when the tribunal met he said 'Yes' to a list of directorships: British Petroleum Co., B.P. Tanker Co., B.P. Trading Co., Barragore Jute Factory Co., British & Chinese Corp., Hunwal Tea Co., Petroleum Steamship Co., and Scottish Oils; he was also joint deputy chairman of Alliance Assurance and a governor of the Hudson's Bay Co.

His younger brother, John Henry Keswick – Eton, Cambridge, member of Boodle's, Bucks, and the Junior Carlton – was having his summer holiday at about the same time, in about the same place. It was 'a rather variable feast', he told the tribunal – 'as work came and went, I came and went too.' He was back in London on 11 and 12 September, and at the office he received two letters. One came from Barton, dated 5 September, written aboard a Britannia aircraft on its way from Hong Kong to Japan: Barton, too, was taking a holiday. 'My only worry on leaving', he wrote, 'is the fear of devaluation – the pressure on sterling seems to increase. I would be grateful if Tony [W. J. Keswick] and you would let me have your recommendations, so that I can take whatever action may be necessary when I return, as naturally I do not want to miss the bus with the firm's Gilts. Sorry to bother you with such problems when you should be concentrating on the grouse!' The other letter was from W. J. Keswick in Scotland – the brothers were staying about eight miles apart at Dumfries – giving, first, the previous day's bag of grouse, followed by a list of the people who were with him at the rented shooting; they included a nephew of the Hambros Bank family, members of the Keswick family, a boy at Eton, and Mr Nigel Birch, Member of Parliament and Economic Secretary to the Treasury. The letter continued: '*Gilts*. I'm worried about the Firm's and Companies' gilt-edged. Remind me next week we must do something about them. Hugh of course will want to clear out of the lot. Perhaps he is right and they should be sold. The future certainly looks murky. I thought Nigel was very depressing' – this last sentence was to be joyfully seized by the Left and hawked about as being Typically Tory.

The letter ended: 'Sorry the hols. are nearly over. I've enjoyed them. See you No. 3 [No. 3 Lombard Street, the Matheson offices] Monday.'

The combination of these letters, said J. H. Keswick at the tribunal, convinced him that they should recommend (they could do no more) that gilt-edged be sold. He knew that Jardines would soon need ready cash for instalment payments on the *Eastern Maid*, a ship just delivered to the Indo-China Steam Navigation Co., and another vessel. A Hong Kong factory also had to be paid for. J. H. Keswick left a note for his brother suggesting they discuss the matter, caught a train back to Scotland on Thursday, 12 September, and resumed his holiday. With him he took the letter addressed to himself from Barton, and an envelope of office mail for W. J. Keswick, among it another letter from Barton, this time addressed to W. J. Keswick, and dated 3 September. Barton wrote in this that 'while I do not for one moment forget that we are a British firm and should therefore support our own currency, I do feel that, with the international nature of our business, we might be wise at this time to transfer part of our sterling investments to North America when there is so much talk of possible sterling devaluation . . .' It was the kind of sentiment that must have been behind many letters, cables, and conversations in September 1957.

The Attorney-General's line of questioning made it clear what he was trying to discover: did the letter from W. J. Keswick about the future looking murky owe anything to the information received from Mynors: did that letter, rather than Barton's, impress J. H. Keswick? The answer was No. Did the two brothers get together on the grouse moor and decide to recommend that Jardines sell gilt-edged? There was some detective-story stuff. J. H. Keswick had to deny that he 'thought matters were so serious that when you received your brother's letter you got on the train and went up to Scotland at once' – he pointed out that his sleeper had been booked weeks before, since 'a special grouse drive, which was a feature of our lives every year' had been arranged for 13 September. Why, it was asked, did W. J. Keswick write 'See you Monday' if he knew that his brother was coming north again, and he would see him *before* Monday? The answer, reasonable enough from the hard-working businessman, was that he didn't want to talk shop on a shooting party. The tribunal concluded there had been 'serious discussion between the brothers', who had decided it was 'inevitable that they should recommend the sale of the firm's gilt-edged securities'. Still, a picture did emerge of two men who worked in adjoining offices, knew one another's views inside out, and, being in sympathy, could drift towards agreement without formally arriving at a decision: the informal harmony that the City's so proud of.

In contrast to the heavy economic undertones, the Keswick holidays, or 'hols' as they were sometimes referred to, had an engaging air of informality that seemed to jar the interrogators at times – J. H. Keswick had to explain that 'my holiday is not an exact number of days. I don't work on an equation of taking one off here and putting one on there.' He was closely questioned about his sleeping-car arrangements (he got them mixed up one day and corrected them the next). It all had a pleasantly free-and-easy flavour. The counterpoint of grouse and crisis and the debonair ripostes at Church House ('Then you shot grouse, I suppose?' 'Shot at them.') combined to make the Keswick world seem a little extraordinary; the information that there were Chinese servants in J. H. Keswick's Scottish house, that one was now in the spacious-living zone, added a further dash of colour.

Holidays continued to interest the tribunal when they reached Monday, 16 September – the beginning of the week in which Bank Rate was to go up, and the day on which W. J. Keswick arrived back at 3 Lombard Street. He was in the office by 8.45, having read the morning papers. He then wrote the following letter to Barton in Hong Kong, who that morning had himself returned from his Japanese holiday:

PERSONAL AND PRIVATE
My Dear Hugh,

I have just returned from Scotland where we had a wonderful time, record shooting and good fun all round. But I return to a very depressed City. I believe the trade figures are dreadful and one hears on all sides ugly rumours about devaluation.

John tells me you are asking for a cable about our views on devaluation, and especially about the merits of selling Gilts. This is not easy, and whatever view one takes one is apt to be wrong. I shall telegraph you today. Personally, I do not believe the Chancellor dare devalue, and therefore he will resort to all measures before so doing. The speculative pressure against Sterling is very severe indeed. It seems a heads-I-win-tails-you-lose bet for the sellers of Sterling short, and I do not see how they can be stopped.

What measures the Government will take to check inflation, which is rampant, and to protect the Pound I do not know. I am certain, however, that the Credit Squeeze will go on and it looks to me as if money will get tighter.

Consequently, it must be right policy to keep as liquid as possible, both the Firm itself and the Companies.

Kadoorie [one of Barton's colleagues] I know is worried about Sterling and is scared. The more people like him who cry down Sterling the weaker it becomes. It happens to be our currency and I feel it is up to us all to support it as much as possible. If Sterling really goes we all go. But these are platitudes.

Now as to Gilt-edged: I know your fears in holding them and, in view of the importance of being liquid during a time of Credit Squeeze and dear money, perhaps the time has come to sell. Reluctantly, therefore, I recommend you to sell the Firm's holdings in case they slide away further, and then to keep the cash in London.

You have payments to make for Indo-China building instalments and you already have an overdraft from the Hongkong Bank because you did not want to take a loss on the Indo-China holding of Gilts. But you might consider taking this decision to sell now. I must say I can see no reason why Gilts should go up. My advice, therefore, all round is to sell.

With regard to the Insurance Companies, I imagine you should continue your policy to switch more into North American Bonds and Equities. Again, this is anti-British and derogatory to Sterling but, on balance, if one is free to do so, it makes sense to me.

Yours ever,

W. J. Keswick

The chairman of Mathesons next drafted a telegram:

CODE. TO BARTON, HONG KONG

For Eyes of Taipan Only

L/B. Confidential. Personally believe in spite pressure there will be no devaluation at least not immediately. Anticipate tighter money therefore as temporary precaution recommend selling majority of J.M. & Co. Ltd holding –

  3 per cent Savings Bonds 1955/1965
  3 per cent Savings Bonds 1960/1970
  3 per cent War Loan 1955/1959

at approximately 87,76,97 respectively, without reinvesting for say 3 months, telegraph if you agree. Indo-China S.N. Co. Ltd should also possibly act similarly.

The Taipan – the Boss, the Principal, literally the Big Class – was of course Barton. Barton, who has been described by a friend, the James Bond author Ian Fleming,* as 'perhaps the most powerful surviving English big shot in the Orient', is one of the personalities of Hong Kong. He lives with his family above Big Wave Bay in the south-east of Hong Kong Island, where (again the source is Ian Fleming) there are orchid trees, turtle doves, and seven Boys in attendance. Barton is a member of the Legislative Council, deputy chairman of the Hongkong & Shanghai Bank, and a steward of the Jockey Club. While W. J. Keswick in London was writing the telegram, Barton in Hong Kong was concluding that he had to act without waiting to hear from Lombard Street. He arranged meetings for the next day, Tuesday, 17 September, of Jardine, Matheson and the Jardine Engineering Corp. Meanwhile, having shown the draft telegram to his colleagues, W. J. Keswick decided not to send it till his brother returned to the office – that morning, as he expected. But, feeling that 'I had not had my full whack of holiday', J. H. Keswick decided to take a couple of days extra, stayed in Scotland on the Monday and Tuesday, and so didn't appear in Lombard Street.

At one p.m. on Monday W. J. Keswick crossed Cornhill and Threadneedle Street, and went into the Bank of England for lunch, as he often did; it was because he knew he was going there, he said, that he had drafted the letter and cable to Hong Kong first thing in the morning. He met Mynors who, while not mentioning Bank Rate specifically, said there might be a 'swingeing rise in interest rates'. Then W. J. Keswick left the

* In the *Sunday Times*.

City to visit his dentist and his barber, and didn't go back to the office till next day. When he did, on Tuesday morning, and found his brother still away, he had the telegram coded and sent off by 12.40 p.m. After all this, the telegram arrived in Hong Kong too late for the meetings of Jardine, Matheson and the Jardine Engineering Corp. Both had already resolved to sell their entire gilt-edged holdings – £539,384 in the first case, £46,500 in the second. The telegram did arrive in time for the meeting, previously arranged for the Wednesday, of the Indo-China Steam Navigation Co., which decided to sell its holding of £300,000 Savings Bonds. Instructions to make these sales, together with another £139,069 nominal of gilt-edged to complete the sale of insurance-company holdings that had been started in August, were sent on the Wednesday, and received by Mathesons just before one p.m. Two firms of brokers handled most of the business, which was done principally with three firms of jobbers. The deals were made by telephone, after the Stock Exchange had closed. By the end of the afternoon Jardines had gone a long way towards getting out of gilts, and three firms of gilt-edged jobbers were left with a quantity of stock on their books that was going to make them feel sick in the stomach within twenty-four hours, when the top-hatted Government Broker left by a side entrance at the Bank of England – the regular Thursday ritual – and took the Bank Rate news into the Stock Exchange.

Because by this time the wheels had started turning. The Governor of the Bank was back, there had been weekend meetings with the Chancellor and Treasury officials, and at the end of Wednesday morning the Treasury was on the phone to Cobbold to say the Government would approve a Bank Rate of 7 per cent – the 'swingeing rise in interest rates' at last. Late on Wednesday afternoon W. J. Keswick was called in to see Mynors again. The Deputy said it had been decided to recommend to the Court of Governors next day – the creaks of traditional machinery were heard throughout the tribunal – that Bank Rate go up; whereupon Keswick, looking worried, disclosed that he had just received some big orders to sell gilt-edged. Mynors told him to carry on with the uncompleted sales so as not to arouse suspicion – as it turned out, it was too late to stop them anyway. The stock had been sold, to produce a total of £841,007.

Again, there was some heavy questioning. First, W. J. Keswick had to satisfy the tribunal that he delayed sending the telegram to Hong Kong simply because he wanted his brother to see it. Then he practically had to parse it. What had he meant by 'tighter money'? Barton, who made a statutory declaration to the tribunal – he didn't appear – said he thought it meant higher interest rates; W. J. Keswick said he intended only to refer to the existing situation, and the tribunal accepted this when it came to report. It was nice to know that jargon like 'tighter money' and 'dear money' and 'need for liquidity' and the rest, tossed about so freely by the financial experts, were vague enough to mean different things to City men. As for W. J. Keswick's integrity, he was found to have 'behaved with complete honesty and propriety in the difficult and embarrassing situation in which he found himself'.

He had disclosed nothing; but there were plenty of voices outside the City to say that a man should never be put in such a difficult and embarrassing situation. His own view of how a person with two allegiances should behave in the small world of the City came in an obviously heartfelt speech, when he was explaining how he felt about the handwritten letter which gave him the scrap of inside information at the start of September. He said:

It is inconceivable to me that [Mynors] was giving me a tip, because he wrote the same letter, I believe, or similar letters to other directors, and a copy was kept in spite of being asked to destroy it. I cannot believe that he wished – and I can only put it in this way – to put me in baulk, so that I could have no freedom of action whatsoever, so I took it at its face value in the simplest way, that it was a courtesy letter to a fellow director, telling me about the situation, that remedies were being considered, that the Governor was away, and there was no need for me to return. . . . That is the first consideration I had to make, and that is what I did. The second is: should I or should I not be influenced by that letter? My decision, right or wrong, was this, that he wrote to me on the third, and I went to London on the sixteenth – badgered by requests and talks with my brother about whether we should sell, or whether we should not sell – and at that time I decided, rightly or wrongly, that I had not had any more communications from the Deputy Governor, that the news was stale, written on the third (I took my decision on the sixteenth), it was unconfirmed and tentative. I also could not at that time go to the Deputy Governor and say: 'What is the position, because I want to advise my colleague whether to sell or not to sell.' It would have put him, I believe, in a most impossible situation. Nor could I, at that time, have written to Barton and said: 'I cannot advise you.' So I took the action that you all know about, and those are my reasons for taking them. If I had to do it again I would not act differently in any way.

Cobbold admitted that a director might be under strain at times when he had to keep his Bank of England knowledge in a watertight compartment. But this sort of thing, he said, happened in banking and accountancy and the law. It was an old problem at the Bank of England; it was also found in the United States. The Bank, said Cobbold, gained by having the benefit of advice from merchant bankers, trade unionists, and industrialists. The Radcliffe Committee happened to be gathering evidence at the time, and was asked to look into the matter of part-time directors; it did, and agreed with the Governor about their usefulness. The exact details of Bank Rate protocol have since been altered, but the basic routine seems the same. No doubt central bankers see a significant difference between the Bank of England announcing a Bank Rate change (old style) and the Bank announcing it *with the approval of the Chancellor of the Exchequer* (new style). The fact that it always has been with the Chancellor's approval, if not actually at his instigation, is presumably beside the point. The Bank can be told what to do by the Government, but is highly sensitive to any idea that it's a mere operating department under the Treasury. Labour's post-war Chancellor, the late Sir Stafford Cripps, once called the Bank 'my creature'. Cobbold brought this up at the tribunal, only to point out quickly that the day after, Sir Stafford assured him that the phrase had been used 'lightly and in jest'.

City protocol generally had an airing at the tribunal, and nowhere so completely as in connexion with Lord Kindersley. In the case of W. J. Keswick, a man with inside information had to sweep his mind clear, because a colleague was pressing him for advice. In the case of Kindersley it was the more subtle problem of a man with inside information, moving among merchant bankers and insurance officials, having to be discreet without being over discreet and so giving the quick-witted a clue to what was happening. It was, in fact, a truly British dilemma.

Lord Kindersley – Hugh Kenyon Molesworth Kindersley, C.B.E., M.C. – went to Eton, served in the Scots Guards, succeeded to the title (which was created in 1941) in 1954, and was fifty-eight years old at the time of the tribunal. He is a heavily handsome man, with a fleeting resemblance to David Niven; there is a light moustache, penetrating eyes, and an air of distinction. In 1957 he had been a managing director at Lazards, one of seven, for thirty years, and the chairman since 1953. He was connected with various other companies – the ones mentioned by *University and Left Review* (see page 11), and the one they omitted, S. Pearson. The name 'Pearsons', which means little to most people, conceals one of those iceberg organizations – massive, silent, and beyond the public view. The Pearson story, full of nostalgia for Englishmen who like the idea of empire-building, runs from the middle of the nineteenth century, when it was founded as a firm of public works contractors. Pearson himself, later the first Lord Cowdray, was one of the early petroleum enthusiasts. He arrived in Mexico in 1889, bought and developed oil-rich land, and early this century formed the Mexican Eagle Oil Co. He sold out after the first war to Royal Dutch and Shell – thus 'Shell-Mex'. (Shell itself began in 1831 as a firm importing mother-of-pearl shell from Japan, founded by a Marcus Samuel whose banker son, the first Lord Bearsted, shipped oil from Baku to the East. The merchant bank of M. Samuel & Co., with the present Lord Bearsted as chairman, is now a leading accepting house. The first Bearsted, a Jew, and the first Cowdray, were the men who did most to put Britain in oil.) Pearsons are almost, but not quite, at the top of the group's pyramid – the apex is a small £1,000 company, the Cowdray Trust Ltd, which acts as trustee to the first Lord Cowdray's will. But Pearsons are the executive company in the group, which includes the Westminster Press (provincial newspapers all over Britain), the pink-newsprint *Financial Times*, the *Economist*, the *Banker*, the *Investor's Chronicle*, a group of china-shops, a bolt-making company, and Lazard Bros. The present Lord Cowdray, one of the richest men in the country, owns more than two-thirds of the shares in the English Lazards, which has associate houses in Paris and New York – it was founded by three Franco-Jewish brothers who went to New Orleans as textile merchants in 1848, though it isn't a 'Jewish house' in the sense referred to on page 78.

Lazards were the Pearson company where attention was concentrated. Like the rest of the merchant banks, Lazards were caught up in the sterling crisis. As fears of devaluation grew, sterling deposited with merchant banks by overseas firms was steadily drawn away, and freshly-earned sterling wasn't deposited at all. At the beginning of July the total on deposit at Lazards was £11,320,000. Through August it stayed above £10,500,000, until the last week, when a million and a half disappeared overseas. Another million went in the first twelve days of September, and the Lazard deposits were down to a little above £8,000,000. In order to be able to meet these demands for money, a merchant bank will keep a high proportion of its assets in a form that can be turned into cash at half an hour's notice – a higher proportion than a domestic bank, with greater assets and, comparatively speaking, fewer foreign depositors likely to be stampeded into a run on the bank. Lazards' ideal was about half. If deposits were £10,000,000, they wanted £5,000,000 in loans to the discount houses ('on call' – see page 64) or held as bank bills and Treasury bills which could be sold to the discount market at any time. The important thing in such cases is to be 'liquid'. Gilt-edged stock wasn't regarded at Lazards as being liquid enough, since on a real crisis occasion the market in gilt-edged might contract, and large sums couldn't be realized in a hurry. Thus as money was taken out of the discount market to repay the foreign depositors who were calling in their funds, Lazards' liquid holdings dropped to around 40 per cent of deposits. To keep the percentages up they called in more than £500,000 that had been loaned to local town and city councils at seven days' notice – some of the loose cash in the City, which may be ultimately cash from Switzerland or Canada or the United States, is always being borrowed by borough treasurers. They sold £500,000 in gilt-edged at the end of August, followed by a further £500,000 a few days later; and by Friday, 13 September, they were wondering whether they ought to sell some more.

Every Friday Lazards hold a 'money meeting' and consider the state of the firm's finances. Any idea that merchant banks weren't such informal institutions as the legends assert was soon squashed. The money meeting of managing directors on Friday the 13th took a look at what they call the 'brown book', which gives a rough idea of deposits, money on call, and gilt-edged stock. Kindersley pointed out how deposits were falling. It was agreed they ought to be more liquid, and there the matter dropped. Everyone understood that the way to achieve this happy state of affairs was to sell some gilt-edged, but there was no detailed discussion. As Kindersley said: 'I think we all decided to sleep on it over the weekend – Friday isn't a frightfully good day to go selling on the market in big amounts.'

At this point Kindersley knew no more and no less about the chance of a Bank Rate rise than W. J. Keswick had known in Scotland. He had seen Mynors twice at the Bank of England, on 2 and 12 September, and there had been general talk of interest rates rising. On the Monday – 16 September – he was to know exactly what was in prospect for the coming Thursday; but by this time an automatic censorship was in operation at Lazards, and Kindersley, as far as his colleagues were concerned, had been enclosed in a wrapper of tact. They knew matters were coming to a head. On Friday 20 September the Chancellor was leaving for a meeting in Washington of the International Monetary Fund; it was a reasonable guess that the Government would act to support sterling before then (even so, the number of poor guessers elsewhere in the City was enough to destroy confidence for all time in financial prognostication). One of the managing directors at Lazards, Mr Alan Denzil Marris, guessed right when he said that as the I.M.F. meeting approached, it was obvious that among the people to be consulted were the part-time directors of the Bank. 'The nearer you get to that point,' he said, 'the more your automatic processes work, and one of our automatic processes, certainly mine, is that I wouldn't dream of trying to embarrass Lord Kindersley by asking his opinion about something that he might have discussed at a meeting I did not know about that he had just come from.' 'Speaking for myself,' said another managing director, Mr Daniel Meinertzhagen, 'I have been brought up always, in times of crisis particularly, not to mention things to Lord Kindersley which might be controversial at that time.'

It was in this atmosphere of self-imposed purdah that the morning meeting was held at Lazards on 16 September. It began as usual with reports from heads of departments. No one mentioned gilt-edged. Like the other morning meetings that were described, it seems to have been a routine that the managing directors wanted to complete as quickly as possible. 'You see people looking at their watches,' said Marris, 'and wanting to go off to other meetings and that sort of thing. The fact is, major decisions that are taken at Lazards are more frequently not taken in the morning meeting. It may seem queer, but it's a fact that they are taken by the people concerned with the particular aspects of the firm's business.' This Monday morning it was around noon that two or three of the managing directors, sitting together in the big partners' room, drifted into a discussion about gilt-edged. There was Mr John Victor Openshaw Macartney-Filgate, who got into conversation with Mr Meinertzhagen, and Mr Marris, who came in later. The idea of selling a good chunk of gilt-edged stock, around £2,000,000 worth, was generated among them – Macartney-Filgate appears to have put the thought into words, but it was what the other two were thinking. It meant the largest sale of gilt-edged stock at Lazards that Macartney-Filgate could remember, though he and his colleagues emphasized that it wasn't a panic decision, that £2,000,000 in the gilt-edged market was a drop in the ocean – like astronomers

airily reeling off light-years, the banking and stockbroking witnesses kept saying there was nothing sensational about these
quantities of Government stock, as indeed there wasn't to them,
till the tribunal and the public were bemused by so many strings
of noughts.

Merchant banking is clearly an art, not a science. There was
nothing exact about the decision to sell the stock. 'My reason
was wholly unscientific,' said Macartney-Filgate, when asked
why he suggested £2,000,000 rather than £3,000,000. 'One plays
this tune according to ear,' said Marris. On that Monday the
foreign deposits had, in fact, started to rise again – it might have
been only a temporary trend, but in any case none of the managing directors noticed it. What they sensed and acted on was a
continuing tension, an atmosphere, as one of them put it, where
'the foreigner was still taking his money away'. The prestige of
the house was referred to more than once. Money needed to be
kept in the discount market not only because Lazards wanted to
be liquid but because with a large quantity of Lazard-accepted
bank bills in circulation, the market *expected* a certain amount of
call money. If it fell away 'there might be some comment – your
prestige, your name might suffer'. A merchant bank needs to
radiate confidence as a fire radiates heat. Nowadays the issuing
and company-nursing and pension-fund-management side of the
business is more important than bill-accepting at Lazards. But
the old need to have a spotless name abroad is felt as strongly as
ever. As Macartney-Filgate wrote in an article about merchant
banking that appeared in the *Sunday Times*: 'The Accepting
Houses provide buyers or sellers not so much with finance but
with assurance in advance that finance will be available for the
trade contemplated.' (I came across the article while looking
through files covering the tribunal period. It was printed on
8 December 1957 – midway through the tribunal, two days
before Macartney-Filgate gave evidence.)

Messrs Filgate, Marris, and Meinertzhagen talked about gilt-
edged and decided to seek formal approval the following day
from the Hon. Thomas Brand, the senior managing director,
and the one generally consulted about investment. ('It sounds a

very unofficial way of doing things,' said Macartney-Filgate, 'but it works.') Meanwhile the chairman was in his office off the main room, leaving it in time to go round the corner for a management committee meeting of Royal Exchange Assurance at 12.15. At 12.45 he was called to the Bank of England, told by Cobbold that it was proposed to raise Bank Rate 2 per cent on Thursday, and gave his formal assent as a director. From this point Kindersley was a man with a burdensome secret. He returned to Lazards for lunch, where a visitor from India had been invited to talk about his country – merchant bankers' lunches are very good as a rule, but meant for talking shop – retiring to an adjoining room at 2.30 to preside at a board meeting of the British Match Corp. At 5.30 he went home by car, giving lifts to Marris, who sat with him at the back, and Meinertzhagen, who sat next to the chauffeur. They talked about the poor old pound but no one mentioned gilt-edged.

By this time Kindersley had a new set of worries. A £30,000,000 issue of stock by Vickers, one of Britain's major steel and heavy engineering firms, was due, and after leaving Cobbold early on Monday afternoon he recalled that 'here was the biggest transaction that had been done in the City or was going to be done in the City for donkey's years, except for the Steel Company of Wales, which had been left something like ninety-two per cent with its underwriters and clogged the market for months.' In these matters it isn't the company that suffers, so much as the banks and insurance companies which underwrite the issue; most issues of stock are guaranteed through the medium of one bank, which then farms out the bulk of the underwriting to City institutions and keeps a little itself. The company collects its money whatever happens; if investors don't apply for the stock, the underwriters have to pay for it, and shed it slowly as best they can. A flop can clog the market for months. Since a higher Bank Rate would depress share values and make the price of the Vickers issue, already agreed upon, unpopular with investors, Lord Kindersley was anxious to save the City from what he described as 'indigestion' and avoid bad relations between the Bank of England and the underwriters; there was no question, said the tribunal in its report, that he was affected by the sub-underwriting that had been passed on to Lazards and the Royal Exchange as usual, and that they were going to find themselves stuck with.

Nothing at the tribunal gave more of an impression of the City as a club, a collection of adjoining offices where matters can be dealt with promptly and without fuss, than the underwriting evidence. The Vickers underwriting was in the hands of Morgan Grenfell, another of the accepting houses, an extremely dignified firm, once controlled by the American bankers, J. P. Morgan, and still associated with Morgan Guaranty Trust Co., with which J. P. Morgan have merged.

(I once read a book by an American writer who described the scene at a Wall Street bank, and mentioned a banker from Morgan Grenfell who was present. Feeling that this gave an opportunity for ice-breaking I wrote to the banker, mentioned the book, and asked if I might call and see him back at Morgan Grenfell to talk about merchant banking in general – I had learned not to say I wanted to talk about anything specific and dangerous like a take-over or a new issue. He wrote back, kind as they all are, to say No, adding that there had been an 'awful lot of undesirable repercussions' from that reference. Morgan Grenfell are among the old guard, and of course lined up with Lazards and Hambros over British Aluminium.)

Agreement to underwrite the issue was formally signed between Vickers and Morgan Grenfell on Monday afternoon, 16 September, and sub-underwriting offers were in the post that evening. The list of people who sub-underwrite in the City is practically the same whatever the issue, which makes for speed. Banks and insurance companies take the underwriting as it comes – if they turned choosy and declined the chancier business, the plums would soon stop coming their way. If the amounts to be underwritten are large, sub-underwriters will be contacted a week or so in advance of the formal offer, but in any case the issue is often arranged on the basis of unwritten guarantees. Sub-underwriting, Kindersley agreed at the tribunal, is 'a sort of a club'; and when, worried at the thought of £30,000,000 of stock being dumped, he was trying to see if there was still time to do something, he had only to cross a few streets and contact a few acquaintances. On Monday afternoon, after the British Match meeting, he went to see the Governor again and asked if a rise in Bank Rate could be postponed. The Governor said that at the end of the week the Chancellor and the top brass at the Treasury were going to Washington and the Prime Minister was going to Ottawa; they had to be present when Bank Rate went up, so it couldn't be postponed.

Next day, Tuesday, Kindersley was at a board meeting of the Bank of London & South America, where he spoke to another part-time director of the Bank of England, Sir George Bolton. Bolton agreed the Vickers business was important, and suggested he see the Governor again. At 3.30 he saw Cobbold, where they went over the same ground and reached the same conclusion; he then got the Governor's permission to go and talk to the senior managing director of Morgan Grenfell, Lord Bicester, who was yet another of the Bank of England's part-time directors, to explore the possibilities of postponing the Vickers issue. 'Morgans and ourselves', said Kindersley, 'are probably closer than any other two issuing houses in the City of London. We discuss intimate details of every kind and description. I don't think Lord Bicester would find it in the least surprising that I should come to him and say to him: "Look here, Rufie, is it too late to stop this business or not?" ' Lord Bicester said it was 'common practice in all the City houses for the heads of the firms to get together, if there is anything, and talk about it'. It might have been possible for the issue to be referred back to the Vickers directors, after Bank Rate went up. But when Kindersley realized that the sub-underwriting was completed, that the whole business was settled, he said: 'Well, that's the end of it. There's nothing that can be done.' The following morning, Wednesday, his chauffeur-driven car had to stop in traffic on the Embankment, on his way to the City, and drew up alongside Mr Cobbold's. The Governor suggested he change cars – London traffic offers plenty of scope – and on the way east Kindersley confirmed that he would support an immediate increase in the Bank Rate.

At Lazards they had been busy selling gilt-edged stock. Mr Brand, consulted by Mr Meinertzhagen on Tuesday morning, gave him authority to sell up to £2,000,000 – he had been thinking himself of around a million and a half, but he was glad his colleagues' ideas were 'higher rather than lower'. Stock with a nominal value of £1,000,000 was sold on Tuesday, and another £400,000 on Wednesday; £500,000 more should have been sold, but Lazards' stockbroker was able to get a reasonable offer for only £50,000 of this block of stock – 3% Exchequer 1960 – and Mr Meinertzhagen told his Stock Exchange dealer to refuse the unreasonable price. This was, in fact, only ⅜ of one per cent below the acceptable price of 96 39/64. On a sale of £500,000 of stock the difference would mean less than £2,000, an amount hardly worth quibbling about if Lazards really had been panicked into selling. (When Bank Rate did go up, 3% Exchequers fell more than 3 points.)

Lord Kindersley knew nothing of these sales till Wednesday evening, when they had all been completed. By this time he had overcome yet another hurdle. As senior governor of Royal Exchange Assurance – where they have had governors since the eighteenth century – Kindersley had to be at the Royal Exchange for a Fire and Life Committee at noon on Wednesday. Then came a meeting of the full court of directors at 12.30, and the Treasury Committee at 12.45. Anxious to have a word with him was the investment secretary, Mr Clyde Algernon Sydney Cooper, who had returned from his holidays two days before to find City talk confirming his fears of a currency crisis. Like many others, Cooper thought Bank Rate should have been raised at least a month earlier. He decided they ought to sell gilt-edged. There was the need to have accessible funds in time of trouble, besides which Royal Exchange had a number of immediate liabilities, including instalments on tanker loans, a fire loss in Manchester, an overdraft in Canada and the underwriting, accepted from Morgan Grenfell, of shares and loan stock for the Vickers issue worth £618,900. So Cooper wanted to see Kindersley. The tradition of avoiding 'controversial' matters in the chairman's presence was, not surprisingly, absent outside Lazards.

Cooper agreed with Lord Justice Parker that he thought it a 'natural thing' to consult Lord Kindersley. He was hoping to be called to see the Governor before the Treasury Committee, but it was a little after 12.30 before the internal phone rang, and the senior assistant general manager, Mr Roberts, said Lord Kindersley would see him. Kindersley was afraid someone would want a word, so he had been keeping the Fire & Life going as long as possible. When they finally came together in Mr Roberts's office, Kindersley put in a quick question about holidays. Cooper, a yachting man, had been to Burnham, a yachting centre in Essex. 'I hear you've been doing nicely at Burnham,' said the Governor and began talking about the winds and the people who drowned there. ('If he felt more like discussing yachting than insurance,' Roberts said at the tribunal, 'I didn't feel I could object.') After a few minutes of this, Cooper tried to get back to business. He said the Vickers underwriting didn't look too good – but Kindersley was on his feet, saying it was time for the court of directors. Cooper went out feeling a trifle angry and slighted at the interruption. At the Treasury Committee his request to be allowed to sell a substantial amount of gilt-edged was approved with little discussion, and no comment from Lord Kindersley. Long after, Kindersley asked one of his fellow directors, the late Lord Weeks, if he had given anything away at the committee. 'Only one thing,' said Lord Weeks, 'I did think that you looked particularly po-faced that day.'

Royal Exchange sold gilt-edged to produce £1,160,000 before the end of the afternoon. It was the combination of this sale, the Lazards sale, and a sale by the British Match Corporation – Lord Kindersley being chairman – of £375,000 nominal gilt-edged, that focused attention on these companies. But every suggestion of impropriety was dismissed. In the tribunal's words:

We find there is no justification for any allegation that Lord Kindersley disclosed, either intentionally or unintentionally, any information about the impending increase in the Bank Rate or about the proposed restrictive financial measures, or that he used that information for the purpose of private gain. We are satisfied that he conducted himself with complete honesty and propriety during a period when he might at any moment have been placed in an embarrassing position.

There was one other principal strand in the inquiry. Mr Oliver Poole was deputy chairman of the Conservative Party, a man of wide City interests. He was a director, though not a managing director, of Lazards; and the day before Bank Rate went up, which was also the day he became deputy chairman of the party after having been chairman – he was making way for Lord Hailsham – he and a couple of Tory research officials saw the Chancellor of the Exchequer. A steady stream of journalists, editors, trade unionists, and heads of nationalized industries went to the Treasury that afternoon and the following morning, to hear from Mr Thorneycroft's own lips a summary of what the Government was going to do, but with no mention of Bank Rate. Thorneycroft, who was later criticized by Labour M.P.s for having seen all these people, explained that he wanted to have them on his side before he left for Washington. (And as Mr Fry of the *Manchester Guardian* wrote at the time, advance information from officials is usually the most effective method known for shutting a journalist's mouth.) Mr Poole was summoned at four p.m. on Wednesday, sandwiched between Sir William Haley, editor of *The Times*, and Donald Tyerman, editor of the *Economist* – the list of journalists and proprietors called in is another of the tribunal's curious by-products, since as far as the Treasury was concerned the only papers that counted were *Financial Times*, *The Times*, *Economist*, *News Chronicle*, *Daily Telegraph*, and *Manchester Guardian*, with Reuters news agency for good measure.

Mr Poole asked for a list of proposals. The only document available was a two-page draft of the Chancellor's public statement, for release after the Bank Rate was raised, headed *Top Secret* and containing nine paragraphs. Paragraph 9 read simply: '(Paragraph to be added.)' The Bank Rate news was to go here – Chancellors' stings are usually in the tail – and Thorneycroft's principal private secretary, using a long pair of scissors, neatly snipped off Para. 9 before Poole saw the statement. Had Poole noticed that page two was two inches shorter than page one? Had he guessed that there was to be a Para. 9 about the Bank Rate? Hardly surprisingly, no, he hadn't. All the ingenious guesswork came after the Thursday, not before. No one seems to have put awkward questions to Thorneycroft, as they might well have done, about the inadequacy of his proposals for curbing overdrafts and carving public expenditure without the stiffening of higher interest rates. Paul Bareau of the *News Chronicle* did ask the Treasury P.R.O. about Bank Rate, but was thrown off the scent by some deft P.R.O.-manship. Neither Poole nor any of the journalists could possibly have leaked anything, because there was nothing to leak in the first place (for the record, the tribunal found 'not a shred of evidence that Mr Poole made any disclosure'). But in the weeks following the 7 per cent Bank Rate, London crackled with rumours. Although total sales of gilt-edged that Wednesday, £16,500,000 nominal against purchases of £14,000,000, were nothing out of the ordinary, a spurt of after-hours selling, coupled with the drastic fall in price next day, caused much grumbling among jobbers. One told a journalist he had been 'shot to pieces'. Another firm issued a circular to say that their readiness to deal after hours – on the telephone, after the Stock Exchange has closed – had been badly abused on 18 September, and put the blame on brokers' clients. (Later it came out that this particular firm of jobbers was reducing its size anyway, and used the 18 September situation as an excuse for announcing that it intended to stop dealing after hours. But at the time it was a juicy piece of evidence for the papers.) The tribunal heard about the 'lonely situation after hours' of jobbing firms – there was something absurd in the idea of jobbers sitting around tables in dealing rooms, picking up the coloured telephones and quoting prices to stockbrokers with no clear idea how prices were moving, in the middle of a square mile where every kind of commercial information is on tap. Anything from the price of pepper in Singapore to the latest in Canadian railway stock is available to those with teleprinters; but stockjobbers don't go in for teleprinters, and rely instead on the brokers to tell them if there has been some turn of events that is going to affect prices.

Explaining why he didn't like dealing after the Exchange closes, a jobber said: 'One is out of touch with the market, and it is so simple for a broker to tour jobbers one by one and almost take advantage of them, one might say. One is out of touch with one's fellow jobbers, and sees very little of what is going on.'

Wednesday often brings a heavy turnover late in the afternoon because it's a day when many institutions hold their board meetings – as Royal Exchange Assurance had done – and don't finish till around the time the Exchange closes, so that any decision to buy or sell must be implemented on the phone. Jobbers took various views of the stock they were offered that afternoon. Some were unworried. 'I went home, like a good many fellow jobbers, with stock on my book, but I was quite happy about it,' said one. When Bank Rate went up, 'my son, who was in partnership with me, said I went very pale.' ('I am sure Her Majesty's Government would desire to apologize for that,' said the examining counsel. 'I accept the apology,' said the jobber, gamely.) A jobbing firm with £500,000 of gilt-edged stock on its books might have lost something like £15,000 – while on the other side, a heavy seller like Lazards made about £32,000 profit (taxable, as Mr Brand quickly pointed out – Lazards are authorized dealers in securities, so in-and-out sales count as income). A dramatic rise in interest rates, some nice profits and some nasty losses, provided ample material for gossip. A series of coincidences brought in the personalities, and once the talk was under way it swept through the City like a trawl, catching fish of all shapes and sizes.

Anyone who ever plans a monograph on rumour in a tightly-knit society, or some such topic, will find the Bank Rate tribunal indispensable. When Labour M.P.s started asking questions in Parliament and pressing for an inquiry, they were inundated with letters and phone calls from people who 'knew' there had been a leak. Some of the tales arose from simple misunderstandings. Susan Chataway, nineteen-year-old sister of Chris Chataway, TV commentator and later M.P., had just gone to work at the Conservative Central Office. She made a light-hearted remark to her cousin, a Civil Servant at the Foreign Office, on the 9.8 from

Woking to Waterloo. It was never altogether clear what was said, except that there was some joke about inside information, and her cousin got the impression she knew about the Bank Rate rise before it happened. On another railway line, a reporter from the Sunday newspaper *Reynolds News* said that at Watford station, north of London, he heard the P.R.O. at the Ministry of Labour say to a principal at the Ministry of Housing: 'We were told in the Press office about the Bank Rate on Wednesday afternoon.' His colleague said: 'I think it's a scandal.' But the Civil Servants, apparently, had misunderstood one another. Mrs Dorothy Campbell, well known in the entertainment world, was attending a cocktail party in the West End on 18 September. Suddenly she announced: 'I hear the Bank Rate is going up one and a half per cent tomorrow.' Stockjobbers would have gone white in the face, but since most of the guests were from films or television, the remark lacked bite. It came, said Mrs Campbell, from the blue; it was 'just a wild thought'. The tribunal decided that Mrs Campbell 'made what she intended to be a sensational remark in order to draw attention to herself'.

Still stranger things happened. Hurrying forward to smash images of perfection that had been bothering them for years came a cheerful band of iconoclasts. The fact that something so near the heart as money was involved sharpened many grievances. If the City had plaster legs, now was the time to reach for the hammer. Mr Harold Wilson, Labour's 'Shadow' Chancellor, received incredible accusations. One of the less lurid came from a City journalist who had been sacked by his paper. He said the paper had made £18,000 out of prior knowledge, and that he had overheard two Japanese bankers talking excitedly (in Japanese, of course) about an impending rise in Bank Rate; but he died before the tribunal sat, and the accusation about the paper was nonsense. The London United District of the Ancient Order of Foresters was dragged in because of a misunderstanding about dates. A stockbroker's clerk and his typist wife were dragged in because of a misunderstanding about times.

On top of this an assortment of smaller deals in the gilt-edged market had been unearthed by the Treasury Solicitor's staff, and gentlemen who had been having a quiet gamble were asked to explain themselves. There was the stockbroker who bought £50,000 Savings 3% on Tuesday and sold them at mid-day on Wednesday when he judged the market to be at a peak. On Thursday morning, as soon as the market opened, he sold another parcel of stock, this time £50,000 Consolidated 4%. He was an uncovered bear – he didn't have the stock and was gambling on a fall in price before he had to deliver it. How often did he have these little gambles? It was difficult to say. 'In the gilt-edged market, when it is moving, obviously we have a gamble there. If it's the industrial, it might also be gold mines, but we have a go every day.' Instead of doing a crossword puzzle on the electric train, he studied the markets with the aid of *Financial Times*, *The Times*, *Mail*, and *Express*, preparatory to having his daily gamble. He had been doing it for nearly thirty years. Had he always been so successful? 'Well, I wouldn't like to say.' And how much had he made? Only a small profit on the Savings 3% – about £150. Rather better on the Consolidated 4%, which he bought back the same afternoon – about £1,250. It was a private speculation, without significance to the tribunal, but not without interest in a land where the mechanics of having a flutter on the Stock Exchange are so badly documented.

The sound of axes being ground went on long after the market had recovered from its jolt. 'The tribunal', said Harold Wilson, not altogether fairly, in Parliament the following February, 'has quite fortuitously provided the country with a valuable insight into many other questions of national concern. One of the impressions which many people have formed is the essentially amateurish way in which vital decisions affecting our whole economic well-being are taken – the "old boy" network, the grouse moors, "Nigel was very depressing".' Other M.P.s were concerned with the effect of such a tribunal on those who were examined. 'They are iniquitous proceedings,' said Harold Lever, another Left-winger. 'They are the nearest thing to a lynching party which is permitted in this country . . . . The idea prevails in some circles that if a man has nothing to hide, he doesn't mind a public inquiry. Of course, nothing could be more false than that notion. Nobody ought to be stood up in public and cross-examined about the intimacies of his private life, have his correspondence turned over and his pockets turned out, unless there is a good case against him for doing so.' Mr Grimond suggested it was 'putting a rather severe strain on people to ask them to bring out their correspondence before a tribunal, and expect it to look as though it was written for publication by a high-grade girls' school'. Certainly, few people would care to face a tribunal; but harsh though it may have been, it's hard to see how the facts could have been elicited without the stripping-and-searching technique.

It was generally agreed that the City's reputation for integrity hadn't suffered, though to those outside the City, let alone outside Britain, there were signs of incipient obsession over this reputation. Anyone who reads the transcript of evidence in a thousand years as a relic of a vanished society might well wonder what half the witnesses were getting at. He might further speculate about the significance of grouse shooting, and the mysterious status of the merchant banker, and even wonder why so many stockbrokers and stockjobbers lived an hour's journey from the City in houses with gentle names like *Tanglewood* and *Willows* and *Fir Trees* and *Hidden Cottage*. Reading the report of the tribunal he might come across Para. 39 and wonder what exactly the tribunal meant when they said: 'Although we have come to the conclusion that there was no general leakage of advance information as to a rise in the Bank Rate, it does not, of course, follow that there may not have been individual cases in which dealings were prompted by the improper disclosure or use of confidential information.' It was like a tiny flaw in a large block of crystal.

8

THE CITY'S GOLD

A BRICK-SHAPED bar of gold fits nicely into a pair of open hands. Solid and dull yellow, lightly scratched as if nails have fought for it, the bar is worth £5,000; and several thousand years after the raw shine of the metal in earth caught the attention of early financiers, such bars remain the one basic international instrument of currency. In spite of advanced mining technology, the sophistication of paper currency, and the progress of economic theory, any of which might have unseated gold from its throne, mankind stubbornly refuses to accept any ultimate substitute for pieces of a soft and industrially unimportant metal. From the start it had the advantage of a certain beauty when refined, coupled with immutability and scarcity – but not an *impossible* scarcity: it was hard to get, but always obtainable in the end. Gold remains the world's best documented mineral. Fairly accurate records of the quantities mined are available from 1493, the year after Columbus found America, and someone calculated that in the next four and a half centuries, to 1940, a total of 1,222,000,000 ounces of refined metal came into existence, a large-sounding figure but astonishingly small when expressed as a pile of gold bars: such a pile, neatly stacked, would be less than fifteen yards along each side, which hardly seems worth the slaughter and misery entailed. A man from Mars, of the kind who used to pop up in B.B.C. documentaries whenever an innocent eye was called for, would take a lot of convincing that gold was ever worth it, let alone that it should continue to be coveted, guarded, and painstakingly passed from country to country, in an age that should be able to afford to write it off as a mineral with limited practical application.

The City of London has its philosophers like everywhere else, who don't always take gold too seriously. They appreciate that its very uselessness in the manufacture of tinplate and nylon and nuclear warheads is one of the points in its favour, since it makes gold independent of demand except the demand for cash, security, and prestige. But the fundamental absurdity of the gold business strikes some of them. A man at Samuel Montagu, the merchant bank which is also a leading bullion house, fingered his spectacles and said the trouble was that man had an inherent desire to possess it. 'Apart from the fact it's on my fingers and in my teeth,' he said, 'it's flaming well useless. Nowadays gold dealings are basically between nations, and as a sideline there's the hoarder, principally in France and the Middle and Far East, living in countries which are basically insecure. The U.K. has a stable political system – if you allowed the Englishman to buy and sell gold he wouldn't bother. But in a country like France, every little farmer has gold under his bed or up the chimney or somewhere. It all ties up with the geography of Europe. The Scandinavians don't hoard gold because they haven't been invaded often enough. But the Belgians do, and so do the Germans, though not as much as the French. The whole story is ludicrous, really.'

Before the war, and again today, London is the world's principal market for gold: chiefly because of the immense South African output, most of which is sold through London. The market adjourned on 1 September 1939, and after the war economic bedevilment kept it closed until 1954, when the news was extruded in typical fashion from Threadneedle Street with the announcement that 'the Bank of England will discontinue the publication of buying-prices for gold as from the 22nd March, 1954, when the London Gold Market re-opens'. Between 1945 and 1954 the Bank was the only source of gold in London, a sad come-down for the market from the hectic days of the 1930s, when political unsettlement in Europe sent large amounts of 'hot' money from country to country, much of it in the shape of gold bars, with most of the movement organized in London. This was before elaborate exchange control arrived to inhibit the market – which, if operated freely, provides a simple bridge between currencies. It was not until several years after 1954, when sterling was in a strong enough position to stand up for itself, that freedom in any way comparable to 1939 had been restored.

Gold is one of the London markets with a specific location: an upstairs room at N. M. Rothschilds, where every morning the ritual of gold-fixing is carried out around a heavy polished table by the representatives of four firms of bullion dealers and two of refiners. Two of the firms present carry most weight: Samuel Montagu, and Mocatta & Goldsmid, a purely bullion house, now owned by Hambros Bank, which is ten years older than the Bank of England. But the greatest weight is, in the best City tradition, carried by someone not present in the flesh. Rothschilds are represented at the meeting as refiners, but their representative is there in a second capacity: agent of the Bank of England. The Bank, as the channel for South African gold, is the power behind the gold-fixing. The Reserve Bank of South Africa is making the sale: the Bank of England is acting as its agent: and the man from Rothschilds is the mouthpiece through which the shadowy central bankers make their pleasure known. Just before 10.30 in the morning the telephonist dials TIM for the speaking clock, so that proceedings can start dead on time. The dealers file in and take their places, either at the central table or at smaller side tables; each has a telephone, with a line open to his office, and a small Union Jack on a stand, the idea being that when the flag is down the verbal dealing must be honoured, but on the words 'Flag up!' or 'Flag!' everything stops until the man who has spoken says 'Flag down' or changes his mind. The origin of the phrase is obscure – the Union Jack ornaments, which came later, were a present to the market by the Rothschilds one Christmas, cautiously interpreted by the market as a joke – but there's a feeling that the custom is decorative and vaguely proper. The dealers indicate whether or not they are buyers of gold (they usually are). The Rothschilds man will probably say: 'Figures, please.' The dealers will indicate the price they offer, which will be in the region of 250 shillings an ounce, and the Rothschilds intermediary passes it on to the Bank. The

Bank may now say: 'No gold', which means the market has to bid more; or, having been asked for a total of 150 bars, it might offer 90, leaving the market to divide them pro rata, or start all over again with a fresh bid, perhaps a farthing an ounce higher. One farthing per ounce makes a difference of nearly ten shillings to the price of a bar; a profit of as little as 3s. 6d. on a bar of gold is common, so that dealers are working to fine margins. Before the second war, the gold-fixing quoted its prices in sterling because this was the natural thing to do; when the gold market reopened, the dollar was the all-important currency, but the gold-fixing clung and clings to a sterling price.

Like the bill brokers' morning visits, the gold-fixing represents only a part of the real work of the market. There are bullion men who dismiss it as a farce, a piece of ritual that goes on and on because no one knows how to end it. More gold is traded outside the room at Rothschilds than inside it, at whatever price can be agreed; perhaps the principal value of a formal gold-fixing is that it provides a price for gold that the City columns can print, a daily yardstick about which there can be no dispute. The rest of the work is done by phone, with demands for gold coming from a wide range of buyers, with central banks at one end of the scale and private merchants at the other. About 25,000,000 of the annual non-communist world production of 30,000,000 fine ounces comes from within the British Commonwealth. South Africa, the major producer, mines 18,000,000 ounces, something over one-third of *total* world production, and bullion men are sometimes scornful of the idea that the South African Government is susceptible to economic pressure from Britain of all places. To have the gold in the earth is not the same thing as having it cast in bars; mining, from shafts sunk as deep as two miles and processing as much as 160,000 tons of rock to produce one of gold, is expensive – if it wasn't, and if the amount that can be mined weren't limited, the Sterling Area's gold reserves could be painlessly replenished. But to have one of the world's principal sources of gold sending it to London on preferential terms is of tremendous importance. There are private arrangements, never publicized, between the Bank of England and the Reserve Bank of South Africa, whereby London has a virtual monopoly of the gold and in turn supplies South Africa with its foreign-currency needs.

Gold mining is an expanding industry in South Africa, with new mines growing in the Far West Rand and Orange Free State. The same is probably true of another major source of gold, the most important after South Africa – the Soviet Union. Russia's output of gold has been a secret since before the second war, but many bullion dealers now put it as high as South Africa's. In 1959 the Russians began sending quantities through London, and more than 8,000,000 ounces of bar gold were consigned direct. This was another result of the market's increasing freedom, specifically of the Bank of England's announcement at the end of 1958 that gold dealings in London could now be permitted against all currencies (except domestic sterling: a U.K. resident may not purchase or hold gold on his own behalf). This made it as convenient for the Russians to sell gold in London as at other European centres, and, to the irritation of the Swiss, who saw their market shrink rapidly, tons of Siberian gold came on offer in the City. This Russian metal is the finest quality gold they see in London. A standard good-delivery bar contains 995 parts of gold in 1,000. South Africa, using the chlorine process for re-fining, sends bars of 996; the Russians, using electrolysis, produce 999 parts of 1,000 pure gold (though this doesn't make Russian gold any more valuable, since payment is for the gold content, not the total weight). One school in the City thinks Russian gold is uneconomic because of transport costs from Siberia; all dealers agree that the Russians combine punctiliousness in delivery with a tough and sometimes paranoiac approach to bullion dealing. The Russian Trade Delegation at Highgate used to handle their gold, but the agent now is the one and only Soviet bank in Britain, the Moscow Narodny at Finsbury Circus. 'They're all terribly keen on secrecy,' said one bullion man. 'They've got a chip on their shoulders, they always think they're being taken for a ride – not unjustifiably sometimes, since there have been instances of dealers trying to take advantage of them.' Another dealer, who I'm sure had never taken advantage of anyone, said:

'There are complications with Russian deals because of the absence of profit motive – in their mentality they possess no profit element. If the Russian can only get thirty-five dollars an ounce because the market is slack, he'll offer his fifteen tons or whatever it is in fifteen different places and depress the market. He doesn't understand this. He'll be offering gold in Prague, in Zurich, all over the place, and in London we get a flood of people ringing up to say they've all got a few tons to sell – the same gold appears time and time again, and the market gets pushed down. Again, if the Russian is leaving money with us pending a purchase, and he thinks the price he's paying is too high, he'll get round this to his satisfaction – and to ours as well! – by leaving the money with us for a week, till he can make a better price. What he doesn't understand is that the better price represents interest at $1\frac{1}{2}$ per cent per annum, and we're lending that money out at $2\frac{1}{2}$ per cent.'

Whether the gold comes from South Africa, Ghana, Southern Rhodesia, Russia, or anywhere else, when stacked in the vaults of a bullion dealer it becomes as anonymous and magical as treasure turned up on a desert island. At one house, where visitors can see the gold but are not encouraged to discuss security, they convey another variety of deceptive City casualness. The loading bay where the armoured van backs in to collect and deliver bullion is either sealed from the street by metal shutters, or conveniently blocked by a parked saloon car. But there is no impression of steel and concrete vaults. The loading bay looks like a dilapidated garage, with bits of chain and a bare electric bulb. The offices, entered through a narrow doorway adjoining, have a stone staircase, brown walls like an old classroom, and, straight ahead, a door with a frosted glass pane saying *Strictly Private*, as though it were felt that *Private* on its own wouldn't be enough to deter a gang of gold thieves. There is an outer grid of bars; and beyond is a back room which seems as if it might have something to do with a forge – tools fixed to the wall, row of teacups, pin-up pictures, smell of solder, and, in a glass case, a balance proudly introduced as being sensitive to the weight of a postage stamp. A coal fire makes the room stuffy – most rooms at this house have an open grate, full of bright red coals and shining fire-irons in winter, as well as central heating. The visitor stands on a square of floor which becomes an elementary lift; it grinds down on an oily metal pole and delivers him to a couple of small underground rooms, carved out when the building was put up at the end of the last century, where a safe in one corner stands open, and the light shines on more than a million pounds' worth of gold: three tons, or about 250 bars. A mass of gold has an orange tint not present in a single bar. Stuffed in among the bars are some twists of newspaper, each wrapping a slab of platinum about the size of a bar of chocolate, but roughly cut, with unequal sides: pieces of heavy, colourless metal, worth about £1,000 each. Why do they wrap it in newspaper? The dealer looks puzzled at the question. 'Why waste money making it look pretty?' Scattered round the room are bags of damp-looking sawdust to pack the gold. Small white-wood boxes are piled ready to receive a bar apiece; metal strip is machined all round, and red seals applied. In the East, where gold has been the subject of careful study and devoted application for longer than anywhere else, they know how to saw around nails and part metal strip, extracting gold in transit without anyone being the wiser; but even the experts have trouble with seals. Elsewhere in the main room are stacks of leadlike bars, larger than the gold. This is silver, looking grimy and unappetizing, in bars weighing three-quarters of a hundredweight each. And in the farthest room are containers with small flat pieces of gold, each weighing 3·7 ounces and worth £45. There is only one reasonable category of use for little bits of gold that can be carried in a waistcoat pocket, sewn in a lining, or passed from person to person while shaking hands: but what happens to gold when it disappears into the economic undergrowth of the East is no concern of the London bullion dealers.

There can be few commodities which leave the wholesaler's storeroom for such a variety of destinations. The most proper are the central banks – they frequently feel it beneath their dignity to deal with one another, even where this would be the natural thing to do, preferring to go through the medium of a bullion firm. Physical movement of gold isn't always involved – a sale between countries may involve no more than moving a label from one safe to another. For some years up to 1957, central banks, wishing to make settlements through the European Payments Union (now defunct), entered the London market as buyers of gold whenever the price fell below the equivalent of $35 per ounce: the price at which the United States Federal Reserve will buy gold tendered to it, and sell to other central banks of which it approves. To buy gold at less than $35 an ounce was to buy a means of settling international debt cheaper than settling direct in dollars. After 1958, with decreased confidence in the mighty dollar, creditors rather than debtors among central banks began buying gold in London, switching surplus dollar balances into metal – they have also withdrawn considerable amounts of gold direct from the U.S. Treasury, though with something like $17,000,000,000 worth in stock, more than the rest of the non-Soviet world put together, there is still a long way to go before the statutory minimum level of $13,000,000,000 is reached. But there has been a steady drain on U.S. gold reserves. In one week near the end of 1961, stocks fell by $300,000,000, largely because Britain, after weathering a sterling crisis earlier in the year, found itself amassing a large quantity of dollars – which were then exchanged with the Americans for their gold. This drain on U.S. stocks has encouraged speculation about the prospect of an increase in the price of gold – a step which might conceivably be taken by the U.S. authorities, and which would push up the world price of gold.

The arbitrary nature of the gold business is emphasized by the way economists talk of the value, or otherwise, of increasing gold prices all round. Radcliffe summarized the case for deciding overnight that the gold in everyone's vaults should be worth considerably more than the day before:

It is possible to argue, as some witnesses have done, that the central fact in the situation is the failure of the world's supply of monetary gold to keep pace with the increase in the value of international trade. In the past twenty years the increase in the gold reserves of all countries has been less than 50 per cent, while the value of international trade has increased fourfold; the stock of gold has been rising at about 2 per cent per annum, while international trade, even at constant prices, has been rising at a rate between two and three times as great. It is perhaps natural, therefore, to regard a substantial increase in the world price of gold as an appropriate method of securing a more satisfactory level of international reserves.

But Radcliffe doesn't see this as the answer; and until some emergency, such as a dramatic dwindling of United States gold stocks, arises, making an increase expedient, gold is likely to remain at $35 per ounce.

One factor that helps to keep central banks short of gold, in relation to world trade, is that so much of the output of mines is snapped up by or on behalf of hoarders and smugglers, who usually absorb as much as central banks, and in some years far more – in 1951, when the Korean war was at its height, only 17 per cent of all gold produced reached national reserves. People in some western countries are large-scale hoarders – the traffic in smuggled gold from Switzerland into France has been so extensive that it could have been maintained only with the connivance of the Customs, if not of still higher authorities – and so are people in the East, which has been absorbing gold for centuries without any sign of satiety. This is the point where high finance shades into bazaar-and-mystery land. Gold bought on the London market leaves England by air practically every day for such destinations as Baghdad and Beirut – purchased, quite legally, for external sterling (that is, sterling as distinct from the domestic variety used in the U.K.), dollars, or most other currencies. Beirut is traditionally the centre for gold merchants. 'There are', said a British banker in the City, 'some clever people in Beirut. It's a port. It's the gateway to the Middle East, at the eastern end of the Mediterranean. It's got a lot of banks and dealers – very clever people. When it comes to trade the Lebanese have got cleverer brains than anyone else. Every port in the world, from Lagos to San Francisco, you always find a group of what are called Syrian merchants. They're not Syrians, they're Lebanese. They're called Syrians because that's the old name, when the Lebanon was part of Syria, before the French split it up. They're all over the world. People speak of the ancient

Phoenicians, the master traders – well, they still exist.' Beirut is the centre where the currency fiddles associated with the Kuwait gap were centred. Beirut and Kuwait accommodate the U.K. resident who is willing (once legally, now illegally) to turn sterling into dollar securities without using the available 'pool' of such stocks in London. The sterling would be remitted to Beirut, but would actually leave the Sterling Area through the little oil kingdom of Kuwait, where there are no currency controls – it suits Britain to look the other way and let wealthy and strategically important Kuwait do what it likes, knowing that much of the oil revenue will in fact be invested in British securities. Beirut, where the presence of so much gold helps the process of exchanging all currencies one for another, is a very accommodating place. The merchants, receiving their plane-loads of gold from Switzerland or London, cut it into convenient sizes if this hasn't been done already, and stamp it with a mark which, in the case of a reputable dealer, carries as much authority in the Middle East as the Bank of England does in Lombard Street. India is the chief destination, because every Indian bride, however poor, needs gold in her dowry. Her father may mortgage himself for the rest of his life, but she must have some kind of bangle or ornament. Before the war gold could legally be imported into India, but Indian exchange control now forbids this, and the way has been opened for one of the largest regular smuggling trades in the world: by Arab dhows from Muskat or some such jumping-off point, and into India through Pakistan, or direct to the western coast. (Bombay is said to be out of favour in recent years, after a spell of unpopularity, because the Customs officials are changed frequently and have become unbribable.) The smuggled gold used to be handed over in exchange for rupee notes, which were, very conveniently, the currency of the Persian Gulf; banks around the Gulf would take the notes, and eventually reimburse themselves by repatriating them to India. The Indian Government's latest retort is to issue special rupee notes for overseas circulation only, making payment to smugglers more difficult; but no one supposes for a minute that the gold will stop coming in, making rich men out of the Arabs who bring it. The profit of the smugglers is, say City bankers, colossal – it has to be to compensate for the risks of prison and of losing shipments, since as much as £2,000,000 may be seized in one interception. The Radcliffe Committee heard evidence about this trade from several bankers – it was marginal to the interests of the committee and found no place in the Report, but when the full transcript of evidence was published early in 1960, the couple of pages that dealt with gold had an eccentric air in such sedate surroundings. 'No country', pointed out one of three bankers answering the committee on the matter, 'has yet devised a watertight control of money. It is beyond the wit of man to invent one.' The leak of gold into India, where it got out of the control of the Indian Government, ran into 'millions and millions and millions of pounds a year, nobody quite knows how much'. Every now and then someone got put in gaol, which helped; but nothing really shook the faith of the smugglers. 'The gold would go to India whatever happened. With the millions of marriages every year in India the demand for gold is insatiable; it will go on for ever.'

As one of these bankers told me later, even a country like Russia, with as near-absolute a currency control as any State is likely to achieve, can't prevent a black market in roubles on its Eastern frontiers. And of all the means of evading regulations and satisfying basic needs, gold is incomparable: anonymous, universally acceptable, and enhanced by its mystique. There is an excellent market for gold coins in the Middle East, but old British sovereigns command a better price than new ones because the new ones bear the Queen's head, and the East is prejudiced against coins with women on them. This is the kind of weird thinking that the London gold market must take into account as a matter of everyday business. Gold is romantic, mysterious, and generally far-fetched, permanently symbolic of what simpletons we all are. At least the dingy basement and old-fashioned trappings of the bullion house achieve the dignity of not appearing to take the stuff too seriously.

9

£40,000,000 FOR A SHOP

No word in finance has become more suspect since 1945 than 'take-over'. The take-over business has already been touched upon – the twilight world of Mr Nickleby, the theatrical attitudes of the British Aluminium affair, and the discreet courtship of P. & E. by Kenwood. Take-overs will continue as long as there are companies to be taken over. By the end of the 1950s it seemed possible that the conditions that put them in the headlines day after day had spent themselves, though the vigour of the principle went on being demonstrated. No one who reads newspapers should be in any doubt about what happened in the previous decade. Amid post-war inflation, prices rose but dividends were kept down: this was because companies faced high rates of tax, because the economic atmosphere bred caution, and because at one time 'dividend restraint' was Government policy. Thus the true value of companies increased more than the apparent value, as represented by their shares – since the size of dividend is the largest factor in determining the price of a share. The difference between real and apparent value was an exploitable margin. A financier could either buy his way cheaply into the company through the stock market; or he could make a public offer to shareholders of a price somewhere between these two values. Once in control he could turn hidden assets into cash, paying special attention to property, which generally turned out to be worth far more than the balance sheet showed. Take-over bidders have been damned for stripping companies to line their own pockets; for disregarding such social assets as hotels and theatres, pulling them down and putting up speculative office buildings instead; for encouraging golden handshakes to ousted directors; for making large sums in tax-free capital gains. The fact that they make money under people's noses, brazenly and legally in broad daylight, is hardly calculated to bring them love and affection. They have been defended as stimulants and catalysts, doing good to shareholders and business generally, at a time when fierce competition in consumer-goods industries and among shops made conditions ripe for weeding out the inefficient.

Towards the end of the 1950s it was felt that most of the obvious plums had gone, or had ceased to be plums because their boards had woken up to the danger. The bidder who was after quick capital gain – and he was the kind the moral and political fuss was about – could find few unsophisticated managements sitting on potential goldmines, either too ignorant or too inefficient to do anything about it. Nevertheless, the last year of the decade provided some spectacular take-over fireworks, culminating in the glorious bangs and cascades of the Harrods setpiece, when the so-called finest shop in the world was fought for through two hot summer months.

As a preliminary to the big event, one of the best-publicized men in the business, Mr Charles Clore of Sears Holdings, tried to buy one of the largest brewery groups in Britain, Watney Mann. Clore, who began his career by buying a roller-skating rink at Cricklewood, built his reputation earlier in the 1950s with a series of take-overs that left him owning more than 1,000 shoe shops – including Freeman, Hardy & Willis, Manfield & Son, and Dolcis – Furness Shipbuilding, Bentley Engineering, Scottish Motor Traction, Shaw & Kilburn (Vauxhall car dealers), laundry companies, and air-conditioning companies. He used the classic technique of selling property freeholds acquired by take-overs to the ever-wealthy insurance companies, renting them back on long leases, and using the cash for further expansion. Little had been heard of him for a year or two when at the end of May 1959 a bid for Watneys was announced by Sears Holdings – which in a former life had been J. Sears & Co. (True-Form Boot Co.), before Clore embraced it, unlocked its assets, and turned it into a holding company to control his enterprises. Clore offered £20,000,000 for the Watney shares, and one of his staff spoke the dreaded words: the plan was to 'redevelop properties, using part as shops and offices'. Pubs would be made more attractive. New restaurants would be opened, and 'the earnings of the group will be improved'. With 3,670 pubs in London and the home counties, a trading profit the previous year of £3,373,743, one of the largest wine and spirit businesses in the country, and the Coca-Cola agency for the south of England, the board of Watneys rose up in fury against Clore, said the offer was 'preposterous' and acceptance would be 'deplorable', sat tight – and won. The price of Watney shares had soared with the offer, taking them to 77s., 17s. above the Sears bid of £3. Clore, instead of raising his offer in the accepted manner, wasn't prepared to go higher. Watneys had been tempting. But there were only limited opportunities for redevelopment of property – the Watney board was aware of this particular goldmine – and Clore must have considered his first offer was near the limit of Watneys' real worth at that time, however much 'redevelopment' ensued.

Before the offer was withdrawn, the idea of a fight for 3,670 pubs had brought the affair down to brass tacks. The Englishman was implicated. Barflies who would not normally consider such things were moved to protest, in a jocose sort of way, at a system that made the walls of their pubs and the fluid in their glasses the abstract counters of tycoons. This may have been sentimental of the barflies, but one of the constant elements in people's attitude to the goings-on of financiers is a widening of the eyes when the business world splits open for a moment, as it does in a publicized take-over, to reveal what a variety of strings the City is pulling. Truisms take on a fresh edge when spoken by men who have everyday experience of them. The remark to the Radcliffe Committee by Sir Ivan Stedeford that 'Money is power – if you have money you can do anything you want to' is elevated from cliché by the fact that Sir Ivan was the chairman of Tube Investments, speaking in the midst of the British Aluminium affair. In the same way, the amorphous idea of a 'Them' who manage our affairs is made tangible by a take-over involving books or beer or bread or clothes. This often hurts, and it's no wonder that the City has been at pains to give instructions on the etiquette of the take-over – not that the *Notes on Amalgamations of British Businesses*, already referred to, are likely to have any effect on the take-over business. It would never do for people's awe of high finance, or high anything else, to turn into a persistent sense of grievance.

The fight for Harrods, which officially opened on the day Clore withdrew his bid for Watneys, brought home the facts of life to many people who had never been inside the place but who would have been willing to admit they thought of it as an institution. Surviving, as the *Observer* said, like 'a dinosaur among wolves', Harrods was a piece of the past that by sheer weight of purpose had gone on living into a shopping age that its founders never dreamt of. The store was in Knightsbridge, south-west of centre in London, in a district that became fashionable when the Great Exhibition of 1851 was held in Hyde Park, and has remained a good address. A great façade of grubby yellow brick overhung the street, concealing a calm, space-wasting interior like the setting for an Edwardian novel blown up to extravagant dimensions. Tradesmen, trading in practically every commodity under the sun except milk – because an early owner disapproved of Sunday work – knew their place in Harrods. Customers were flattered in various ways; notices on the walls referred to them as *visitors*, presumably in case the word 'customer' suggested they were being pressured into buying; credit was extensive. Whenever the papers reported a case involving fraud on London shops, Harrods was likely to be mentioned because it was the natural place for high-livers to open an account. (There was the case of Mr P, a young Scot who came to London and started living it up in 1957. While working as a £9-a-week clerk he opened an account at Harrods and obtained goods worth £600, made up of little items like a typewriter and a gold watch, all of which he promptly sold, before the law overtook him.) With 100,000 account customers, bills took time to emerge from the Harrods counting house.

The sober-suited salesmen and pretty salesgirls among the 5,500 employees were discouraged from hard selling by lower commissions but higher salaries than is usual at stores. Staff addressed one another formally on the shop floor. In ten years up to 1959 the only developments had been a casual wear department and a wedding gift bureau – though one explanation for this could be that the service was already too good for improvement. Available for telephone orders twenty-four hours a day, every day of the year, Harrods summed itself up with its telegraphic address: *Everything, London*. It had a banking hall with its own bank; butcher's department with meat in frills and master butcher in high-buttoned Victorian overcoat; fish department with beautiful slabs, beautiful fish, and archetypal fishmongers; grocery department with, someone calculated, 45,000 different non-perishable items; boys' shop, young man's shop, man's shop; waiting room for customers' dogs; one of the best bars in London; wedding service, funeral service; bakery; shoe repairers, clock repairers; silver-plating shop; tea-blending house; antique workrooms; sweet factory, trunk factory, cardboard-box factory. 'You can', wrote John Gale when the battle was warming up and Harrods was collecting enormous amounts of free publicity in every newspaper, 'walk miles below ground, down Hans Crescent Corridor, Brompton Passage, and Chinatown, past endless stockrooms and the potato stores. Africans or West Indians drive past on trolleys towing basket trailers. You can visit the fur cold-storage room ("he may not *die* down here," says the white-coated attendant, referring to the moth, "but he won't do any damage"), where Father Christmas's cloak hangs up with Coronation Robes.' Over all Harrods lay the mark of quality, crystallized in the painted letters on one corner of the building, 'By Appointment to Her Majesty the Queen Suppliers of China, Glass and Fancy Goods', signifying that Harrods held a Royal Warrant of appointment to supply goods to Buckingham Palace. The Harrods writing paper balanced this message, in the top left-hand corner, with another on the right: 'By Appointment Suppliers of China, Glass and Fancy Goods to H.M. Queen Elizabeth the Queen Mother.'

Harrods was a group, not just the one Knightsbridge store: built up by some shrewd take-overs of its own into the third largest department-store group in the country. It began with a tea merchant, H. C. Harrod, who took over a grocer's shop, and handed it on to his son when Knightsbridge was becoming fashionable. Charles Harrod expanded like a good Victorian. He refused to dress his windows, fined assistants when they were late, and for years allowed customers no credit; but when he left it in 1889, it was one of the leading stores. He was followed by Richard Burbidge, a rising man in the rising business of department stores. Burbidge came in as general manager after serving with Whiteleys, the once famous store that still survives in Bayswater, long after the district has ceased to be superior. For the twenty-odd years until the first war, department stores were in their prime. Most of them began as drapers. (Harrods began as grocers: hence their emphasis on food.) They gave small drapers and grocers their first taste of ruthless competition, drawing in the middle-class customers with large stocks and dignified service; but between the wars the stores slid into decline, as suburban shopping grew and the new formidable mass-market of the working and lower-middle classes took shape, catered for by the 'multiples', with Woolworths and Marks & Spencer in the lead. Amalgamation was the obvious answer, and after the second war many stores coalesced into groups, where central buying and a balance between quality shops and popular shops gave them a chance of competing with multiples.

By 1959 the largest group was Debenhams, with total assets estimated at £56,000,000. It contained 130 shops and stores, including several large stores in London: Debenham & Free-body, Harvey Nichols, Marshall & Snelgrove, Woolland Bros, Swan & Edgar. Second came the House of Fraser, which had been a mainly North of England and Scottish group till 1956, when half a mile of stores in Kensington High Street – Barkers, Pontings, Derry & Toms – were taken over to make the group worth, in round figures, £28,000,000. Third was Harrods. It was thought that not more than half the Harrods profits came from the Knightsbridge stores. Included in the group were the London stores of Dickins & Jones and D. H. Evans, and assets were put at £23,000,000.

When rumours that someone was after Harrods began in June, City and Press did the obvious equations. Debenham + Harrods

= Fraser × 3, which would make Debenhams unassailable fo
years to come. But Fraser + Harrods = Debenhams, or ver;
nearly – which would leave two giants of comparable size t
compete for a shrinking slice of the cake. Between 1950 an
1957, department stores' share of retail trade fell from six to fiv
per cent; multiples' share rose from twenty-three to twenty-fiv
per cent. With their single-minded avoidance of slow or unusua
lines of goods, bulk purchase of articles made to their own rigi
specifications, and drastic economies in space, the multiples were
and are, encroaching all the time. But the fight for Harrods wa
more than a matter of equations and budgets. Like all the bes
City occasions it was also a matter of personalities. At Harrod
itself was the kindly, courteous chairman, Sir Richard Burbidge
Bt, grandson of the Burbidge who came from Whiteleys. Bur
bidge had lived in a flat backing on to the store since he was ;
baby, and toured the departments every morning. He ha
recently been unable to decide whether to keep Harrods inde
pendent, with the risk that someone might buy him out, or t
make the best of a bad job by merging with Debenhams. Bur
bidge liked Debenhams, but he kept hesitating. For some tim
he had been talking with John Bedford, the Debenhams chair
man: another quiet man, who had risen inside the business, an
who could claim that he had never made a bid over the heads o
sitting directors, or gone into the market and bought share
anonymously. All Bedford's take-overs had been kid-gloved
Burbidge and Bedford spoke the same language; unlike th
hotter arenas of industry, shopkeeping has continued to produc
a species of milder tycoon, combining efficiency with a stron;
distaste for ruthlessness. When take-overs generally were in th
news, one Debenhams' man told me: 'There seems trouble in th
City distinguishing between a take-over bid and a merger – it'
said that if a merger is justified, then so is a take-over. I'd hav
thought that was just as true as to say that when people ge
married they have intercourse, and therefore that justifies rape
Debenhams' attitude has always been that in nine cases out of ter
we are approached by the company – perhaps the managemen
are getting old, and they're going to have a death-duty problem

and then we do say to them: "Any time you want to sell, we'd be interested." But all our mergers have been done on a friendly basis. Of course, you've got to decide in all these things what you're in it for. If you're some men you're in it to make money. If you're a Fraser you're in it more for the glory.'

Fraser was the third man: Hugh Fraser (now Sir Hugh), a Scottish millionaire, a comparative newcomer to the front rank of take-overship. While Burbidge advanced towards the plunge with Debenhams, then retreated a step, hesitating on the brink while the months went by, Fraser began to make careful preparation. In the third week of June Harrods Ordinary £1 shares went from 97s. to 114s., and Fraser told the Press: 'I have put in proposals for Harrods.'

Fraser was born into shopkeeping, and a less ambitious and original man might have been content with the modest family draper's in Glasgow, founded by his grandfather, that he inherited in 1926 at the age of twenty-three. It took him a long time to get going; the old theory that drive in business is lost by the time of the third generation had every chance to be proved true in the depression-ridden twenties and thirties, especially in Glasgow. But he managed to expand even before the war, buying up shops for a song, and after 1945 made the company public. Fraser was the first to perfect the property technique of selling freeholds to insurance companies. With financial expertise went a tough approach to draping, on multiple-store lines, and a burning sense of personal mission. The first take-over to put him squarely in the headlines was in 1953, when after a fight with the directors he bought Binns of Sunderland, a company with department stores in north-east England and Scotland, for £4,600,000. Fraser was moving south, but before he reached London in 1957 he swallowed stores in Glasgow, Dundee, and Aberdeen, and paid £3,000,000 for Seager, Evans & Co., the distillers. This was thought to be a personal purchase – Fraser is extremely rich. He came to London with a bid of £10,500,000 for John Barker, a Kensington store with two associates, Pontings and Derry & Toms – all next door to one another – and the Zeeta chain of restaurants. It was expected that Debenhams would make a counter-offer, but at the last minute they said they would do nothing. So Fraser won Barkers. As a group it was bigger than Fraser, but he was able to retain control of his empire, as he had retained it in the past, by issuing virtually voteless 'A' shares to the Barker shareholders in exchange for their stock. It was the sale of Barker properties that helped finance the Harrods bid two years later.

Fraser hasn't always been successful. His two most notable defeats have both been put down to Scottish patriotism, a curious but not improbable suggestion for a man who styles his company House of Fraser, and has the scrapbooks in his office bound in tartan cloth. In 1956 Charles Clore made a bid for Scottish Motor Traction, a company whose main business was distributing Vauxhall cars. There was resentment at the thought of control in a Scottish firm passing over the border – unlike Wales, where industry has been almost invariably developed and owned by the English, Scotland retains some industrial and commercial autonomy. Fraser was approached as the man to help save S.M.T., and flew back from the United States to intervene. But he admitted that 'I am not after S.M.T. in the way I went after Binns'; and it was Clore who won. The other failure, in the case of Lyle & Scott, the Scottish knitwear firm, was less obviously connected with national feeling; but when they asked why he wanted Lyle & Scott, Fraser told the directors who opposed him that the company obviously needed more capital, and he 'didn't want to see it go to the financiers in London'. Fraser lost this fight because the chairman of Lyle, a blunt and dour individual called Charles D. Oliver, fought him with the anger of a man defending his hearth. I met one of Oliver's London directors, and later Oliver himself, who sat in the bar of his hotel with a look of crumpled iron, and said he never stayed in London a minute longer than he had to. Seen through their eyes a take-over was an enormity, an assault on a way of life; if their feelings were anything to go by, a year's crop of take-overs and attempted take-overs must generate an amazing amount of heat in the upper reaches of industry. Lyle & Scott were a private company, founded 1878, making high-class knitwear in Hawick; they held the British licence from Coopers of Wisconsin to make men's Y-front underwear, described as 'the fastest selling line in underwear in the country'. Fraser made an offer which was accepted by a small majority of the shareholders, who included investment trusts; but Oliver and the directors who were with him invoked one of the company's articles of association which laid down that if a shareholder wished to transfer his shares, he must first offer them to other shareholders. Those who supported Fraser tried to get round this by keeping their shares, but accepting money – £3 for each £1 share – from Fraser, and binding themselves to vote for him. Whether by so doing they had virtually sold to Fraser, in contravention of the articles, was a question that dragged through the courts for three years, until the House of Lords, reversing earlier decisions, finally came down in favour of Oliver.

'My chairman', one of Oliver's directors said to me, a few weeks after they had won, 'insisted that we shall win. He said if he spent his last penny he'd do it. He wasn't going to lie down and be squashed.'

I would have liked Fraser's view of the Lyle & Scott affair, not to mention Fraser's view of Harrods, and Fraser's view of Fraser. But he proved to be one of the inaccessible tycoons. The descriptions are interesting: lives outside Glasgow, family man, tends orchids and wears one in buttonhole, drives fast cars, shrewd, defiant, misses nothing, makes all directors resign when he takes over and re-seats them only if they prove their worth, likes whisky and pink champagne, talks quietly with Scots accent, visits London weekly for meetings of Automobile Association of which he's hon. treasurer, runs a newspaper, is a Justice of the Peace. A man who had a short life as his public relations adviser told me he was 'dead contemporary, with an unexpected amount of natural charm and good manners'. Fraser has enclosed himself within the walls of tycoonery, and the nearest I could get was an assistant who was courteous and hopeful but eventually produced a *No*.

Approaching tycoons is either very easy or very difficult, and in difficult cases a great deal of finesse is called for. Another of the tycoons I approached while writing this book had shielded himself with an official who gave me a strange interview – he asked what I might expect from the book, and continued without waiting for an answer: 'You're writing this presumably as a principal with a royalty, presumably 12½ or 15 per cent. You may be very happy to say: "I acknowledge thanks to Mr X for his help" – you may not even be prepared to say that. On the other hand, if we give you the information, if we're really helpful, you might feel inclined to say: "Well, it's only a very small section of the book, so it hardly qualifies for a contribution, any division of royalty – but I should like to do something in recognition of the help given me here. If my books does well, I'll give something to the Blankshire Home for Stray Birds" – which you've never heard of, but which happens to be before me at the moment. What's your reaction?' I said I thought it was an extraordinary thing to suggest. The assistant murmured something about his embarrassment. He intimated that he was handling other matters on a larger scale at the moment. 'We'll let it pass,' he said. We shook hands at the lift, but I never did see Mr X.

Neither did I see Mr Fraser – who, a letter told me six weeks later, felt we were 'somewhat too close to affairs'. Still, it was a well-publicized take-over. Rumours of a bid for Harrods had cropped up before, but at the end of June 1959 two potential buyers came into sight together: Fraser and Debenhams. From the start there was strong feeling. Fraser had been talking to Burbidge since 9 June, but said he hadn't known Debenhams were in the field; he was understandably narked to have been kept out of the secret. Bedford said that 'friendly discussions' with Harrods had been in progress for months. On 23 June, a few days after the news broke, the Harrods board unanimously recommended a Debenhams offer worth £34,500,000, against Fraser's informal proposal of £32,600,000. Both proposed a mixture of cash and shares for the 4,000,000 Ordinary and 4,000,000 Preference Harrods shares – Fraser included substantially more cash – and the value of the offers fluctuated with the value of the shares. June 23 was Sir Richard Burbidge's sixty-second birthday. Pictures showed a kindly Edwardian face, with neat moustache and bushy eyebrows. The story went round that Burbidge had said to Fraser: 'I should much prefer Harrods to remain independent, but if it must be taken over I want it to be by a draper and not an outsider.' Fraser thought 'draper' meant himself; but Burbidge meant Bedford. The other alleged Burbidge-to-Fraser remark had a still rougher edge. It was: 'No, sir. Not you.'

While Fraser was complaining that he hadn't been fairly treated by the Harrods board, and providing the usual determined reactions, the financial Press was busy wondering whether Harrods was worth more than thirty times its annual net earnings of around £1,000,000. There was also speculation about the behaviour of Harrods shareholders: would they, when the time came, go against the advice of their directors, or would they put up a show of 'shareholder loyalty' and go for Debenhams? It was confidently expected that they would be loyal. Institutional holdings in Harrods were not large. On 23 June the biggest holding appeared to be 'London office, Royal Bank of Scotland Nominees' (this might have been Fraser), with 57,856 Ordinary shares and 68,000 Preference. The Cooperative Insurance Society held 13,848 Ordinary, 67,500 Preference. The Church Commissioners for England (who are into everything – they made a nice profit out of British Aluminium) 34,000 Ordinary and 10,000 Preference. Harrods was not, said stockbrokers, a very dynamic business. They were rather dull stores shares, steady and unspectacular, of the kind that would appeal to the middle-class ex-urbanites who made up a good proportion of those 100,000 account customers. The large number of young, elegant women shoppers to be seen any morning at Harrods would not be expected to hold shares; the older, tweedier, up-for-the-day-from-the-country women would. 'Harrods', said one stockbroker, 'was just the place for them to put their money. It was something specific. They could get off the train at Victoria and take a taxi and *look* at it.'

A stronger reason for expecting Fraser to lose was that the shares he offered in exchange were House of Fraser 'A' – almost, but not quite, voteless shares, with one-twentieth of a vote apiece. Voteless shares have been regarded with displeasure by the City for some years, though in compensation they are always cheaper than vote-carrying shares. Two other take-over groups have used them – Sears Holdings and Isaac Wolfson's Great Universal Stores. The argument that it's wrong to take investors' money without giving them a say in the company's affairs, and the fact that insurance and investment companies often refuse to buy them, hasn't deterred concerns like Marks & Spencer, Rootes, Express Dairies, and British Electric Traction. But opinion has been flowing hard against voteless shares, and the Debenhams offer of four 10s. vote-carrying shares for every £1 Harrods Ordinary looked better, to most City columnists, than Fraser's 2½ 5s. 'A' shares plus 20s. cash – though with Debenhams standing around 31s., the Fraser 'A' at 41s., the total amounts offered were now practically the same. Offers for the other half of the Harrods stock, the 4,000,000 7½% Preference shares – which carried a vote apiece, and so were as important to the buyer as the Ordinaries – were similarly close, both around 40s. a share. But a certain amount of pleasure could be detected in the way people explained how difficult Fraser would find it, how this time he had bitten off more than he could chew. Once more there was the old City feeling that behind the scenes, subtle alignments were taking place. Lazards were acting for Debenhams. Morgan Grenfell, their best friend among merchant bankers (*vide* Lord Kindersley) were advising Harrods – and one of Morgan's managing directors was on the Harrods board.

A week after the first offers were published, a third bidder appeared in the shape of a tailor-and-draper group, United Drapery Stores, offering the equivalent of 138s. 3d. for each Harrods Ordinary, and putting a total value of £36,000,000 on the Harrods stock – £3,000,000 more than Fraser or Debenhams. A new personality floated into view: the chairman of United Drapery, Mr Joseph Collier, a bald, soft-spoken Jew with heavy glasses and a sad way of talking about money. Mr Collier had begun with a shop near the Elephant and Castle and gone on to own the John Collier shops, the Alexandre shops, the John Blundell shops, the Richard shops: altogether the best part of a thousand, though with few department stores. Collier was particularly interested in a Harrods store that was being built in Birmingham, on one of the few central sites left in a large English city. Like Fraser and Bedford, he was anxious to let it be known that he didn't want to *change* Harrods: put together, the expressed intentions to leave Harrods untouched sounded like the minutes of a society for the preservation of ancient monuments. The Collier bid was highly thought of; so was the fact that United Drapery were known to be backed by the Eagle Star Insurance group. Yet talking to people in the City, one got the idea that besides the arithmetic of the bids, some indefinable quality attached to the Fraser offer. 'Some people just believe in Fraser,' said one stockbroker. In an office outside the Stock Exchange I heard a man say that jobbers of Scottish extraction were doing their best to spread pro-Fraser rumours because they wanted a fellow-countryman to win -- it sounded improbable, but the rumour was significant. Fraser was being thought of as a man under a star.

Over the last weekend in June, Fraser enhanced his magic with a practical move: he announced that he would give full voting rights to all Fraser 'A' shares. This removed the small black cloud of disapproval, and also increased the value of the Fraser proposals, since the shares would be worth two or three shillings more when enfranchised. The move, said Fraser, had been under consideration for 'a great number of years': it was nothing to do with the Harrods bid. 'We are now', he said, in a voice that must have been heard with alarm in the boardrooms of Great Universal Stores, Marks & Spencer, and the rest, 'becoming a share-owning democracy, with unit trusts and so on, and I think it is only right that shareholders in any business, should the occasion arise, should have a vote at the shareholders' meeting.' They were impeccable sentiments, impeccably timed, and were followed on 7 July by a formal Fraser offer – so far they had been only 'proposals' – which showed the extent of Fraser's determination. For every Harrods Ordinary he was now offering £3 in cash and 2¼ Fraser 'A's – worth another 90s. But for the Preference shares his offer was lowered to 30s. cash; it was assumed he had been buying heavily in the market, and already held a large quantity of Preference stock. The revised terms meant that Fraser was committed to finding £18,000,000 in money, and the Cassandras got busy again. The sound of men caught on the wrong foot came from Philip Hill, Higginson, United Drapery's merchant-banker advisers: '£18,000,000 cash is a lot of money. How can Mr Fraser justify it? We shall have to consider our next move.' (Philip Hill, admitted to the Accepting Houses Committee only the month before, were the one merchant bank to make informal statements to the Press. Debenhams, they said, proposed 'the marriage of two large lumps of Victorian masonry'. Fraser was 'like Jonah swallowing the whale'.)

Time passed. July was a hot month. People went on holiday and the papers got bored. So far only Fraser had made a formal offer, and investors waited patiently, or decided to call it a day and sell through the market. Already there were nice pickings for Harrods Ordinary stockholders, whose shares had risen from 74s. to 130s. in a few weeks – the shares refused to rise any nearer the value put on them by bidders because investors and specula-tors were suspicious of them, afraid the whole affair might have a Watney-style ending, with the bidders backing out. The Pre-ference stockholders were already beginning to curse. Before Fraser's formal offer they could have sold through the market for more than 40s. a share; now the Preference were worth little more than 30s.

Fraser's annual accounts were published, and seemed to bear little relation to his offer. According to the balance sheet House of Fraser had £884,020 cash, less than its current tax liability, and not far towards £18,000,000. But sales of John Barker property were expected to realize £1,500,000, and the rest would no doubt come from sales of more freeholds, including those of Harrods, and bridging operations from the Fraser bankers who 'just believed in Fraser'. In the letter columns of the *Financial Times* a lively correspondence was in progress on non-voting shares. They were, said one man, protection for the family business which was forced to issue shares because of high taxation; they saved him from take-overs. The average investor with a vote never

used it anyway, and when he bought 'A' shares he knew what he
was doing. To try and alter his contract by howling for a vote was
dishonest; the Psalms described a righteous man as one who
'sweareth unto his neighbour and disappointeth him not, though
it were to his own hindrance'. An angry retort came from a
Glasgow investor who thought it was 'plain cant and humbug to
speak of democratic principles and our way of life in the same
breath as non-voting shares', adding a cryptic quotation from
Jeremiah: 'The heart is deceitful above all things, and desperately
wicked: who can know it?'

At the end of July several things happened at once. The
Fraser offer was posted to stockholders. Debenhams announced
they had increased their offer for the Ordinary stock, which
made it worth a few shillings per share more than Fraser's (the
Preference offer remained a full ten shillings higher). And
United Drapery withdrew. U.D. shares immediately rose, on the
principle that whoever won Harrods was going to pay dearly
for it, and so was well out of the struggle. From now on the
Fraser and Debenham shares see-sawed as each in turn looked
like winning; with the likely winner's falling, and the likely loser's
rising, since it was assumed that the winner's shares, issued in
part-payment to Harrods shareholders, would be promptly sold
for cash. The market, crystal-gazing busily, discounted the shares
in expectation of this selling. Special-buying operations, designed
to keep up the price of sagging shares, were said to be in progress.
There was plenty of excitement, and, day by day, the feeling that
Debenhams were in trouble. When the formal Debenhams offer
went out on 5 August, and the formal recommendation to support it followed from Harrods, the nine Harrods directors revealed how much of their own stock they held: the princely
amount of £17,454 Ordinary and £1,250 Preference. Another
omen was that United Drapery were found to have sold 500,000
Preference shares to Fraser, after Debenhams had turned them
down. Collier told me afterwards how he warned Bedford to
make up his mind quickly if he wanted the shares, and how a
phone call came from Fraser's solicitors in Scotland at 8.15 one
morning, asking if it was true that the shares were for sale.

Collier sold to Fraser, probably at a special price around 45s. a share. Bedford explained later to the Press why he had refused to pay 45s. It meant, he said, putting two values on a share, one in private and one in public. Bedford's attitude may have been theoretically admirable, but it was a fact that he had missed the chance to buy outright 6 per cent of the Harrods voting power.

The closing date for the Fraser offer was Saturday, 22 August, for the Debenham offer Wednesday, 26 August. Well before the Fraser date the air was thick with circulars and counter-circulars. Fraser's growth, said Bedford, looked 'positively slow' beside United Drapery. Debenhams knew more about the luxury end of the business. Debenhams would be able to finance the purchase without selling any Harrods properties. But in the market they began to think that Fraser would win. He was buying every share that came in sight, and his offer had more cash in it – very important, since the thought of cheques instead of other people's shares is a powerful persuader.

On Tuesday, 18 August, Lazard Bros were buying space in the papers to print a letter from John Bedford. 'Our offer', he said in heavy type at the end, 'has the goodwill of (i) Harrods' Directors (ii) Harrods' staff (iii) Harrods' customers. I regard these last two items as being of the utmost importance as I cannot see any merger being successful without them.' The same day Fraser added 6s. 8d. per Ordinary share to his offer. Bedford made no comment. On Wednesday the former chairman of John Barker, now 'hon. president', was declaring that he had had nothing but the friendliest relations with Fraser, and was sure the staff would say the same. There were rumours that Debenhams were withdrawing – but on Thursday morning Bedford gritted his teeth and added another 10s. per Ordinary to his price, which meant finding another £2,000,000 and made his bid worth, at current prices, more than £37,000,000. People were losing count of what was happening. The cash content was still better with Fraser, though some investors who wanted to see the colour of money right away, and were weary of the interminable contest, sold in the market. But on paper the Debenhams offer was now well ahead: 156s. 9d. per Ordinary against Fraser's 141s. 6d.

Fraser did nothing more. Confidence began to radiate from his Scottish headquarters – yet what was he confident *of*? No doubt he recognized the value of sounding like a winner well in advance of victory. Perhaps he knew that investors who were tired of calculating and recalculating would keep their eyes on the hard, finite cash. His superior strategy was emphasized by the way he concentrated on the Ordinary shares. And he certainly knew that by fixing the closing date for their offer four days later than his, Debenhams had played into his hands. On the Friday afternoon, stockbrokers' desks were stacked with parallel bundles of acceptances, one for Fraser, the other for Debenhams, both signed by Harrods investors who had left the final decision to their brokers. There was still time for Debenhams to win – but it needed a spurt of confidence, and confidence was lacking. 'We didn't know where we stood,' said one broker. 'The more ups and downs there had been, the more I'd advised clients to sit tight. But when it got to the Friday we were in a cleft stick. There was a mild story going round that "If you don't accept Fraser you may be shut out". There were people who said he'd be satisfied with 51 per cent of the shares. If we didn't accept on Friday, in time for the post, it might have been too late. The Debenhams offer didn't close till the following Wednesday – the time to decide about Fraser was *now*. People who might have held out were afraid of being left in a minority, holding shares that no one wanted. It's true that some of the merchant bankers were putting their weight behind Harrods and Debenhams. (How do they do that? Well, they influence the broker.) But by that Friday afternoon the psychological atmosphere was that Fraser was winning. I kept the forms on my desk till three o'clock, then I sent off the acceptances for Fraser and threw the others in the basket.'

The fear of being stuck with unwanted shares was enough to decide many investors, and many brokers. They accepted the Fraser offer – or they sold in the market, where Fraser's brokers were still busy. Debenhams were thought to have made few if any purchases that day, and by next morning jubilation reigned across the border. The number of acceptances, Fraser said from Scotland, was fantastic. The weather had broken and violent storms followed by flooding affected many parts of England. 'I would have thought the mails would have been held up,' Fraser was quoted as saying. 'But no. We have had three mail vans full. I have never seen so many letters in my life.' Even the elements and the G.P.O. were no match for the master draper; and no one had anything to say about shareholder loyalty. Fraser was now safe in extending the Ordinaries offer to Wednesday, the same day as Debenhams: his strategy had done the damage. By Monday night, having lost a stone in weight in two months, he was flying from Glasgow to the South of France for a few days' holiday; he paused on the way to tell reporters that he had paid more than they supposed, and left the impression that Harrods would cost him something like £40,000,000. Bedford was still refusing to admit defeat. He said he thought Fraser had jumped the gun, and was reported to be meeting Lazard Bros to discuss Fraser's claims. He said that 'four and a half million shareholders have not cast their votes. They are probably waiting to hear our statement tomorrow.' But it all had an academic ring. Fraser had been the one who desired Harrods. He had long since satisfied what Dr Johnson called every man's 'lurking wish to appear considerable in his native place', and had swept into London with all the passion of the stranger. Only an equal depth of passion could have beaten him.

That week the 'Bids and Deals' columns were full of the usual good things. The Universal Winding Co. of the United States had made an offer to acquire the assets and liabilities of Thomas Holt, the wholly-owned textile machinery manufacturing subsidiary of Thomas Holt Holdings (Rochdale), for £375,440. The Dinkie Heel Co. were offering to acquire the £10,000 share capital of Colburn Metal Producers for £80,000. Morgan Grenfell & Co. announced that their offer on behalf of Cerebos, makers of Bisto, for Brand & Co., makers of A1 Sauce, had succeeded. The take-over business was proceeding as usual, as it had been all summer – in July, for example, partly obscured by the Harrods smokeclouds, Mr Clore had got control of Mappin & Webb, the jewellers and goldsmiths, another Royal Warrant holder. Harrods now went the way of Mappin & Webb and A1 Sauce.

Formal admission of defeat came from Bedford a few minutes after noon on Monday, releasing Harrods shareholders who had accepted the Debenhams offer so that they could go over to Fraser. Jonah had swallowed the whale, and Sir Richard Burbidge was left with the melancholy task of telling his senior executives, assembled in a lecture hall, that House of Fraser were the new proprietors. He remained chairman for a few weeks more, then stepped down to be joint managing director when Fraser took over. Later still he said good-bye to the plushier end of retailing and went to be chairman of British Home Stores. Bedford told a special meeting of Debenhams shareholders, called to approve the increase in capital that would have been necessary in the event of victory: 'We could have won, but I felt that Debenhams ought not to resort to take-over methods. We started off on a friendly basis. It was only the intervention of other people that turned it into a bear garden. I do not like take-over bids and I do not like the people who make them.' Later he said Debenhams would have won but for the 'premature Press comments that Hugh Fraser had made it'. It didn't sound convincing. The one piece of material consolation was that although it cost Debenhams £46,917 in advertising, circulars, and other campaign expenses, the eventual sales of Harrods shares in the market made money and gave an overall profit of £17,077.

It was the end of the year before I met Bedford. He sat in a large office, a dark-eyed man with greying hair, not intimidating; with very white hands on the desk, resting among leather cases for scissors and letter-opener, stamped with his initials. 'We take the view – we may be old-fashioned,' he said, 'that we've no right to go buying in the market without the knowledge of the people from whom we're buying. We take the view that it isn't right for me, knowing I'm going to see Sir Richard Burbidge and offer him £7 for his shares, to go and buy them in the market at £4 10s. At the time we negotiated we didn't own one share in Harrods. We may be old-fashioned – I don't know. As far as I'm concerned I should do the same again.' He had all the figures in his mind: what Barkers cost, what Binns cost, United Drapery profits, what the Harrods-and-Debenhams dividends would have

been. He was a very likeable man. He said he came from War-
wickshire; originally he was going to be a lawyer, but joined
Debenhams after being apprenticed as a draper, against the
advice of people who said the business was choked with relatives,
and he'd never get to the top. His happiest time, he said, was in
the days when he would be sent to take charge of a new store.
It turned out that he knew a lot about the history of Debenhams,
and the district where the head store stood, to the north of Oxford
Street. 'Debenhams have been here since 1778,' he said. 'This
was fields, and the little brook, the bourne – that's how you have
Marylebone, from St Mary on the bourne - ran through Regent's
Park, across what was Tyburn Way – Oxford Street – through
Green Park, and into the Thames. This was the village of Marylebone, and Debenhams have had the same site since they started.
Where Marshall & Snelgrove are now was Lord Derby's town
house. From Wigmore Street to Regent's Park were fields. It
was a good ride to the village of Kensington . . .' Presently he
remembered a point about Fraser dividends, and buzzed his
secretary for the Fraser annual report. As I was going he gave a
small smile and said: 'You'll see the others and get a different
story, I expect.' In Oxford Street the shoppers milled around with
determined expressions in the rain. All villages, all brooks, were
far, far away. It was a hard old world.

10

THE OPTIMISTS OF LLOYD'S

ON a thin sheet of crinkly paper sixteen inches square, which is attached to all policies issued by the ancient and truly British insurance institution of Lloyd's, upwards of sixteen thousand names appear in miniscule print, marshalled in fifty columns under numbered headings that run from '2 & 49' through '999' to '031'. This is a complete list of the gentlemen admitted to membership of Lloyd's, grouped in the syndicates to which they belong. There are over five thousand individual members, most of them on several syndicates apiece, which accounts for the sixteen thousand. In each syndicate of which he is a member, the lucky gentleman holds a percentage interest. Thus the 1961 list shows Lord Poole, who appeared in a previous chapter as Mr Poole, in Syndicate No. 56, with a '29' beside his name, and the legend '779ths of 39.52%' outside a long bracket enclosing his name with that of others in the syndicate. This means that Lord Poole's share of the profits – and of the risk – in Syndicate No. 56 was 29/779ths of 39.52% of the total. At the cost of some eye-strain one may recognize the names of politicians (Labour as well as Conservative), stockbrokers, bill brokers, gold merchants, textile manufacturers, shipowners, and numerous peers of the realm. I happen to know of a reputable haulage contractor who started with one lorry and a shed in a provincial town, and a not so reputable business man, who are on the list.

Most of the 5,000-odd are 'underwriting members', generally known as 'names' – these are sleeping partners in the syndicates, and normally never go near 'the Room' at Lloyd's, the enormous open chamber where business is done. An 'underwriting agent' (or simply 'underwriter') heads each syndicate, and, with a small staff, handles the actual business; like his 'names', he takes a percentage of the profits, is probably paid a fee by his members in addition, and will himself be a member of other syndicates. The brokers who place insurance business with syndicates – the public aren't allowed to deal direct with Lloyd's – supply a good many 'names'. Some syndicates are under the wing of a firm of brokers, and there are innumerable underwriter-broker family and business connexions. Gardner, Mountain, D'Ambrumenil & Rennie, for instance, is one of the large and distinguished broking firms; Syndicate No. 507 in 1961 contained the name D'Ambrumenil eleven times, Mountain four times, and Rennie and Gardner once apiece.

But no rule applies to any of this. Lloyd's, handling one-fifth of British insurance business – one-third if life insurance is excluded – is potent, clever, honest, successful, and can safely be described as unique. At Lloyd's the City's supposition that there is no place on earth to compare with it comes to full bloom. Consider the ordinary insurance company. Among the good works of civilization, insurance companies are a model of solid bureaucratic prosperity. They have a finger in every pie – and they are where much of the City's wealth and power are now to be found. When Alliance, already mentioned, merged with the Sun, besides the seven peers on the board there were a couple of Rothschilds, a man from Hambros, W. J. Keswick of Mathesons, and the president of Joe Lyons the caterers. But along with the old guard, a new race of insurance officials is taking over much of the authority once wielded by flamboyant individuals. Insurance companies in Britain are increasingly run by sober-faced men in offices that overhang streets like Cornish cliffs lined with windows. There is a cold immaculacy about insurance. Even senior officials give the impression that they are the minions of some other and greater race of officials higher up the liftshaft. In good times or bad a fortune in premium income descends on them every week and is poured into the Stock Exchange, to be switched from stock to stock by expert, impersonal managers. When the City wonders what 'the institutions' will do – whether 'the institutions' will look with disfavour on voteless shares, or sell their stock to a take-over bidder, or turn down their thumbs on a new issue – insurance companies are at the heart of the phrase. They are logical, impartial and give the impression that if every member of every top management dropped dead playing golf the same weekend, quick-fire promotions from the promotion-hungry lower ranks would take immediate effect on Monday morning; by Tuesday there would be fresh names in the slots of the doors, and policy-holders would be none the wiser and none the worse.

At Lloyd's it is still a business of individuals. There is no limited company, no air of bureaucracy, no feeling that to track down one's affairs in the building would lead through nests of offices to a punch-card operator. Lloyd's is simply a collection of men who provide piecemeal insurance – a slice from one syndicate, a slice from another, until the full amount is covered – spending their day on hard wooden benches at open stalls under one high roof. The underwriters travel up from the country each morning and work a comparatively short, hard day. Behind them is the capital and unlimited personal liability of the 'names' – the politicians, merchants, peers, and the rest – who, in return, may get an annual return of 10 or 20 per cent on their money, besides the tremendous social kudos that goes with membership of Lloyd's. It establishes a man's financial integrity, and provides a passport to practically every exclusive club in London.

They are very keen on history at Lloyd's. Most City publicity doesn't recognize the need to reveal what's been happening since 1900, and at Lloyd's one of the easiest things to discover is detail about the coffee house that Edward Lloyd opened in the 1680s. At the time of the Festival of Britain in 1951, a replica of a seventeenth-century bow-fronted coffee house opening on to a cobbled street was built at Lloyd's, complete with quill pens, hat-racks, fireplace, and special glass in the windows. Insurance, like banking, spread north from the Mediterranean, and a Genoa policy, probably the oldest insurance document in existence, preceded the coffee house by three centuries; dated 23 October 1347, it covered a vessel called the *S. Clara* on a voyage from Genoa to Majorca. By the fifteenth century, marine insurance was well established in Venice (Shakespeare's *Merchant of Venice* has been called implausible on the grounds that any Venetian merchant in Antonio's position would have taken elementary precautions and insured his marine enterprises). In London in the seventeenth century insurance was still a haphazard business, with plenty of enthusiastic amateurs among the merchants who were willing to add their names to the policy of insurance – one below the other, thus 'underwriters' – until the total amount was covered. From meeting at Lloyd's coffee-house the underwriters moved to premises of their own and expanded on the lines of a club. It was another hundred years before 'coffee-house' dropped out of the title, in the 1840s, by which time the system of Lloyd's Agents in every large port, to report on shipping movements, appoint surveyors, and generally look after the underwriters' interests had been established, and Lloyd's had made its reputation for paying up promptly. Marine insurance, with a little fire cover, was all they thought of until 1887: then a humorous broker who was insuring some furniture against fire asked the underwriter if he would cover him against burglary, and the underwriter accepted. Expanding business has burst the seams of several buildings since then – the latest move was to Lime Street in 1957 – and every kind of insurance can be placed by brokers at the underwriting 'boxes' with the exception of full-life policies: Lloyd's will cover a life for up to five years only (no binding contract for longer periods is made by Lloyd's, regardless of the type of insurance, lest future members of syndicates inherit risks they dislike and can't shed). But although non-marine insurance now provides the bigger part of Lloyd's business, marine underwriting is still looked on as something special. To be an underwriter at Lloyd's is good but to be a marine underwriter is better.

For all the popular (meaning very successful) syndicates there is a permanent waiting list of outsiders who would like to get into Lloyd's. Theirs is the most expensive form of entry. For the privilege of becoming a 'name', that is, an underwriting member, a sleeping partner in a syndicate – a man who neither does business with Lloyd's (say a broker) nor brings business there (say a shipowner) – must first submit to detailed personal audit and show that he is worth something like £75,000. His banking affairs are examined, his mortgages, his Stock Exchange dealings. The autocratic Committee of Lloyd's begins as it means to go on, by refusing any financial privacy. It would no doubt be possible for an individual to arrange some window-dressing at the time of an audit, in the way that banks call in money just before the balance sheet is struck and make themselves look even richer than they are; but the Committee must come reasonably close to the truth about a man's fortune. A less gold-plated means test is applied to applicants who take business to Lloyd's, and for the 'inside' applicant, such as a broker, there may be no means test at all.

It depends who the applicant is and how much is known about him; but whoever he is and whether or not he has to pass the £75,000 means test, he must put up a further amount of cash in proportion to the premiums that the syndicate intends to accept on his behalf. An £8,000 deposit would cover a yearly premium income in the marine market of something like £26,000. But £8,000 would be looked on as the minimum. With premium income working out at about £55,000 per underwriting member, £15,000 to £20,000 would be nearer the mark for the deposit of most names. This money is invested by the Committee on the members' behalf; he draws the dividend but mustn't touch the capital. Until a few years ago the money was invested entirely in gilt-edged stock, but a half can now be put in equities. (Large amounts of cash have also traditionally been invested in gilt-edged when underwriters are building up their syndicates' reserves. At the Bank Rate tribunal it was said that in 1957 the Committee's advice to members to sell gilt-edged stock was taken as a good tip outside Lloyd's, and contributed materially to the market's weakness that summer.)

Besides the cash qualification there are rules befitting an exclusive club. Election to Lloyd's must be proposed by six members. There is an entrance fee of up to £1,900 and an annual subscription of £88. The member must be a British citizen. He agrees to abide by the Committee's ruling, and of course must accept unlimited liability for the losses of his syndicate. The claim on him in the event of the syndicate losing money will be in the same proportion as his claim to the profits; and if the syndicate is overwhelmed by some combination of bad underwriting and dreadful misfortune, he is, as underwriters like to say with a cheerful relish that disguises the awfulness of the possibility, 'liable for the shirt on his back'. Land, house, furniture, cars, and clothes can be sold to realize money to meet claims on the syndicate. In practice the possibility is reasonably remote. A central guarantee fund of several million pounds exists as an additional buttress behind policies, and has been used to help sinking underwriters. Members' cash deposits can be used to meet exceptional claims. Still, the contentment of members gets an occasional jolt. In 1954 a syndicate of fifteen ceased to accept risks after 'adverse experience in hull insurance', and each member had to fork out about £17,000. Infrequently an underwriter is temporarily barred from Lloyd's because he has compromised the syndicate.

The atmosphere at Lloyd's is very different from the Stock Exchange. Strangers are allowed inside the Room, suitably accompanied. Marine underwriting is on the ground floor, where in mid-morning several thousand people may be coming, going, or sitting still with a telephone glued to one ear and a finger jammed in the other to keep out the din. Above is a gallery, and here the non-marine underwriting is done. The dimensions – 340 feet by 120 – make it probably the largest commercial room in Europe. It's like a cleaned-up version of a railway hall, with marble pillars and high ceiling, taken over in wartime by a bombed-out group of offices who set their clerks down in rows of desks with broad aisles between. The air is conditioned; an attendant, red-robed and looking from a distance like a lord mayor on a dais, intones an endless singsong chant, the names of people who are wanted by other people, into a stick microphone; but underwriters and their all-male staffs sit in traditional, unalterable discomfort on narrow wooden pews. Sometimes there is a car cushion or a pneumatic pad; usually not even that.

Horse-play is less pronounced than at the Stock Exchange. There, in any ten minutes in the public gallery, you're sure to see half a dozen pieces of paper crumpled into balls and flung at the backs of heads: a mock uppercut: a mock necklock from behind. (Debagging, that grand old sporting custom, takes place after the public gallery closes at three.) Time drags for the jobbers, poor fellows, sitting with their backs to the pillars and waiting for something to happen.

At Lloyd's the view from the gallery would gladden the heart of a Samuel Smiles. The queues of brokers at the boxes melt and re-form; there is a continual flux of paper, hands, and well-combed scalps; not until late in the afternoon, when smoking is allowed and work is dying down, is there much sign of leg-tripping and paper-slinging. There are fewer Jews than at the Stock Exchange, and for some reason a more athletic-looking kind of man. It may be the better light and brighter surroundings, but the average underwriter seems a little thinner and unfustier than the average stockbroker.

'My dear chap,' said a City man who has worked inside Lloyd's, 'there is no business in my experience where such an agreeable income can be earned in such agreeable surroundings with a minimum of output. It's a golden business. The under-writers sit there and see a good many brokers, agreed, but the amount of intellectual effort involved is small. It's the flair that counts.' He pointed out that not all the underwriters were as fortunate as they appeared. Brokers with a syndicate in tow may appoint a salaried underwriter; or they may lend him money which he has to repay over a period of years. 'It keeps a good man on a tight rein,' he said. 'It'll pin him down for twenty years – pin him down for life – and it makes sure that all the profits are kept in the same stable.' However, most underwriters draw a fee from each name in the syndicate, as well as being names themselves, of their own and other syndicates. In a good year since the war it's said that one or two leading underwriters have collected a gross income from all their activities in the region of £100,000. This sounds like an exaggeration: under-writers, like stockjobbers and coal-miners on overtime, have to put up with a lot of nonsense about earnings. Syndicate accounts are made up three years in arrears – the profits of Year 1 are paid out in Year 4, so as to allow 'run-off' time for claims and settlements to be made. In 1961, when the 1958 figures were published, they showed that the marine, aviation, and transit sectors of the market drew £128,000,000 in premiums; after providing for reinsurance and reserves the profit was £6,200,000. 'All Other Business', which turns out to be all other business but motor and life insurance, brought £167,000,000 in premiums, and ended up with a profit of £6,100,000. Motor insurance, strangely enough for this unprofitable field, made £1,600,000, and a small life profit gave a total return of £14,100,000. This works out at close on £3,000 per underwriting member, which is far from being a record among post-war years. The underwriter, with all his fees and percentages, should be getting considerably more than this. There's no doubt that a few flourishing underwriters have been up to the £50,000 mark, before the Inland Revenue took its £40,000 or so.

But there have been some bad years, with falling profits caused by a combination of long-term competition and short-term misfortune. Tempest losses in the States were heavy in 1956, and then and the following year there were heavy personal-liability claims from the U.S. Lawsuits against doctors and hospitals, often handled by lawyers who take a cut of the damages as a fee, have cost Lloyd's a small fortune. Premium income has been kept down since the war because of cut-throat competition with insurers all over the world, particularly in countries where insurance has been encouraged by governments as a means to commercial independence. A young underwriting member who is also a broker said over his glass of wine and stale ham sandwich that internationally Lloyd's would never regain its pre-war importance. 'There are a lot of people who think they're living in that era,' he said. 'In fact both the Germans and the Swiss are fast trying to muscle in. The Americans are retaining more and more of their own good business, but they're not as yet trying to take business from other countries. I think it's a good thing it should be ventilated. Some of the underwriters live in a dream world and don't realize what's happening. It would be a bloody good thing if they were woken up.'

Wherever insurance is placed, a good proportion of it finds its way back to London as reinsurance. American companies have long been in the habit of laying off risks with Lloyd's, and large quantities of dollars are earned in this way. (British insurance has holdings worth nearly $900,000,000 in the U.S., about half the total British investment there. This fact was told me almost in confidence by an insurance official, who said that while it was a matter for boasting in Britain, it was wiser not to brag about it in New York. 'If we do,' he said, 'we're obviously asking for fellows to get up in the Senate and say, "Why the hell should all this good American money go over to London when we've got perfectly good American insurance companies?" Mind you, in the last year or two underwriting results in the States have been so awful that earnings have been much lower, but over the years we've done rather well. In the war those funds were collateral for Lend-Lease. But if we start saying too much, we get a manager in New York asking what we mean by it.')

In recent years, Lloyd's underwriters have been inclined to turn up their noses at the increasing amounts of the less profitable reinsurance – less profitable because the cake has already been nibbled. The broker/underwriting member said this was the kind of thing that happened:

Through a broker a professional insurer offers Lloyd's a participation in its original business, less certain commissions. Now, the Lloyd's underwriters' reaction is to say: 'We don't want to write this business because if we refuse to reinsure these risks, the business will come to us direct and we'll get it on much better terms – we'll only have to pay out fifteen per cent of the premium, whereas if we do it as reinsurance it'll be twenty-five.' But being committed on various other contracts, the next thing the underwriters know, they get the business through another contract already accepted – in the end it may come to them as reinsurance of reinsurance, via Switzerland or somewhere.

Insurance is always a complicated business, but Lloyd's can claim that they handle the guts of the matter in the simplest possible way. Policies are prepared in the brokers' offices and signed at the policy signing office. Claims are handled centrally, often without reference back to the underwriters. Underwriters have their offices elsewhere in the building, but the important places are the boxes, working on the corners of desks with waistcoat buttons clicking on the woodwork, elbows hovering near ribs, and a box of sweets under the seat waiting to be kicked. The underwriter sits at one end with his assistant and a couple of clerks, separated from the facing desk and bench, which may house an extension of his own syndicate or a rival, by pigeon-holes and shelves loaded with loose-leaf files, a set of *Lloyd's Register of Shipping*, and an atlas or two. An underwriter may be seen looking intently at a *Handy General Atlas* published for the benefit of schools, scale 1 : 15,000,000 or 240 miles to the inch, trying to locate an obscure ore port in South America. Full sets of charts are available, but for most purposes 1 : 15,000,000 would be held sufficient. (As with the merchant bankers and the money-market men, you can never be sure that self-deprecation isn't part of the public act, indicating the English devotion to amateurism. This underwriter took a sly pleasure in saying an atlas was good enough for *him*.) When asked if there isn't a great deal of inconvenience in the physical arrangements, underwriters agree vaguely, but obviously feel that any fundamental change is out of the question. Devotion to tradition infuriates the contemporary-minded, but how can the man who makes a profitable living out of a traditional business be sure what parts of the tradition he can afford to throw away without harming the machinery? Here as everywhere else in the City, 'flexibility' is what they're most proud of. 'The good underwriter's got it all in his head,' said a name. 'He's got to know which part of the business is paying and which part he's losing money on.'

Out of the blue come brokers, most of whom he will know by name, with 'slips' – narrow-folded sheets of thick paper with brief details of the risk to be insured at the top, followed by the initials of underwriters and the percentage they are willing to underwrite. Privacy is out of the question. Everyone sees what everyone else is doing. Many of the brokers are juniors, taking round routine risks – 'placing brokers'. The heads of important broking firms are rarely seen in the Room, though a senior broker will be needed to launch a difficult or unusual slip by finding an underwriter who will provide a 'lead', the first name on the slip. Most of the really big underwriters, with syndicates running up to more than two hundred names, are recognized leads in certain kinds of insurance – war risks, trawler risks, hurricanes, and so on. The best underwriters are often the ones willing to speculate with a new type of risk: they break the ice, the gamble pays off, and the grateful brokers repay them by offering a good share of profitable business. It cuts both ways – a broker may tell an underwriter that he can write only 1 or 2 per cent of a profitable risk, or an underwriter may be offered 20 per cent and refuse to touch it. 'There's a great art in knowing exactly the number of bad risks you'll accept,' said an underwriter, 'and also how you'll turn the man down in such a way that he isn't offended.'

Details on the slip are often too sketchy to answer all the questions that might be raised among suspicious men, and underwriters trust brokers not to pull a fast one. Relations between the two are generally good, though tempers can fray by the end of the afternoon. Various methods of broker-approach are recognized: the hail-fellow, the funny-story, the business-like, the talkative. 'The rule is,' said a businesslike broker, 'when the underwriter picks his pen up, shut up.'

Streams of brokers, coming in from their offices elsewhere in the building, or if not then within half a mile of Lime Street, give the Room a feeling of endless small excitements. 'The important thing,' said a top underwriter, 'is that people's reaction will be: What will Lloyd's do about this? They must never be able to look in a little book and *know*.'

An underwriter who let me sit at his box kept assuring me that the risks being brought round by brokers weren't typical, until it occurred to someone to point out that none of the risks ever are. An American engineering contractor was insuring his property in Liberia. Next came a consignment of Irish wool being sent from Leipzig to Poland – no one at the box appeared to know what Irish wool was doing in Leipzig in the first place.

Then came a consignment of bar gold from a London bullion dealer to Colombo; I caught '2/6%' scrawled in heavy blue figures before the slip went on its way, and the next broker, mildly embarrassed, produced a little matter of cover for some Brazilian green coffee that had found its way into Paraguay without an import licence. Cover was required for transit from Paraguay to New York; the broker had a letter about it. He was shaking his head when he showed it to the underwriter. They shook their heads together. It was out of the question. 'It smells,' whispered the underwriter, and they wished one another good afternoon. A straightforward renewal of some hull insurance – insurance of the ship itself – followed; at the head of the slip was typed, 'Warranted no Macareo and Orinoco rivers and tributaries' and someone said this had saved underwriters about $2,000,000 in four years. The vessels were under charter to a steel company, and were being used for carrying ore from Venezuela; he wasn't sure what kind of ore, but it must be a metal ore, mustn't it, since this was a steel company? The Macareo and Orinoco rivers and tributaries were bad places for claims because ships kept going aground. If you had an eighteen-foot draught and a seventeen-foot bar, something had to go.

I waited to see one more broker. This one had a cargo of Russian benzine, 4,400 tons valued at nearly £200,000, in drums, coming from Russia to Britain. 'This insurance', said the slip, 'to pay claims for leakage up to 1 per cent on the whole shipment in each drum.' The broker, a middle-aged man in a blue suit, leaned his elbows on the desk. 'The importers send chemicals to Russia,' he explained, 'and now Russia's turned round to them and said: "You've got to take this benzine from us." Well, the importers don't usually deal in benzine. I believe they've been selling it at a loss.' We all nodded sagely: applying the screw in business was the same whatever your politics. The broker explained that the importers were buying the benzine c.i.f. – 'cost, insurance, and freight', the price to include all three. But the Russian policy didn't cover war, or, what was more to the point, the first 1 per cent of loss; so, since the importer was losing money anyway, he thought he might as well make a proper job of the insurance. 'The question is,' said the broker, 'is there a premium for it?' He looked up at an uncomfortable angle into the eyes of the underwriter; his elbows slipped another inch apart. 'The Russians've told him it'll be in steel drums, but I should have thought it would be in a tanker. In drums there shouldn't be any leakage, but in a tanker the normal loss is between half and one per cent, isn't it?'

The underwriter cleared his throat and said 'Yes, yes, yes,' not impatiently but as though each 'Yes' belonged to a separate question. He turned the slip over; there was nothing on the back. 'The only gamble here is what kind of a leakage there's going to be,' he said. 'A lot depends on the drums,' admitted the broker. 'Now, if it's acetone, some people have magnificent drums for that, two inches thick. There's no evaporation in those – absolutely tight. But I don't suppose Russia's got drums like that.'

No one seemed sufficiently well informed on the drum situation in Russia to contradict. Suddenly the underwriter said: 'Suppose I quote you a thousand pounds in full for that?' The broker stood upright, held up his hands and smiled. 'Well, I mean, it's anybody's guess.'

'I'll quote you a thousand pound,' said the underwriter. 'It's a sporting offer and it might tempt other people to write a little bit. Shall I pencil something down?'

The broker paused a moment till the pencil was in the underwriter's hand. Then he went on conversationally: 'I thought, if they're *good* steel drums they can't evaporate.'

The underwriter wrote his idea of what the premium should be, so that the broker could put it to his clients and perhaps to other underwriters. 'I think leakage has got to be interpreted in the widest possible way,' he said.

'Oh, it's got to be, it's got to be,' said the broker. He took the slip. 'Thank you very much.' A queue had grown, and the next man craned forward as he left. The slip was thrust out ready. It had something to do with insuring against beetles in a consignment of Turkish figs.

Such variety of risks, especially when it reaches the fringe area of pianists' hands and actresses' breasts, is the aspect of Lloyd's that comes in for most publicity. Nowadays British insurance companies are probably as ready as Lloyd's to quote a rate for a curious or sensational contingency; but no single company ever could or probably ever will gather such an assortment of gaudy insurances under one roof, from cricket matches and garden parties (against rain) to Hitler's personal plane, baseball teams (against forged admission tickets), Jimmy Durante's nose, and film-company expeditions. Even the Loch Ness Monster, trusty friend of journalists, was involved in one Lloyd's policy. When Monster fever was at one of its periodic peaks a few years ago, and practically everyone who passed the Scottish loch thought he'd seen something below the surface, Bertram Mills, the circus people, offered a £10,000 reward to anyone who produced the Monster alive in London. Then they prudently decided to insure against the possibility of anyone collecting. The underwriter who was approached for a lead had no objection to writing the risk, but didn't want some joker turning up with an oversized pike; in the end he defined Monster as 'more than six feet long and unknown to the Zoological Society'.

If a risk can't be placed with Lloyd's it can be written off as uninsurable. This fact, coupled with the Lloyd's reputation for coping in war as well as peace, gave an edge to the new principle of 'Automatic Termination of Cover', adopted by Lloyd's in October 1959. When war broke out twenty years earlier, marine insurance could be cancelled at forty-eight hours' notice; by the sixties two days' notice has become as old fashioned as a sword. 'This insurance', reads the new clause, 'will terminate automatically upon the outbreak of war or upon the inception of a hostile act or occurrence which results in a state of war (whichever may first occur and whether there be a declaration of War or not) between any member of the North Atlantic Treaty Organization and any of the Contracting Parties to the Treaty of Friendship, Co-operation, and Mutual Assistance signed at Warsaw 14 May 1955, or the Central People's Government of the People's Republic of China; and this insurance is warranted free from any claim arising from such outbreak of war, hostile act, or occurrence.' Two paragraphs later the document adds that in the event of such automatic termination, 'pro rata net return of premium shall be payable to the Assured'. Lloyd's looks ahead not only to atomic holocaust but to the need for stumping up amid the ruins, which is either noble or crazy, depending which way you look at it.

Its wealth, its solid unity, its air of a long-established dynasty, keep Lloyd's secure from most mortal nightmares. It takes a real disaster, or the possibility of one, to fracture the confidence and let alarm leak out – since the second war there has been one such crisis, and the details are still remembered with the nearest thing to a collective shudder that the Room is likely to see, short of Automatic Termination of Cover.

The Indonesian affair, which crept up on the marine market and nearly cost it £11,000,000 because of one clause in an insurance policy, began at the end of 1957, when anti-Dutch nationalism flared up in Indonesia. For years this enormous spreadeagled country – several thousand miles from either end of the chain of islands – had lurched from crisis to crisis, to the detriment of national morale and economy. Till 1939 it had been a Dutch colony – the Dutch East Indies. In the war the Japanese occupied it, and after 1945 it was caught up in the flood of nationalism and became the independent State of Indonesia. The Dutch stayed on, with a stake in oilfields and tobacco plantations, operating plane services and keeping their ships busy along the enormous coastline. By 1957 there were serious and growing divisions in Indonesian nationalism, and military commanders in parts of the islands of Sumatra, Borneo, and Celebes had proclaimed autonomous provincial governments. When President Sukarno, in the capital of Jakarta on the island of Java, campaigned against the Dutch for the return of 'West Irian', or what the Dutch in their old-fashioned way still insisted on calling Dutch New Guinea, political commentators in Europe suggested cynically that he was simply concerned to divert attention away from his crumbling power. The call to liberate West Irian – a land with an impenetrable interior but of prestige value to the Dutch – was revived in Jakarta in October

1957. Anti-Dutch slogans were painted on foreign shops and cars, an effigy of a red-faced man was burned in front of the residence of the Netherlands diplomatic mission, and even non-Dutch foreigners came in for attention – the American Standard-Vacuum Oil Co. had slogans painted on the building, though this was quickly recognized as *lèse-majesté* by the anti-imperialists and the words were scrubbed off.

It takes a major Pacific crisis to arouse interest in Britain, and London paid little attention, even when the Indonesian Foreign Minister, Dr Subandrio, meeting his Australian counterpart at Saigon, said that if the United Nations didn't look favourably on his country's case, the matter might lead to world war. By November the Jakarta Club, used by both European and Asian businessmen, was closed and guarded by fixed bayonets and machine guns – accused, in the old familiar phrase, of being a 'centre of subversive foreign activities'. Rumours began to circulate of measures to be taken against Dutch property, valued at between £400,000,000 and £500,000,000, and on 1 December the Indonesian Cabinet published the first stages of its plan for getting rid of the Dutch. K.L.M. Royal Dutch Airlines were forbidden to use Jakarta airport. All Dutch-language publications, including half a dozen newspapers published throughout the archipelago, were banned, and so were papers and magazines from the Netherlands. The rumours, still one jump ahead, now said the Government meant to do something about the Dutch ships that ran between the islands: more exactly, they said that the Dutch shipping company K.P.M., which maintained three-quarters of the inter-island services, was down on the list for the nationalist chopper.

K.P.M. – Koninklijke Paketvaart Maatschappij of Amsterdam – were a leading Netherlands shipping company, with more than a hundred vessels listed by *Lloyd's Register*. A large proportion of them were in the East Indies trade; many had been built for the shallow Indonesian harbours; often they had Indonesian crews with Dutch officers. When the 1957 troubles began, K.P.M. were an obvious target for the nationalists. Confused reports came out of Jakarta, but there was no doubt that the heat as on. Dutchmen were spat on – literally; car tyres were deflated, street traders refused to sell food to Dutch housewives, Dutch businessmen had their office and car keys seized, commercial contact with firms' headquarters in Holland was broken; and at the K.P.M. offices, the mob moved in, hauled down the company ensign, and hoisted red flags. At first this invasion of K.P.M. premises didn't seem to be official. The Government was afraid of going too far too quickly, and the anger spilled out mixed up with apologies. While Dutch estates were being put under Indonesian rule, and Indonesian youths were entering Dutch houses, sitting in the best chairs, and demanding to listen to the radio, the Government was regretting the high-handed methods that were being used, and explaining that the Dutch weren't being expelled: they were, said the Information Minister, Mr Sudibijo, being 'kindly requested to leave'. But the Dutch started queueing to buy airline tickets, and at the Hague the Netherlands destroyer *Drenthe* was made ready to sail east. As for K.P.M., the Indonesians seized and boarded every ship they could reach, and by the middle of December they had more than forty vessels, about half the inter-island fleet, bottled up in harbours.

At Lloyd's they showed the usual interest in anything maritime, as news of the ships' detention was posted on the boards inside the main entrance. But the Loss Book, the volume like a family Bible that stands open on a lectern, its entries carefully penned in letters that can almost be read from the gallery above, received no additions. It was only after some weeks, when the Indonesians gave no sign of releasing the K.P.M. ships, that the first wave of uneasiness went through the marine market. Like most foreign fleets, K.P.M. were insured against war risks. But the company's policy included an unusual clause. It arose when the owners of Dutch vessels trading with Russia and the Baltic States wished to cover themselves against the risk of ships being held behind the Iron Curtain – this was in the post-war period when no one knew much about trading with Russia. The clause became popular with several owners, among them K.P.M. In the case of K.P.M. it said simply that should the vessels be seized or captured by

anyone, not simply East European States, and held for a period
of four months, the owners could recover total loss from the
underwriters, giving underwriters in exchange the rights of
recovery and salvage. Most of the K.P.M. insurance was placed
direct in London, either with Lloyd's or companies; and of the
smaller amount placed with underwriters in Holland and elsewhere, a large part had as usual found its way back to London as
reinsurance. No one was ever sure of the exact figure, but the
London marine market's obligation for the forty-odd ships
detained in Indonesia was put at more than £11,000,000.

Underwriters were faced with the distant but dreadful possibility of the worst marine loss in history. American windstorms
have caused larger claims, but these have been more widely
spread. One syndicate was committed for nearly £500,000, an
average of £2,000 per name. The point was that no one had ever
envisaged such a loss when the policy was underwritten. When a
fleet of ships is being insured, the system is that each underwriter
will indicate what he is prepared to take of the largest vessel,
then automatically receive an equal proportion of the rest – 'top
value and pro rata'. His commitment is scaled down to the value
of each ship, but it means that should two ships of the same fleet
be involved in collision, he will have a double claim to meet; no
underwriter could envisage anything worse than a head-on
collision at speed between two of the Cunard *Queens*. The detention of the K.P.M. ships was almost as bad. 'It was so bad,' said
one underwriter, 'that at first it seemed too big a catastrophe to
be true. Really and truly you don't do that sort of thing nowadays, seizing dozens of ships and locking them up in harbours.
Many of us felt it was alarmist nonsense. But a few nervous
underwriters kept saying the fleet was in danger, and there was
some reinsurance to lay off the risks.'

The size of the ships ranged from a few hundred tons gross
to nearly 6,000. Rows of them lay silent along the K.P.M.
wharves at Tandjong Priok and Surabaya and Bitung, watched
by rows of dock workers squatting on their heels. They were a
source of bitter frustration not only to their Dutch owners but
to many Indonesians, who, while disliking K.P.M., saw trade

and communications between the islands and with Singapore
and the rest of Asia being rapidly strangled. The guards on board
experimented with electricity and the plumbing, which didn't do
the fittings any good; the sun baked down on the wooden decks;
and in London it dawned on the underwriting community that
amid the Indonesian atmosphere of stubbornness and confusion
and pride and spite, forty well-found and expensive ships might
stay tied up till they dissolved in rust – or until the underwriters,
having paid up, exercised their rights of subrogation and claimed
the ships for themselves.

Following the first rule of men in trouble, a committee was
set up to look into the matter. The committee looked and
debated, aware that nearly two months of the four had now
expired. No one had any idea of the intentions of the Indonesian
Government, and it was soon obvious that the only answer was
for someone to go and find out – and to put the case for the
London underwriters. It was a ticklish business. Unlike merchant
bankers, who as a rule prefer not to become involved with the
bales of cotton and cargoes of oil in which they're interested as
bankers, underwriters expect to deal in materials when they come
to salvage ships and cargoes. But the K.P.M. ships would have
presented a unique kind of salvage. If the Indonesians refused to
surrender them, Lloyd's might end up with a claim against the
Indonesian Government. Yet there could be no question of using
a big-stick technique. The Indonesians were understandably
touchy about Western reactions to their nationalism; and the
arrival of a party of immaculate London underwriters with polite
threats in their briefcases could have been disastrous. On the
other hand there were certain facts, overlooked in the fervour,
that Lloyd's desired to impress on the Indonesian Government.
The Dutch had suffered a bad blow in Indonesia, to their pride
and to their pocket. They had been kicked out wholesale, and it
was already fairly clear that even if the ships were returned, and
even if K.P.M. wished to continue trading, the Indonesians
wouldn't have them back. This meant that the forty ships, plus
an equal number idling at Singapore and Dutch New Guinea,
would be banned from the trade for which most of them were

built or converted. There was a world surplus of shipping. It was certain that the company would have to send many of the ships to the breakers; from which it followed that whoever stood to lose from continued detention of the ships and subsequent payment by the underwriters, it wasn't Koninklijke Paketvaart Maatschappij. It isn't clear what official advice, if any, the British Government tendered in all this; certainly the Foreign Office knew of the proposal to send an insurance delegation, and a Foreign Office man, familiar with Indonesia, told one of the underwriters that he thought they had little chance.

But no one had a better plan, and early in February the delegation set off. It was led by Roy Merrett, one of the biggest Lloyd's underwriters, with a peer-studded syndicate nicknamed 'the House of Lords'. With him went Harold Hopwood, a company underwriter, then chairman of the Institute of London Underwriters; Paul Dixey, another Lloyd's underwriter, though with a smaller syndicate; A. W. Green, of the Salvage Association; and Hugh Mitchell, of the Lloyd's Claim Bureau. None of them knew much about the Far East or Indonesia, but in the Essex village where he lived, Dixey was friendly with a family that knew some of the Indonesian Government. It was a contact, and this was another of those occasions when contacts might be important.

The five had their inoculations, flew to Karachi where they stayed briefly to get used to the climate, and arrived in Singapore to be greeted by the cheering news that a rebel government was about to be proclaimed in Indonesia. Everyone advised them to wait and see which way the cat jumped, but after some hesitation they decided to press on, arriving at the floodlit Jakarta airport with no idea whether yesterday's rebels would turn out to be tomorrow's government. They had arrived unofficially. They were greeted unofficially, by insurance contacts, and taken to stay at private houses, where Merrett promptly fell ill. Their stay began and continued against a turbulent background. The rebellion was centred on Sumatra, led by four colonels who said they 'wanted to free Indonesia from the Communists'. The rebel government asked the three oil companies operating in Sumatra –

Royal Dutch Shell, Caltex, and Standard-Vacuum – to stop paying revenues to the central Government and to stop sending their
products to the refineries – these included the paraffin which kept
Javanese kitchens going. At the same time the rebels complained
that the West Irian campaign had been mishandled. They asked
K.P.M. to resume normal operations with Sumatra, declaring
that 'the people's stomachs are becoming thinner and they are
eating broth'. Jakarta replied by threatening to blockade Sumatra,
and doing a little machine-gunning from the air. The rebels were
trying to buy old French naval craft that were up for sale at
Singapore. A Jakarta gunboat intercepted a British-registered
coaster bound from Sumatra to Singapore with a cargo of
paraffin wax. Another gunboat, or perhaps the same one, stopped
a K.P.M. coaster north-east of Singapore, though it wasn't
bound to or from an Indonesian port; the coaster sent out an
S.O.S., a Royal Air Force flying boat went out to investigate,
and the gunboat sheered off. There were reports that the Indonesian Navy was to buy some old craft from Italy. There were
reports that, negotiations with Japan having broken down,
Russia was to deliver ten cargo ships totalling 35,000 tons for the
inter-island services. By early March Moscow had come out
against the Sumatra rebels, and there were more familiar sounds:
Britain had sent the rebels 'several hundred armoured cars' and
the U.S. had supplied 'large amounts of heavy weapons'. Russian
jets were reported to be on their way, Jakarta parachutists landed
in Sumatra, operations at the Caltex oilfield were suspended,
and units of the U.S. Seventh Fleet were rumoured to be in the
vicinity. Most strange of all, the Dutch were said to be furious
because one of their warships had intercepted a K.P.M. vessel,
one of the few impounded ships that were still being operated,
in the Straits of Macassar. The K.P.M. master had been replaced
by an Indonesian, but the vessel, a 2,000-tonner, was flying the
Dutch flag and carried Dutch papers. The warship escorted it to
Dutch New Guinea, and got cursed in private.

Through all this the London delegation moved as delicately
as men in a minefield. They made what contact they could with
civil servants, let it be known discreetly that they were anxious

about the impounded vessels, and sat back patiently. They gained a reputation in Jakarta for being willing to *listen*; it pleased and flattered the Indonesians to find that these nice Englishmen, having flown across the world, were apparently interested to hear the case for Indonesian nationalism. Their intermediaries among the Indonesian insurance men carried elaborate messages – from a Third Secretary here, a Second Secretary there. 'It sounds a damned silly thing,' said one of the delegation, 'but what we had to do was establish that we were nice people.' While they waited they drafted a Standard Hull Form, one of the basic marine insurance documents, for the Indonesians to use. They saw the British Ambassador. Occasionally at weekends they went out into the country for a drive, but most of the time they remained on the spot: patient, polite, sending gentle reminders through their intermediaries that to keep the ships would bring the whole weight of the loss crashing on to the London market. After a month of this, with only a few weeks to go before April produced a bill for £11,000,000, the Indonesians had given no sign that they were convinced. There would probably have been nothing to prevent them stalling a little longer, then apologizing profusely for such a heavy loss, having the ships valued by someone who knew the ropes, and offering London a few million pounds compensation for the whole fleet.

But the delegation kept its nerve, and at last, after five weeks, came a definite response from the Government. Was it absolutely certain, the Indonesians inquired politely, that the K.P.M. insurance policy did include this four-month detention clause? Was it absolutely certain that the Dutch weren't going to suffer? Would the underwriters please produce the original policy or an authenticated copy? Again, it might have been a delaying tactic. It was decided that Dixey should fly back to London and show the Lloyd's copy of the policy to the Indonesian Ambassador. The day before he left, Dixey played his one personal-contact card; he rang the Foreign Minister's wife to tell her he was going home, hoping it would produce an invitation to see her husband. It did. 'Oh, don't worry,' said the Minister, 'we're going to release the ships.' But it was a slender piece of encouragement to take back.

The policy was produced in London, but in Jakarta the waiting went on for another fortnight. No doubt the idea that if Indonesia helped Lloyd's now, then Lloyd's would be able to help Indonesia in future, had taken hold by this time. No doubt the Indonesians were nervous of what might happen if the underwriters claimed on them. On 20 March, just over a fortnight before the time-limit expired, the delegation were told at 3.30 in the afternoon that the Prime Minister, Mr Djuanda, was going to sign a decree releasing the ships in half an hour. The decree was short – two foolscap sheets. 'The present circumstances', it said, 'do not permit any more the presence of K.P.M. vessels within the territorial waters of the Republic of Indonesia.' Administration of the vessels was returned to the management. The sting was in Article 3 – 'To the K.P.M. Ltd no more licence is granted to undertake the interinsular shipping in Indonesia.'

One of the delegation hurried round to the British Residency to tell the Ambassador, who had been watching discreetly from the sidelines. But the Ambassador's manservant said that not even an earthquake would be permitted to disturb His Excellency's sleep. The bringer of good tidings did the next best thing and made for the Commercial Secretary. 'His reaction', said the delegate, 'was typically English – absolutely overjoyed. He just looked at me and said: "Good. Let's have a drink." So in the middle of that steaming heat we broke all the rules. *We had a drink in the afternoon.*'

Next day the official Indonesian news agency, Antara, was explaining why the K.P.M. ships were returned. It said wildly that with the release 'the Lloyd Insurance Company in London dropped its claim on the Government, amounting to £12,000,000'. K.P.M., it explained, had 'insured its fleet with Lloyd in London. In connexion with the Indonesian action the shipping company claimed compensation from the insurance firm. Lloyd in turn made a claim on the Indonesian Government. Indonesian authorities made it clear that the K.P.M. ships held up were old vessels. They said the Government considered it more profitable to return the ships to their owner, rather than being confronted with Lloyd's claim.'

Perhaps this report was slanted for home consumption. Certainly the British version of what happened is more kid-gloved. However, with the decree signed, niceties didn't matter. A Government representative had already flown across to Sumatra to square the rebels. The Indonesian Press suspected the country had been sold down the river – returning the ships was 'a moral defeat' and 'a bitter lesson to us', wrote one mixed-up columnist. The Left-wing denounced the hand-over, urging the Government to 'turn down any more demands such as have been made by the Dutch shipping company's insurance firms'. But at the harbours, skeleton Dutch crews, cooped up in hostels since the end of the previous year, were going aboard the K.P.M. ships. It was more than a week before they were ready to sail and cables from Merrett arrived at Lloyd's, to be transcribed on to the Casualty Reports and pinned up for all to read the beautiful £11,000,000 messages. 'Witnessed sailing motor vessels *Ophir*, *Leksula*, *Lariang* from Tandjong yesterday', said the first. 'Remainder expected clear here today. News satisfactory all other ports except one at Padang and small one at Rengat.' Some of the ships arrived at Singapore, the nearest port where they were demonstrably safe, on the very last day of the four months. One ship had been sunk in Padang harbour, in rebel country, and couldn't be raised; and a small one sank up a river. The under-writers had to meet a claim for these, and for damage done aboard the rest of the fleet. On the list were jettisoned cargo, broken electric light bulbs, stopped wastepipes, torn mosquito nets, stolen cabin keys, and general pilfering; the entire claim came to £1,500,000, unpleasant but bearable. 'The claims', said an underwriter wryly, 'were paid in a spirit of generosity.' As for the ships that returned to their exasperated owners, a subsequent Lloyd's report gives a dismal catalogue. Passenger vessel *Bontekoe* (4,925 tons): broken up. Passenger vessel *Plancius* (5,955): broken up. Passenger vessel *Swartenhondt* (4,904): broken up. Passenger vessel *Ophir* (4,255): sold to be broken up. *Bandjarmasin* (1,279): sold. *Blinju* (1,330): sold to be broken up.

And so on for twenty or thirty names. K.P.M. insurance continues to be placed in London; but the four-month clause has disappeared.

A great deal of Indonesian insurance business comes to London now, and relations with Lloyd's are very good. The opportunity for a *quid pro quo* from the underwriters came a year later, in 1959, when the Indonesians, having transferred their tobacco market from Amsterdam to Bremen in West Germany, were threatened with legal action by the former owners of the tobacco plantations, who said they would seize tobacco bought in Bremen. With this threat hanging over them, few buyers were likely to attend the auctions. Lloyd's underwriters were asked if they would insure the tobacco against seizure; they did, and extended it to cover the liability of English and Danish buyers. When it was obvious that the sales would go ahead in any case, and that it was the Dutch cigar makers, running short of tobacco, who would suffer, the threat was withdrawn a couple of days before the auctions. Dutch buyers turned up in force, and the sales were a great success.

Indonesia is a popular word at Lloyd's. It was a tricky business while it lasted; but what problem does the City ever face that can't be softened and eliminated by patience, skill, and the personal touch? There was a solid core of expediency, yet everything was sweetened by the general air of good temper. All insurance is a matter for optimists. At Lloyd's they have the special optimism that goes with confidence in the handshake, the smile, and the promise. Establish yourselves as nice people, and the rest is easy.

11

LORD MAYOR OF LONDON

THE origin of the City of London is older than the records; by the time Tacitus gave it its much-quoted mention in A.D. 61 it was already 'a town of the highest repute and a busy emporium for trade and traders', and the couple of millennia since then have produced a handsome edifice of tradition and ceremonial. The City runs on ancient lines, with its own judicial courts and a private income, a flourishing collection of guilds, a nationally important lord mayor, and one of the richest bodies of voters who ever put their marks on a ballot paper. City ceremonial provides the vulgar fascination of seeing hard wealth translated into a soft, creamy spectacle of robes, chains, carriages, invitations, banquets, flunkeys, and trumpets. It hoists just the right kind of expensive, decorative backcloth behind the money-making.

The central figure is the Lord Mayor, and the process of choosing him involves the whole administrative apparatus of the City – part real, part make-believe. The basic instrument of local government is the Court of Common Council, whose common councilmen are elected annually by the voters of the City – residents, and those who own or rent property with a rateable value of £10 or more. The property qualification gives a vote to shopkeepers and other sole traders, and partners in firms, but not to directors of limited companies – which occupy the greater part of the City. This is easily dealt with by banks and insurance companies who feel it would be a bad show not to be represented. By sub-letting a room to an individual for £25 or £30 a year, and screwing a brass nameplate on the door, the managing director is enfranchised and everyone is happy. The qualification as resident applies to a permanent population of around 5,000, most of them iving in flats. The City reached its maximum population about 630, with 130,000 residents. In the eighteenth century came the irst emigration of merchants who had made money and were moving into the countryside; but it was the growth of the suburbs and railways with fast services that shifted the bulk of the population out of the City. Between 1861 and 1871, residents fell from 13,000 to 74,000. The day population has risen steadily, and is now about 400,000 (it seems more at rush hours).

The Common Council is the body with the statutory powers, and does the usual work of a local authority: rates, roads, drains, and the rest. But besides the Common Council the Corporation of London embraces the Lord Mayor and the aldermen. The aldermen (all staunch City men of sound background and good manners) are elected by the voters, one apiece for twenty-five of the twenty-six wards; the twenty-sixth, Bridge Without, is reserved for the senior alderman. They sit as aldermen till they die or retire through old age, having been approved not only by the electorate but by their fellow-aldermen, who can and occasionally do blackball an elected candidate. This happened twice between 1945 and 1960, to the chagrin of the ward clubs where the candidature had been sponsored in the first place; no reasons are given, but it's always assumed that the aldermen have spotted some particle of imperfection which might render the candidate unfit to be Lord Mayor of London. This is the point of the fine mesh provided for inspection of would-be aldermen: once elected they are in the running for the mayoralty, and barring accidents will move steadily up the list till their time comes.

To be considered for the mayoralty, a man doesn't have to begin as a common councilman; but most do. Then he has to be an alderman. Next he has to be a Sheriff. There are two Sheriffs per year, chosen on midsummer's day by the liverymen of the City, sitting in Common Hall – which is the title of the gathering, not a building. One of the Sheriffs is usually chosen from the aldermen; the other, non-aldermanic Sheriff may become an alderman *after* his year as Sheriff if he aspires to be Mayor. About 10,000 liverymen are entitled to vote in Common Hall, though fortunately they wouldn't all try at once. They are the senior members of the City guilds or livery companies – the trade associations of the past, surviving without economic or political importance but still possessed of dignity, rules, often fine buildings (many of them rebuilt since the Blitz), and sizeable incomes from property and investments. Most of their money is spent on schools, charities, and good food and drink. There are eighty-one companies, each with a limited membership. Probably smallest is the Waxchandlers, with thirty-four liverymen; among the newest is the Guild of Air Pilots and Air Navigators; the senior and wealthiest is the Mercers, 206 liverymen and an annual corporate income of more than £100,000 ten years ago – it will be higher now, but of late the companies have become secretive about their income. The Mercers' Company heads the twelve 'Great' London companies: Grocers, Drapers, Fishmongers, Goldsmiths, Skinners, Merchant Taylors, Haberdashers, Salters, Ironmongers, Vintners, and Clothworkers. Some companies died before it was fashionable to preserve them as relics, so there are no longer Silkthrowers, Pinmakers, Woodmongers, Long-bow Stringmakers, or even Tobacco Pipe Makers.

The Sheriff's office is the oldest in the City, and Anglo-Saxon laws mention it 1,300 years ago. In the ritual the Sheriffs' principal duty is to attend the Lord Mayor; they also keep up appearances at one of the City's meeting places between ceremony and real-life: the Central Criminal Court at the Old Bailey, the most famous court in Britain, where major cases may come from all over the country as well as from Greater London. There the Sheriffs look after juries when they have to be locked up, and one Sheriff must be present when sentence of death is passed. They act as permanent hosts, which costs them thousands of pounds out of their own pockets (judges eat well); the Corporation makes each Sheriff an allowance of £350 for his year, but this is soon swallowed up. The Sheriffs Breakfast, which is a lunch for 200 or more, and a share in the cost of the Lord Mayor's Banquet, add to the bill. A Sheriff, in fact, must be a man of means – and so must a Lord Mayor. Once over the hurdle of the shrievalty, the alderman has only to wait till he is most senior on the list of potential Lord Mayors. He could still be blackballed, but no one with a blemished record would be likely to get so far, and anyone who lost his reputation after joining the select company of aldermen and Sheriffs would be sure to resign 'for health reasons', as happened not long ago to an unfortunate bank director, in the running for the mayoralty a few years in the future, who became embroiled in the Exchange Control Act and was fined £20,000. The case was heard before the Bow Street magistrate, outside the City, instead of at Mansion House court where most financial cases go: perhaps to avoid embarrassment, since another alderman would have been sitting at Mansion House.

When his time comes the Lord Mayor is chosen first by the liverymen, then by the aldermen. The Liverymen meet on Michaelmas Day, 29 September, and select two aldermen, who are passed on to the Court of Aldermen for them to make the final choice. In practice the seniority rule is applied at both levels, and everyone knows what is going to happen, though liverymen would regard it as a sad breach of protocol to say anything in public before the formal election. Common Hall (the meeting) held in Guildhall (the building) is frequently a noisy affair, with rows of bald heads and bright robes, a holiday atmosphere, and speeches made between friends. ('It is the fashion these days among some of the silly, nasty men of this world to cast aspersions on the City. The City can shake them off easily. Its reputation still stands high in the world. . . .') The Lord Mayor elect is almost certain to be a liveryman himself. As a Corporation official put it: 'Any man who wishes to be in the swim, so to speak, finds it *prudent* to become a liveryman.' City ceremonial, like the City generally, derives strength from being so interlocked.

Between his election at Michaelmas and his assumption of office in November, with its crowd-catching, street-jamming procession known as the Lord Mayor's Show, now wisely transferred to a Saturday, the elected alderman drops discreetly out of public life, so as not to mar the tail of his predecessor's year. Behind the scenes the administrative machine is hard at work, grinding out the programme for the coming year, and the Lord Mayor elect, should he be the worrying kind, will have already sat long into many nights preparing some of the thousand-plus speeches he will have to make. The awful prospect of daily speechmaking, much of it to rearrangements of the same people who are sure to be speechproof by the end of the year, begins to loom up, for a nervous man, years before he takes office. There will be banquets and luncheons with Cabinet Ministers and royalty at the top table. Bankers and bishops will sit with buttons loosened, waiting for wisdom or, worse still, jokes; nothing sounds pleasanter, in a broadcast from a Lord Mayor's Banquet, than the banging of hands on tables and the cries of 'Hear hear!' when the speaker makes a popular point; nothing sounds more dismal than the silence, followed by a reluctant sigh of patronizing laughter, when a wisecrack falls flat. The prospect of the speeches so unnerved one alderman a few years ago that he resigned within sight of the mayoralty.

I have met two Lord Mayors. One carefully wrote speeches for every function and filed them ready for use. The other prepared nothing. I happened to meet him at Mansion House, the Lord Mayor's residence, beside a massive table piled seven or eight feet above the ground with every conceivable variety of fruit: the gift of the Fruiterers' Company who were holding a dinner there that night, and had presented the fruit to the Lord Mayor, who would pass it on to hospitals. Every apple, apricot, cherry, grape, and banana seemed to have been pumped up above normal size and varnished; a man was on a step-ladder, arranging pomegranates. The Lord Mayor had just returned from a luncheon. His round pink face shone above the morning coat, and he said, when asked what he did about speeches, that he didn't think people wanted to have oratory with their dinner: they wanted to see their pals. He must have enjoyed every minute of being Lord Mayor. The one thing that nettled him, he said, was the thought of money being collected at a Mansion House meal. It was a private house, where 'I invite my brothers', and he wouldn't allow cheque forms to be passed round, no matter how charitable the cause. 'After all,' he said, 'this is the next place after Buckingham Palace.' As he drifted off he said he intended to have a little rest before his next engagement; time didn't worry him; he could shave and dress in twenty minutes.

A day's engagements, as listed on the sheets prepared by the Mansion House secretariat, reads:

11.30. Lord Mayor receives 90 residents from Boston, Mass, U.S.A., at the Mansion House. M.C. & B.

12.45. Lord Mayor and Sheriff leave Mansion House for Bury Court, St Mary Axe. M.C. & B.

1.00. Lunch with the President of the Chamber of Shipping.

5.40. Lord Mayor leaves Mansion House for 11 New Fetter Lane. M.C. & B.

5.45. Reception of Messrs Sweet & Maxwell.

7.30. Lord Mayor and Sheriffs leave Mansion House for Tallow Chandlers' Hall. O.B.B.C. & D.

7.45. Dinner of the Tylers and Bricklayers' Company.

'M.C. & B.' is 'morning coat and badge': a diamond badge, worn round the Lord Mayor's neck on a blue ribbon. 'O.B.B.C. & D.' is normal dress for Lord Mayor and Sheriffs, six nights a week: 'Old Bailey, breeches, chain, and decorations.' The Old Bailey is a cutaway coat, of a style traditionally worn there.

The Lord Mayor's private secretary, a central figure in organizing Lord Mayors' lives, is usually a retired Army or Navy officer with a flair for administration; he's a permanent official, watching Lord Mayors come and go, and has the delicate task of fitting a diversity of masters into the same pattern of ritual. The amount of money a mayor spends from his own pocket during his year of office is never less than £6,000 or £7,000, and men who want to make a splash have spent more than £30,000 in recent years. This is on top of a basic £15,000 tax-free allowance by the Corporation, plus other undisclosed amounts – it wouldn't be the City if there was no secrecy about these things – allowed to entertain overseas guests and help pay for the Mansion House staff, which runs to butler, under-butler, steward, two platemen, three footmen, front door man, usher/porter, housekeeper, two maids, and daily helps. The size of the purse and the temperament of the mayor have to be taken into account in all the planning. The Lord Mayor is in great demand, often from hopeful secretaries of charities, fellowships, societies, and leagues who are unaware of the economics of a cocktail party. The organizer who rings brightly, eighteen months in advance, to ask if the mayor can entertain 500 ladies to cocktails for half an hour is suitably chastened to learn that this is going to cost £150 from the mayor's own pocket. The secretary has to weigh money against tact against goodwill.

Unavoidable functions include dinner with every livery company, which takes care of eighty-one evenings, and either lunch or dinner with every ward club, which covers another twenty-five occasions. All the receptions of all the mayors of all the London boroughs must be attended, which means that on nearly thirty occasions the Lord Mayor will meet the same concourse of mayors for the same purpose. Then there are the great occasions like the Bankers' Dinner, officially 'Dinner to the Chancellor of the Exchequer, the Governor and Directors of the Bank of England, bankers, and merchants of the City of London', where toasts would include 'Prosperity to the public purse and the health of the Chancellor of the Exchequer', and speakers might be the Chancellor, the Governor of the Bank of England, the Chairman of the Stock Exchange, the chairman of Lloyd's, and of course the Lord Mayor. The menu is good without any wild extravagances. Typically:

HOCK Liebfraumilch Hans Christof Wein 1949	NATIVE OYSTERS/SMOKED SALMON
MADEIRA SHERRY	CLEAR TURTLE
CLARET Chateau L'Angelus 1947 CHAMPAGNE Pomméry & Greno 1943	ROAST BREAST OF PHEASANT GAME CHIPS CAULIFLOWER MORNAY

BRANDY   GATEAU ST HONORÉ
Otard V.S.O.P.   PETITS FOURS
LIQUEURS

PORT   DESSERT
Taylors 1935

COFFEE

Round the Lord Mayor's neck hangs, on all State occasions, the Collar of SS: made of fine gold in the shape of twenty-eight richly worked letters SS, with a diamond-mounted pendant of gold attached. It was left to his successors by a Lord Mayor of 1535, Sir George Aleyn; what the SS stand for is unknown (guesses include St Simplicius, martyred A.D. 287, Saints, or Sovereign). Light from the chandeliers and television arcs glistens on metal, flesh, and china, while in the background the orchestra works it way through 'Melodies from *The King and I*' and 'Excerpts from *No, No, Nanette*'. Hospitality is being dispensed along old-fashioned lines, to a list of dignitaries that changes little over the years. Lord Mayors run to a pattern – recent ones include a master printer, a chartered accountant, a wool merchant, two stockbrokers, and a paper magnate – and so do their guests: the Diplomatic Corps, the Church, the Law, the Government, and the City. The Admen's Dinner or even the Pressmen's Dinner is yet to come.

The planning staff under the private secretary includes a man employed full-time on seating plans. The system provides a file for every day of the year and a file for every livery company. Each function has its own sheet, listing details of time, attendance, dress, toasts, speeches ('Special Refs. or Persons to be Named') and principal guests. The list of 'Items to be Checked' names Agenda, Seating Plan, Table Plan Distrib., Afternoon Teas, Cloakroom, Gents and/or Ladies; Wines, Before/After; Music, Entertainers, Flowers, Photographers, Toastmaster, Gratuities, and Car Calling. There is space for Special Notes and Comments after Event. The end product of it all is generally to feed and flatter people, often to aid distress of all kinds – the Lord Mayor is the central figure in many national appeals – and things are handled good-humouredly. But when every move involves a piece of protocol, walls spring up and mark this out as a world of its own. Mansion House planning extends beyond Lord Mayor and Sheriffs to such officials as Swordbearer, Sergeant-at-Arms, and City Marshal, whose duties include waiting on the Mayor in turn, and organizing their own functions. The Sergeant, in 1960 a retired naval captain, runs a fancy-dress party for the children of diplomats and other mayors. The Swordbearer, a retired colonel of Marines, runs At Homes for the Lady Mayoress (who has no official standing, and no badge or chain). The City Marshal, a retired brigadier, has to challenge all troops entering the City – the nightly Bank of England picquet is excluded, fortunately for him, but apart from this no soldiers are supposed to pass through the City without the Lord Mayor's permission. Another of the private secretary's preoccupations is the password at the Tower of London – passwords arrive quarterly, a three-monthly supply of one per day, usually uninspiring place-names like Southampton, Aberdeen, or Cornwall.

Helping to keep the ritual oiled are the City's private means. Instead of having to rely wholly on income from the rates, supplemented by grants from the national exchequer, like other local authorities, the City of London has built up its own reserves. Under the heading of 'City's Cash' is an annual income of, at present, £1,300,000 after tax, drawn from market rents, land revenue, legal fines, and investment. The City's investments, partly in gilt-edged and partly in blue-chip equities, are worth £18,000,000, a solid inheritance from centuries of careful management by experts in these things. A great deal of City's Cash goes to ease the burden on the rates; some of it is spent 'in its own discretion'. It maintains schools, the Guildhall, the Mansion House, the Central Criminal Court; and if it wants to spend £1,000 on buying food and drink in honour of a distinguished visitor, that's no concern of a sharp-nosed Government auditor – especially if, as often happens, the visitor happens to be a guest of the Government.

Because it's useful as well as colourful, City ritual flourishes under everyone's approval. Politically the Lord Mayor can be a godsend when it comes to finding a neutral figure who will represent the nation, perhaps on an overseas visit, without having to choose between parties. He will be superbly correct, an elegant gentleman without, in theory, political affiliations. Like the Common Council, which has no political parties but is in practice a fairly solid bloc of Tories, the Lord Mayor is presumably a shade closer to the hearts of the Right than of the Left. But when the Labour Party, in power after the war, virtually suspended the practice of awarding baronetcies, they continued to bestow the traditional Bt on ex Lord Mayors. The past is persistent. London without City, City without Lord Mayor: both are inconceivable.